SWEET

Real Leaders Negotiate!

Also by Jeswald W. Salacuse

Negotiating Life: Secrets for Everyday Diplomacy and Deal Making

The Three Laws of International Investment: National, Contractual, and International Frameworks for Foreign Capital

The Law of Investment Treaties

Seven Secrets for Negotiating with Government

Leading Leaders: How to Manage Smart, Talented, Rich, and Powerful People

The Global Negotiator: Making, Managing, and Mending Deals around the World in the Twenty-First Century

The Wise Advisor: What Every Professional Should Know About Consulting and Counseling

Making Global Deals: Negotiating in the International Market Place

The Art of Advice: How to Give it and How to Take it

International Business Planning: Law and Taxation

(With W.P. Streng, six volumes)

Social Legislation in the Contemporary Middle East

(Co-editor with L. Michalak)

An Introduction to Law in French-Speaking Africa: North Africa

An Introduction to Law in French-Speaking Africa: Africa South of the Sahara

Nigerian Family Law (with A. B. Kasunmu)

Jeswald W. Salacuse

Real Leaders Negotiate!

Gaining, Using, and Keeping the Power to Lead Through Negotiation

palgrave
macmillan

Jeswald W. Salacuse
The Fletcher School
Tufts University
Medford, Massachusetts, USA

ISBN 978-1-137-59114-2   ISBN 978-1-137-59115-9 (eBook)
DOI 10.1057/978-1-137-59115-9

Library of Congress Control Number: 2017941708

Cover image © Diana Johanna Velasquez / Alamy Stock Vector

Printed on acid-free paper

This Palgrave Macmillan imprint is published by Springer Nature
The registered company is Nature America Inc.
The registered company address is: 1 New York Plaza, New York, NY 10004, U.S.A.

FOR LIVI

Preface

To lead is to negotiate. All leaders have to negotiate to achieve their goals. The centrality of negotiation to the process of leading groups, organizations, and nations is not, however, widely acknowledged. Books on leadership and leaders devote little attention to the role of negotiation in leadership and the ways that leaders negotiate. Courses to train leaders hardly ever consider the importance of negotiation in actually leading. Search committees seeking new leaders for their organizations always look for "vision" and "charisma" in leadership candidates but rarely concern themselves with a candidate's effectiveness as a negotiator. To compound the problem, scholars and consultants seem to have constructed the subfields of negotiation and leadership as two separate water-tight compartments that have little contact with one another. Thus there are negotiation teachers and leadership teachers, negotiation books and leadership books, and negotiation courses and leadership courses, all of which often seem to consider the two activities as having little to do with one another.

A close examination of leaders' actual day-to-to day activities reveals that they are constantly negotiating in order to carry out the tasks of leadership. Indeed, one may say that without the ability to negotiate skillfully leaders would not be able to lead. Effective leaders have to negotiate their leadership to make a difference. I make that statement based not only on my research but on my nearly four decades of experience as a former dean of two very different university graduate schools, leader of several professional associations, chairman of corporate boards, and president of international judicial tribunals. In each of those capacities, I was negotiating all the time. In fact, the boundaries between leadership and negotiation became indistinguishable from where I sat.

The purpose of this book is to draw on my research and experience to examine leadership as a process of negotiation throughout the entire leadership lifecycle, from the actions needed to acquire the power to lead, through the exercise of that power to carry out the specific daily tasks required of a leader, and ending with the negotiations that leaders must engage in to address threats to their leadership. It is my hope that both actual and potential leaders will find in the pages of this book useful advice and ideas to enable them to negotiate their leadership effectively.

In writing this book, I have had the able research assistance of Araya Arayawuth and Stephanie Shaffer to whom I express my profound thanks.

The Fletcher School of Law and Diplomacy   Jeswald W. Salacuse
Tufts University
Medford, Massachusetts
January 6, 2017.

Contents

List of Figures

1

Leadership and Negotiation — Dichotomies and Definitions

According to conventional wisdom, real leaders don't negotiate. Leading people requires charisma, vision, and a commanding presence, not the elusive tricks for making deals. Discussions of leadership often consider the ability to lead groups and organizations as a special quality that one is either born with or gains through long, hard experience. Negotiation is not seen as central to a leader's job. For many executives, negotiation is a tool to use *outside* the organization to deal with customers, suppliers, and creditors. *Inside* the organization, it's strictly "my way or the highway." Accounts of the leadership of Jack Welch at General Electric, Steve Jobs at Apple, Lew Gerstner at IBM, or Bill Gates at Microsoft rarely focus on their qualities as negotiators. That's because most people think leadership and negotiation are two different skills that don't have much to do with one another. For them, strong leaders command and weak leaders negotiate. Leadership is about inspiring followers by giving them a vision. Negotiation is for cutting deals that may or may not work out.

The conventional wisdom is dead wrong. As this book will show, real leaders do negotiate.[1] In fact, they *have* to negotiate if they hope to achieve their leadership goals.

Business and political science literature reflects this conventional dichotomy between leadership and negotiation. There are books on leadership and

---

[1] For an early, preliminary exploration of this theme, see Jeswald W. Salacuse, "Real Leaders Negotiate: Leverage Three Negotiation Fundamentals to Boost Your Power and Persuasiveness as a Leader," *Harvard Management Update* 12, no. 6 (June 2007): p. 11.

© The Author(s) 2017
J.W. Salacuse, *Real Leaders Negotiate!*,
DOI 10.1057/978-1-137-59115-9_1

books on negotiation, but no book closely examines the relationship between the two. That division is also deeply embedded in academia. Thus, leadership and negotiation have given rise to two separate fields of study. Each has developed a distinct, ample body of literature and a separate, large group of scholars. Libraries collect both "negotiation literature" and "leadership literature," and university faculties include both "negotiation teachers" and "leadership teachers." Business schools offer leadership courses and negotiation courses. Despite seeming to have common preoccupations, two of the most significant of which are understanding how to influence the behavior of other people and how to manage groups and organizations, the two bodies of literature and the two groups of scholars historically have had little connection and little interaction with one another. Leadership literature rarely considers negotiation scholarship, and negotiation scholars rarely draw on works of leadership. If you want to verify that statement, just take a look at the index of any well-regarded leadership book and search for the entry on "negotiation." You'll find little. Similarly, a search under "leadership" in the index of standard negotiation books yields not very much either.

The Dichotomy between Leadership and Negotiation

More substantively, the two bodies of literature and the two groups of scholars seem to have different preoccupations. Leadership scholars and negotiation scholars tend to focus on and to emphasize different things. Leadership scholars stress the importance of **power, structure**, and **personality** in their studies because they believe that these are the elements that allow leaders to achieve their goals. On the other hand, negotiation scholars tend to focus on **process, party interests**, and **bargaining tactics** since they consider that an understanding and mastery of these elements is fundamental to the work of negotiators. In addition, the two groups employ different, basic units of analysis or frameworks in their studies. Leadership scholars focus on the organization or institution to be led while negotiation scholars concentrate on the dynamics and relationships between contending parties in conflicts.

The traditional view that negotiation has little to do with leadership misconceives what it actually takes to lead an organization or group. An examination of what leaders do, whether in the headquarters of a multinational firm or the town hall of a small community, reveals that negotiation is the very essence of leadership. In order to do their jobs, leaders must negotiate all day long. Equally important, to stay in power leaders have to negotiate. I make those statements based not only on my research but also on my own experience as an organizational leader. In my tenure as dean of two different graduate schools at two separate universities over a period of 15 years, I was negotiating constantly—with faculty, students, university presidents and provosts, alumni, university trustees, donors, foundation executives, professional associations, and other deans, to name just a few. My life during those 15 years was a constant process of negotiation, an endless dynamic of deal making. Furthermore, as chairman of corporate boards of directors, president of professional associations, lead director of mutual funds, and president of international tribunals, I also had to negotiate to carry out my responsibilities.

My conversations with leaders in other domains—government, business, and the nonprofit sector—revealed that they have had the same experience with negotiation and leadership as I. They all had to negotiate to achieve their leadership goals. Effective leaders are those who negotiate, so it's important for people in leadership positions to see themselves, not as "commanders" as many do, but rather as "negotiating leaders." As this book will demonstrate, leaders who forget that perspective often fail to achieve their goals and sometimes lose the power to lead.

The relationship between negotiation and leadership does not flow only in one direction. Just as leaders must negotiate to do their jobs, negotiators also must lead to make deals. They must lead in at least two important respects. First, they have to lead people on *their* side of the bargaining table—that is, people for whom they are negotiating and the members of their own negotiating team; second, they have to lead people on the *other* side of the table—those with whom they are seeking to make deals on behalf of their organizations, their companies, or their countries. Mediators of disputes, like Jimmy Carter at the Camp David Negotiation between Egypt and Israel in 1979 and George Mitchell in the negotiations between Catholic and Protestants in Northern Ireland in the late1990s, also had to draw on the skills of leadership and negotiation as they sought to help contending parties arrive at a settlement of their conflict. It was only through the wise use of leadership skills, honed as experienced politicians, that Carter and Mitchell successfully led the disputing parties in those two longstanding and seemingly intractable conflicts to accept and engage in processes that led to the 1979 peace treaty between Egypt and Israel that has lasted for almost four decades and the 1999 Good Friday Agreements that laid the foundation for a new era of peace in Northern Ireland. George Mitchell, for example, at a private luncheon in 2016 specifically acknowledged to me that to forge the

Good Friday Agreement in Northern Ireland he drew heavily on his experience as Majority Leader of the U.S. Senate. A close examination of other negotiations, particularly large multilateral efforts such the 196-nation 2015 Climate Change Conference in Paris and the eight-year Uruguay Round of trade negotiations that led to the creation of the World Trade Organization, also reveals leadership techniques at work. Indeed, without appropriate leadership in global meetings of that sort, no agreement can ever be reached. In general, the greater the number of parties in a negotiation the more effective leadership is needed to achieve agreement.

Despite the convergence of negotiation and leadership in practice, the two domains remain largely separate in theory. No book has specifically looked at leadership as a negotiation process or has applied negotiation theories and principles to explain how to lead organizations and groups effectively. In short, no book has asked: what can leaders learn from the field of negotiation? Similarly, no work has directly addressed and explored another important question: how can negotiators benefit from the study of leadership? This book will address both questions. To begin that exploration, we first have to define two fundamental concepts: leadership and negotiation.

Searching for the Meaning of Leadership

It was only *after* I was appointed dean of the School of Law of Southern Methodist University (SMU) in Dallas, Texas, that I began to think seriously about leadership. As dean, I would be the chief academic and executive officer of an institution of some 800 students, a faculty of over 50, and a budget of over 15 million dollars. After the University President, James Zumberg, offered me the job and I had accepted, he gave me what I came to call the "leadership speech," a pep talk designed to tell a newly appointed leader the wonderful things that will happen under his or her leadership. As President Zumberg expressed his confidence that the law school faculty would be strengthened, the student body improved, and the endowment increased under *my leadership*, I remember thinking, "What is this man talking about?"

Leadership was just not a word I associated with myself. Leadership was what Winston Churchill did in World War II, what Martin Luther King, Jr. did during the civil rights movement, and John F. Kennedy did when faced with the Cuban Missile Crisis. It had not occurred to me that leadership would be required of me at SMU. Manage, yes. Administer, sure. But lead? During my conversation with the president, two questions came to mind that I have continued to think about to this day: What is leadership? and What must a person actually do to lead other people? Over the next 35 years, in a variety of other leadership jobs, including the deanship of Tufts University's Fletcher School of Law and Diplomacy, chairmanship of two corporate boards, lead independent director of mutual funds, and president of international tribunals and academic organizations, among other, I have looked for answers to both questions through my research and in my own experience. This book is the product of that exploration. The short answer to both questions, in case you want to stop reading here, is that leadership is a process of negotiation and that to lead other people you must negotiate.

The search for the meaning of leadership has become the modern alchemy of organizational management. Although everyone agrees that leadership is important, indeed vital, for the success of organizations, a clear understanding of its nature has eluded scholars and practitioners, just as the means for turning lead into gold eluded medieval alchemists. In the search for the meaning of leadership during the past century, scholars have developed and pursued a series of theories. One of the first of these was the "great person theory," sometimes called "trait theory," that sought to explain leadership by focusing on the personal characteristics of famous leaders and how they differed from people who were not leaders. Much of this work assumed that leaders had special personal talents denied ordinary mortals that enabled them to lead groups, organizations, and nations. The great person theory not only influenced organizational scholars but also seemed to animate scholarly histories, as well as folklore, that told the stories of famous national leaders from Alexander the Great to Nelson Mandela.

Eventually, trait theory would cause scholars to focus on what leaders actually did, prompting the development of a new orientation that concentrated on leadership style. Further study led to the realization that the ability of a person to lead effectively depended on the circumstances in which that person was called to lead since a person with admirable theoretical leadership traits might succeed in one situation while failing in another. In short, the ability to lead was contingent on circumstances. Thus, scholars looked for the explanation of leadership in the situations that give rise to effective leadership, and less to the personal traits or the styles of the leaders concerned.[2] A person who is an effective leader in one situation, for example, as CEO of a multinational corporation, could prove to be a disaster in another, say as president of a university.

---

[2] William A. Welsh, *Leaders and Elites* (New York: Holt Rinehart and Winston, 1979).

More recent scholarship has sought to explain leadership in terms of the relationships that exist between leaders and their followers. For example, in his seminal study *Leadership*, the eminent historian James MacGregor Burns relied on a relational theory of leadership in drawing a fundamental distinction between *transactional leadership*, which focused on leading others by mediating among their competing interests, and *transformational leadership*, which leads people by changing their attitudes and beliefs.[3] This multiplicity of explanations and definitions of leadership has only served to complicate the search for its essence. But while fashions of studying and interpreting leadership have changed over time, no one has yet seriously suggested that leadership study be abandoned as alchemy finally was.[4]

The word "leadership" expresses a complex and at the same time flexible concept that has allowed scholars and practitioners to define it in many ways. The English word "leader" is derived from the old English *laedan*, which meant to show the way, to be ahead of—a word that conjured up images of shepherds walking in front of their flocks in order to lead them to a particular destination. It also implies the notion of sheep willingly following a shepherd. In this respect it is therefore to be distinguished from the idea of driving a herd of cattle from the rear by using force. Leadership also suggests the action of showing the way, of moving a group of people willingly toward an objective. Many languages, including French and Spanish, have no precise equivalent for the English words "leader" or "leadership." As a result, the English words for these terms have found their way into those languages. So French books and articles on politics and management often refer to "*le leader*," and French libraries have titles like "Comment Trouver Le Leader en Vous" ("How to Find the Leader in You") and "Le Leader de Demain" ("The Leader of Tomorrow"). In Spanish, the word *el líder*, which seems to have supplanted the more indigenous "*jefe*," is also derived from English.

Leadership implies the existence of followers. To be a leader you need people who will follow you. One person alone on a desert island could never be a leader. The arrival on that island of another survivor from a shipwreck creates the potential for leadership. Not only does leadership

---

[3] James MacGregor Burns, *Leadership* (New York: HarperCollins, 1978).

[4] For brief histories of leadership scholarship, see Lee G. Bolman and Terrence E. Deal, *Reframing Organizations—Artistry, Choice, and Leadership*, 5th ed. (San Francisco: Jossey-Bass, 2013), pp. 337–369; Deanne den Hartog, "A Serious Topic for the Social Sciences," *European Business Forum* (Summer 2003), p. 7; and Robert Goffee and Gareth Jones, "Why Should Anyone Be Led By You?" *Harvard Business Review* (September–October 2000), pp. 63, 64.

require the presence of others, it also requires that they are willing to follow the leader in an indicated direction.

Leadership, as we understand it today, is of course much more than merely showing the way. It also implies the ability to persuade or cause people to whom the way is shown to actually move willingly in that direction. History is filled with prophets who have tried to show the way but have failed to move their potential flocks. We may revere their wisdom today and lament the ignorance of those who rejected them, but we cannot say they were leaders. They were not leaders precisely because no one would follow them. To be a leader, you must have the ability to cause other people to move in the direction that you want them to go. Leadership is not accidental, but a willed, deliberate activity. The test of leadership is followership.

For the purposes of this book, I define leadership as "the ability through communication to cause individuals to act willingly in a desired way to advance the interests of a group or organization." The precise action desired of followers and the needed acts of leadership to achieve that action will vary according to the situation and the circumstances.

My own experience with leadership and my observations of leaders in action have led me to conclude that the essence of leadership is not a quality at all. It is a relationship—a relationship between the leader and the people led (the followers). It is the existence of that relationship that causes people to act in ways indicated by the leader as being beneficial to the group to which they all belong. The basis of any relationship is some perceived connection that exists between leader and follower. The nature of that connection varies with time and circumstance. It may be psychological, economic, political or cultural. Thus, in the 2016 US presidential election, Donald Trump, despite his wealth and privileged background, succeeded in building that connection by convincing millions of people that he was one of them, that he understood their lives and aspirations, and that therefore they should follow him and elect him president of the United States. Whatever its basis, leaders work hard at creating that connection because they know that effective leadership depends on it. Whether a leader in Burns' terminology is transactional or transformative, underlying the ability to lead is the existence of a relationship—a connection—with the people to be led. As will be seen throughout the book, one of the basic tools used by leaders to forge relationships with followers is negotiation.

Relationships enable leadership because they often contain two vital forces that move people: trust and self-interest. The relationship between leader and follower often tends to create trust in the leader. Trust, as we shall see, is essential to leadership. People do not follow individuals whom they do not trust, and a person cannot develop trust in another individual without believing that they know that person. Taking action to follow any leader always involves risk, uncertainty, and vulnerability, whether that action is a corporate restructuring, the invasion of a foreign country, or merely a decision to hire an politically controversial professor at a university. Having trust in the leader allows followers to accept proposed action more readily than if no trust existed because trust in the leader has the effect of reducing their followers' perceived risk and uncertainty in the proposed course of action. People believe that a trusted leader will protect their interests.

In addition to trust, self-interest arising out of relationships can also facilitate leadership. Many relationships entail an expected flow of mutual benefits, tangible and intangible, between leader and follower. A person's desire to receive that flow of benefits in the future becomes a powerful incentive to accept the leadership of another individual. Political leaders have traditionally used this dimension of their relationship with intended followers to secure support for their actions. For example, Donald Trump's strength as a leader in the 2016 election was that his followers ardently believed that he would make their lives better. And Lyndon Johnson's mastery as majority leader of the U.S. Senate in the 1950s was due in part to his reputation of rewarding senators who supported him and punishing those who did not.[5]

One must not, however, exaggerate the metaphor of the shepherd and sheep in analyzing the relationship between leaders and followers. Followers are, after all, complex human beings, each with their own perspectives, interests, ambitions, and wills. As a result, the intensity of their willingness to follow a particular person will display a broad spectrum of variations from active loyalty to passive acceptance, from unquestioning idealism to skeptical pragmatism. Moreover, particular followers may support a leader on specific issues but intensively object to his or her positions on others.[6] For example, certain New York bankers may have wholeheartedly approved of President Reagan's free market economic policies but condemned his social policies on gay rights and abortion. All leaders should also remember that followers' loyalties are capable of sudden abrupt change, depending on how followers evaluate changing circumstances and their own personal interests. Thus, the British loyally followed Winston Churchill throughout the hardships of

---

[5] Joseph Caro, *Master of the Senate: The Years of Lyndon Johnson* (New York: Vintage, 1991).
[6] Joseph S. Nye Jr., *The Powers to Lead* (Oxford: Oxford University Press, 2008), p. 34.

World War II, but once the war appeared to have been won they immediately voted him out of office by choosing another leader and another party that would bring them the economic benefits of the welfare state after years of sacrifice caused by the war effort.

Different leaders use different methods to create a relationship with the people they seek to lead. Some rely on their personal dynamism and charisma. Others use effective strategies and techniques of persuasion. Still others employ manipulation and deception. And of course, many leaders create a relationship with their followers through their special ability to articulate compelling visions, grand designs, or glowing future visions in which their followers would share.

Leaders like Winston Churchill, John F. Kennedy, and Martin Luther King created relationships with millions of people through their speeches and public appearances. Churchill successfully rallied an attacked and wounded British people to meet the Nazi threat in World War II. Kennedy, with those ringing words, "Ask not what your country can do for you; ask what you can do for your country," moved a whole generation of young Americans to commit themselves to the Peace Corps and government service. King, by declaring his dream to millions of people gathered in Washington, D. C. and around their television sets throughout the United States, mobilized an entire nation in the cause of civil rights. The followers of these three dynamic leaders were moved to act as they did because of the relationship—the connection—that they felt with an aging British politician, a young American president, and a courageous African-American minister. How did these three men create relationships? They did it through communication. Churchill, Kennedy, and King created relationships with their followers through their extraordinary communication skills. Communication is fundamental to building relationships and therefore to the ability to lead. Indeed, leadership could not exist without communication.

Leaders communicate with their followers in many ways, but one can basically divide leadership communications into two types: mass produced and tailor made. Mass-produced communications like speeches at conventions, television appearances, and tweets, are designed to reach and move large numbers of people at one time. Tailor-made communications, like those that happen in private meetings and telephone conversations, are shaped and directed at influencing specific individuals. In addition to making eloquent speeches, Churchill, Kennedy, and King had to engage in thousands of tailor-made communications in order to achieve their leadership goals. And many leaders with unremarkable oratorical skills have nonetheless been highly effective at one-on-one communications with their followers.

For example, while Lyndon Johnson, who followed Kennedy in the US presidency, was not a great orator, he was a master of the one-on-one encounter– a mastery that led directly to his major achievements, including his dominance and transformation of the U.S. Senate and later, as president, to the passage of Medicare and the Civil Rights Act of 1964.

Defining Negotiation

The word "negotiation" usually conjures up images of high-stakes international diplomacy or multimillion-dollar business deals. But if you've ever haggled with a teenager who wants to use the family car, argued with your partner over where to go on vacation, or tried to figure out who will pick up the kids from school, you've negotiated. The English word "negotiation" is derived from two Latin roots, *neg* and *otium*, which together literally mean "not leisure." For most people, a negotiation is anything but a leisure activity. They usually see it as a time of stress, tension, and anxiety. People engage in a negotiation because they have decided that they can improve their situations in some way through an agreement, whether that agreement is a peace treaty between countries, a strategic joint venture between companies, or a contract with a dealer to buy a new car. Achieving an improvement in the situation necessitates desired actions from the other side. The cause of the stress, tension, and anxiety for a negotiator is the fear that he or she will not be able to persuade the other side to make an agreement on desired terms and that in the end, after much effort, the situation will not be improved and may in fact be worse than before the negotiations started.

The context in which a negotiation happens certainly affects both the way the negotiation is conducted and the results achieved by the parties. Negotiations among warlords at the end of a civil war and those between corporations over a merger may seem on the surface to have nothing to do with one another, let alone with the deals and agreements you negotiate every day with partners, children, business associates, clients, customers, and trades people. Yet an examination of the dynamics of those very different types of interactions reveals that participants rely on similar approaches and techniques to achieve their goals. So, whether you are sitting at a polished conference table in London, trying to secure a loan from a group of bankers, or at your kitchen table, seeking to convince your kids to give more attention to their school work, there are common principles, strategies, and tactics on which you can rely to make the deals and build the productive relationships that you need. Thus regardless of the context in which it takes place, negotiation may be defined as *a process of communication by which two or more people seek to advance their individual interests by agreeing on a desired course of action.*

Negotiation and Leadership: A Definitional Comparison

I have defined leadership as "the ability through communication to cause individuals to act willingly in a desired way to advance the interests of a group or organization" and negotiation as "a process of communication by which two or more people seek to advance their individual interests by agreeing on a desired course of action." After engaging in this definitional exercise, one may well ask: What do these two concepts have in common? Superficially, the two processes both have at least five common elements. First, both rely fundamentally on **communication** between two or more people. Neither leadership nor negotiation can take place without communication. Second, both are driven by a desire to advance someone's **interests**—often, but not always, group interests in the case of leadership and individual interests in the case of negotiation. What is an "interest"? It's what a person or group cares about; it's what people consider important to attain their goals. Within the realm of diplomacy, the importance of interests is underscored by the often quoted view that "nations don't have friends, they have interests." Like nations, individuals also pursue their interests, although for some people friendship is an important interest in itself. Individuals, organizations, and nations negotiate to secure desired benefits or advantages from other individuals, organizations, and nations, so as to be in a better place than before negotiations began. On the other hand, whenever an improvement in your situation is impossible, the option of negotiation becomes pointless. At that point, you are therefore usually faced with two difficult choices: either abandon the negotiation or find another negotiator. Whenever a leader fails to advance the interests of the group, the group has the choice of changing leadership or in extreme cases disbanding the group.

While both leaders and negotiators pursue interests that they think are important, the pursuit of that goal is vastly complicated by differing, indeed conflicting, interests of people on the other side of the bargaining table or within the organizations they seek to lead. Effective leaders and negotiators must know how to understand and manage that diversity of interests in ways that allow the organization to achieve its purposes and desired deals to be made.

A third common element is that both leadership and negotiation seek to induce some sort of **action** by other people, to bring about a change in human behavior in a particular area. For negotiators, just reaching an agreement, that is, simply "getting to yes," is not their real goal. Similarly, for leaders, approval by their followers is not the ultimate goal, but only an intermediate step. For both negotiators and leaders, the real goal is to secure desired action by the parties on the other side of the negotiating table and by the people they seek to lead.

Fourth, practitioners and scholars of leadership and negotiation view both activities as a **process**, a progressive series of actions that culminate in a particular, desired end. That conceptual framework causes both practitioners and scholars of the two processes to employ similar methods of inquiry and address similar questions. For example, as will be seen, both are concerned about strategies and tactics as they go about their work.

Fifth and finally, questions of **power** are deeply imbedded in the way scholars and practitioners think about both negotiation and leadership. Indeed, for many people the ability to lead and the ability to make deals is intimately connected to the leader's or the negotiator's access to power. Power is a key element in leading people and in making deals. Effective leadership and successful negotiation requires the skillful application of power. Both leaders and negotiators need to understand its uses and it limits, its sources, and its mechanisms.

So what is power, anyway? In essence, power is the means by which an individual, an organization, or nation attains a desired end in its relations with other individuals, organizations, and nations. While many people consider power to refer to the physical resources—the size of the army, the amount of wealth, the extent of land occupied—that an individual, organization, or nation commands, an emphasis on physical resources distorts and limits the nature of power in leading a group or in negotiating a deal.

The goal of both negotiation and leadership is to persuade other people to agree to and support an action that the negotiator or leader is seeking. From this perspective, power means the ability to influence or move the decisions of other people in a desired way, whether those other people are negotiators on the other side of the bargaining table or followers in a particular group, whether the subject is a joint venture contract with another company or a decision to go to war against another country. In some situations, a party's physical resources, such as its military, its wealth, or its organization, may indeed influence that decision. But in other cases, less tangible factors, such as an original idea, a strong relationship, or a reputation for honesty may also be sources of influence and therefore power at the negotiating table or in leading groups. For example, U.S. President George H. W. Bush, as a result of significant experience in international affairs as vice president, head of the CIA, and US ambassador to the United Nations and to China, had developed strong relations with the world's leaders and was able to mobilize those relations effectively to persuade them to join the US-led military coalition to drive Iraq out of Kuwait during the 1991 Gulf War. On the other hand, his son, who did not have similar experience and relationships was considerably less successful in negotiating an international coalition to invade Iraq in 2003.

Leading and negotiating thus have at least five elements in common: (1) **communication**, (2) **interests**, (3) **action**, (4) **process** and (5) **power**. They are the common tools and preoccupations of both leaders and negotiators and are therefore important concepts in exploring the links between negotiation and leadership.

Negotiating the Three Phases of the Leadership Lifecycle

Every individual's leadership has a lifecycle that passes through three phases: birth, life, and ultimately death. In each phase, negotiation is fundamental. The basic premise of this book is that leaders will do their jobs more effectively by using negotiations to achieve their goals. In short, they need to negotiate leadership. More specifically, they must negotiate to carry out each phase in a leadership's lifecycle.

The first phase, **leadership attainment**, concerns the use of negotiation to attain leadership. While books about leadership focus on what leaders do, they often do not treat the process by which individuals become leaders. In Part I: Leadership Acquisition: Negotiating the Road to Leadership, this book will examine that process in a variety of situations to see how and to what extent the effective use of negotiation allows a person to achieve both the "leadership deal" and the leadership role that are necessary to give that person the power to lead.

Part II: Leadership Action: Negotiating the Leadership Road, explores the various ways that leaders use negotiation to further the interests of the organizations and people they lead, as well as their own. In order to lead an organization, you must first understand what a particular organization needs and wants. The diversity of organizational forms and cultures requires people contemplating a leadership position to make a demand-side analysis by asking a fundamental question: What does this organization need? Too often, leaders and books on leadership take a supply-side approach to leadership by emphasizing what a specific individual can do or did do for the organization. This book will take a demand-side approach to the subject by asking what groups and organizations need and how their leaders can provide those things. Accordingly, it identifies seven daily tasks of leadership that all leaders must carry out and explains how the skills of negotiation enable the effective exercise of those leadership tasks.

A leader's position is never permanent. No matter the circumstances in which leadership is exercised, it is always subject to a variety of challenges and threats. Sometimes a leader is able to withstand the threats and challenges for a time; in other instances, he or she is unable to do so and must yield the powers of leadership to another person willingly or only after severe struggle. In either case, the challenged leader will invariably employ negotiation techniques and strategies to hold on to a leadership position or, when that is not possible, exit leadership under the most advantageous conditions possible. Part III of the book, Leadership Preservation and Loss: Staying on the Leadership Road examines this, the third dimension of negotiating leadership.

In considering the role of negotiation in leadership, this book will therefore examine its use in the three phases of the leadership life cycle: (1) *leadership acquisition*, the processes by which a person gains leadership of an organization or group; (2) *leadership exercise*, the ways in which leaders use negotiation to do their jobs; and (3) *leadership preservation and loss*, how leaders use negotiation to preserve their power and, when necessary, yield it. These three dimensions form the basic structure of this book, which devotes a separate part to each of the three. Let's begin with negotiating leadership acquisition.

Part I

Leadership Acquisition: Negotiating the Roads to Leadership

2

Negotiating Leadership Positions

The Dual Roads to Leadership

How do you become a leader? What road do you need to follow to get to leadership? If you do decide to make the trip, where do you start the journey? And what about organizations seeking leadership? What road should they follow to obtain the leadership that they need? What is the best way of making that journey? What are the potential pitfalls and traps along the way? For both people seeking to be leaders and for organization that want leadership, the ultimate goal is to negotiate a leadership deal that will meet their respective interests. In reality, however, the two sides must negotiate two deals, not just one. The first is a negotiation that secures the leadership *position* for a particular person; the second concerns the specific leadership *role* that the person selected will play in the organization. Both deals have to be struck if the organization is to obtain the effective leadership it seeks and the chosen leader is to be empowered to lead effectively.

Leadership is not just a *position*, not merely a place on an organization chart. Leadership is also a *role*, a set of functions that a leader is expected to fulfill to facilitate the operation of that organization. More generally, leadership is a social *role*, a set of behaviors that an individual is expected to carry out in a particular group or organization. The difference between your position as a leader and your role as a leader is important to understand. Your position refers to your place in an organization or group and the legal and theoretical powers, rights, and privileges to which you are entitled in that organization or group. Your role concerns what you actually do in and for the

© The Author(s) 2017
J.W. Salacuse, *Real Leaders Negotiate!*,
DOI 10.1057/978-1-137-59115-9_2

organization. The first is the product of your negotiation with those who have the authority to hire you, to grant you a leadership position. The second is also the product of negotiations, often a much more complex and lengthy negotiation that must continually go on between you as leader and the people you are supposed to lead. To travel the road to leadership successfully, to actually lead an organization in the way you think best, you need to succeed at both of these negotiations. Inexperienced leadership candidates tend to focus their negotiating efforts on and give high priority to the first, but sometimes neglect and even overlook the second—an error that can eventually put their leadership in jeopardy.

This chapter will consider the processes of negotiating leadership positions; the next will examine the equally important challenges of negotiating leadership roles. Let me begin that exploration by sharing my own experience in starting out on the road to leadership because it illustrates many common issues that arise in negotiating a leadership position.

Negotiating a Leadership Deal in Texas

My own road to leadership was not the product of a grand design or carefully made plan. In retrospect, it seems more like an accident than a deliberate journey. It began in the late 1970s when I returned to the United States with a wife and two small children but no definite job prospects after spending nine years working in Africa and the Middle East on a series of Ford Foundation development projects aimed at strengthening the region's legal systems. For the last three years of that stint, I was the Foundation's representative in Sudan.

I spent the first year of my return to the United States as a visiting scholar at Harvard Law School writing a study of Arab capital institutions and looking for a permanent job. Having taught law in connection with my Ford Foundation assignments, as well as a Peace Corps volunteer at a new law school in Nigeria in the mid-1960s, I decided to try teaching at an American law school. After several months' effort, I managed to secure a one-year appointment as a visiting professor at Southern Methodist University (SMU) Law School in Dallas, Texas. When I signed on at SMU, the dean, Charles Galvin, made clear that the school could not assure me a teaching position beyond that one year since I would simply be filling in for another professor who was on leave. After that year, my future appeared very uncertain.

About a week before I arrived in Dallas in June of 1978, Galvin announced his resignation after 15 years as the School's dean. I therefore started teaching at SMU as the school began organizing a search for a new dean and creating a "dean search committee" consisting largely of faculty members to conduct the search, a leadership ritual that I would observe and participate in at other institutions during the next three decades. The job of the committee was to identify and evaluate candidates for the deanship and recommend at least two of the most appropriate to the University's president, James Zumberg, who would appoint one to the position.

The first SMU faculty meeting I attended was devoted to deciding on the membership of the search committee and the appointment of its chair. As I listened to the discussion, it became clear that the faculty considered those decisions very important in selecting their new leader and that their divergent visions for and interests in the school led to strong differences on who should serve on the committee and who should lead it. They understood that the members of the dean search committee could influence the president's choice of the next dean either positively or negatively, not only for the future of the school but also for their own individual interests as faculty members. It was also clear that as a visiting professor, a virtual outsider with little possibility of continuing as a faculty member, my participation in that decision was neither wanted nor needed. So I listened to the discussion in silence and abstained from voting on matters relating to the search.

As the year progressed, a parade of dean candidates from other universities visited the school. Based on my non-existent experience of selecting deans, I found none very impressive. Apparently, neither did the search committee since the entire year passed without a recommendation from the committee as to who the University's president should appoint. On the other hand, the good news, as far as I was concerned, was that in the Spring of 1979 the school offered me a three-year contract as a professor and at the same time promised to consider me for appointment as a permanent tenured faculty member. At last, I had prospects of long-term employment.

One morning in the late fall of the next academic year, as the dean search continued to crank on with no visible results but with my teaching and research program in high gear and the process of my tenure appointment apparently proceeding very smoothly, a group of four faculty colleagues, two or three of whom were on the search committee, arrived at my office unannounced. As soon as the door was closed, one of them said, "We think you might make a good dean. Would you be interested in talking to the search committee?"

The question prompted three nearly simultaneous emotions in me: surprise, ambition, and caution. I was first of all surprised. I had never before thought about becoming a dean of this school or any other. Although I had been involved with other law schools in various capacities, I had never considered the possibility of leading one. At the same time, the suggestion from a group of respected colleagues that I could be dean somehow ignited an ambition in me that I never knew I had. Becoming dean of SMU Law School suddenly became an exciting possibility, a captivating challenge that, on the basis of no information whatsoever and with virtually no reflection, I felt I could meet. And finally, having learned something about academic politics at other places, I was cautious that my ambition to become dean not provoke any opponents to obstruct a favorable decision on my tenure as a professor as a way to prevent me from reaching the deanship. It is well to remember when you seek the leadership of any group or institution, you are also likely to encounter opposition that you never suspected existed for reasons you may never have guessed. As a result, when you set out on the road to leadership, you need to think about strategies for dealing with roadblocks and obstacles.

When I asked the group in my office why they thought I was capable of being dean, they pointed to my experience in managing Ford Foundation programs and also to the fact that they knew me and that I had established good relationships with most of the faculty in the year I had been at SMU. While their answer was flattering, it was hardly convincing. None of the factors they mentioned seemed, from a purely objective point of view, compelling reasons to appoint someone who had never taught at, let alone led, an American law school to head a large, complex institution like SMU Law School. Although I didn't realize it at the time, what I had been doing during my first year at the school was developing the basic elements of what every leader needs—a coalition of supporters.

Nonetheless, I did meet with the search committee, agreed to be a candidate for the deanship, and then over the next few months engaged in a series of meetings with faculty, students, alumni, and other university administrators—and so took my first steps on a road to leadership. The meetings consisted largely of answering the questions they asked. The purpose of their questions, I soon realized, was not just to gather information about me and my background, but also to send me messages about how I ought to lead the law school if I were chosen dean. Here is an example: *Question*: "Do you think you will like fund-raising?" *Message*: "Fund raising is an important part of a dean's job. We expect you to raise lots of money for the School." *Answer*: "I think I'll like fund raising if I am successful at doing it."

From that experience and others in the years to come, I learned that, just as in any other negotiation, as you negotiate the road to leadership, it is very important to listen hard for the messages embedded in the questions asked by people involved in the process and to try to discern the unexpressed interests that prompted the questions and the expectations embedded in them.

Eventually, in the spring of 1980 the dean search committee formally recommended two names to the president to consider for appointment as dean of the law school—mine and Kenneth Penegar, then dean of the University of Tennessee Law School with 10 years' experience in the job. Faced with deciding between a seasoned and successful American law school dean and an inexperienced novice with a dubious background in Africa and the Middle East, a candidate who had never taught at let alone *led* a US law school, President Zumberg made the obvious choice: he offered the leadership of SMU Law School to Penegar. The two men then began negotiating a leadership deal.

As negotiations between them progressed, it became clear that Penegar, for family reasons, could not assume the dean's position until the fall of 1981, which would mean that the law school would have been without a dean for three years. The SMU president decided that to leave the school with no leadership for that length of time was unacceptable and he therefore ended discussions with Penegar and began negotiation on a leadership deal with me in late April 1980.

In undertaking any negotiation, it is important to develop as part of your preparation good alternatives to the deal you are trying to make, especially what some negotiation scholars refer to as a "Best Alternative to a Negotiated Agreement" (BATNA)[1] and others call a "no-deal alternative."[2] Developing a good BATNA has several benefits. First, it gives you a standard against which to measure any proposal that the other side puts forward. Obviously, you do not want to accept any option at the negotiating table that is worse than what you can obtain elsewhere. Second, knowing your best alternative to the transaction will often help build your confidence and bargaining power at the negotiating table. Sometimes it may be possible to improve

---

[1] Roger Fisher, William Ury, and Bruce Patton, *Getting to YES: Negotiating Agreements without Giving In*, 2nd ed. (New York: Penguin, 1991).

[2] David A. Lax and James K. Sebenius, *3D Negotiation: Powerful Tools to Change the Game in Your Most Important Deals* (Boston, MA: Harvard Business School Press, 2006), pp. 85–97.

your best alternative to the deal thereby increasing your confidence and negotiating power even more. Indeed, the power that negotiators feel at the negotiating table is often directly proportional to how good they judge their BATNA to be. Third, if your alternative is particularly good, you may want to let the other side know it in the hopes that it will persuade them to make a deal with you. It was for all of those reasons that President Zumberg had insisted that the SMU dean search committee give him at least two candidates from which to choose. As things turned out, I was Zumberg's BATNA. As he evaluated the choice between Penegar's offer on the negotiating table, which meant giving the school an experienced dean but having to wait nearly another a year and a half for that to happen, and appointing a novice who could take over the school's leadership immediately, he decided to go with his BATNA.

The Leadership Deal Negotiation Agenda

In negotiating a leadership position as an aspiring leader, you need to be sure that the negotiation agenda addresses at least two basic sets of issues: (1) issues that relate to your compensation and benefits and (2) issues concerning your specific powers, responsibilities, and resources to do the job. Many newly minted leaders, thrilled by the prospect getting the job they want and the related benefits, naively rely on the "job descriptions" and recruiting ads and information provided by the organization and devote all their negotiating efforts to the first set of issues but forget about the second. Once well into the job, they often come to regret their failure when they realize that their leadership position does not automatically bring with it the resources and the powers needed to accomplish their leadership goals. So if you are about to be appointed CEO of a corporation, you need to negotiate with the board of directors not only your salary and other perks but also your anticipated powers to make changes in the corporate organization and personnel, including the right to fire vice presidents obstructing your efforts at change. If a university president is prepared to name you a dean of one of its schools, you certainly will want to nail down in advance the size of the school's budget for the next few years and your powers to remove academic and administrative dead wood before you accept the job.

Experienced negotiators know that timing is a key to successful deal making. In negotiating your way to leadership, the time to engage in negotiations about your leadership powers and resources is when you are chosen for the leadership job because you will probably never again have as much leverage with the board of directors, the university president, or other appointing authority than you have then. Having expended considerable effort and money on searching for and finding a leader that will meet their organization's needs, they have a strong incentive to close the deal so that they can get back to their other activities and concerns, and the institution for which they are responsible can once again proceed under a stable leadership. In both my own leadership deal negotiations, at SMU and Tufts University, I used the process to advance issues that I believed would be important to my success as dean. At SMU, I was able to increase the law school budget in important ways and six years later at Tufts University to assure deanship control over fundraising as it affected the Fletcher School.

To conduct those negotiations successfully, a newly selected leader needs to do significant research about the specific problems facing the organization that he or she will lead. To prepare for my own negotiation with President Zumberg, I delved deeply into the financial condition of the school, spent hours meeting with the school's financial officer, and carefully read the law school's last accreditation report prepared by a team sent by the American Bar Association (ABA) and the Association of American Law Schools (AALS). The report strongly criticized the university for not giving its law school sufficient funds to hire new faculty and maintain its library at a satisfactory level. I would rely heavily on that report to persuade Zumberg to increase the school's budget for faculty salaries and library acquisitions, reminding him that the next ABA/AALS accreditation was just three years away and that I would have the responsibility for navigating the school through that process successfully. We finally reached agreement on additional money for the school, so I accepted the job as dean in late May 1980.

You should also reduce such agreements to writing since the people who appointed you a leader may no longer be in a position of authority later on when you need to claim the benefits of your leadership deal. A signed written document will be more compelling to that person's successor than your bland oral assertions that you and the former president or board chairman had made a deal. In my case, one month after I took over as dean of SMU law school, James Zumberg, the person who appointed me, moved to the west coast to assume the presidency of the University of Southern California. In my budget negotiations with the provost and acting president the following year, I used my written agreement with Zumberg on more than one occasion to support my demands.

The Nature of Leadership Positions

The position of leader of a group or organization may be either formal or informal. Most established institutions, like corporations, government departments, and nonprofit agencies, have formally constituted leadership positions with titles and more or less well defined powers and responsibilities, as well as specific procedures for identifying and appointing people to hold those jobs. Laws, regulations, and internal organizational documents usually structure these matters in some detail.

On the other hand, in many settings, people without a formal leadership position may nonetheless exercise leadership powers in the sense of having "the ability through communication to cause individuals to act willingly in a desired way to advance the interests of a group or organization." They gain this power to lead not from formal documents, rules, or regulations but from the relationships that they have developed with people in those organizations. Thus, in a corporation, a senior executive with long experience in the company, specialized knowledge, or important relationships with special constituents, like controlling shareholders, may have more leadership influence with the board of directors on certain issues than the company's CEO. Similarly, a high-profile lawyer with close ties to important clients may have more leadership influence within a law firm than the firm's managing partner. And an army officer with command over key military units may have more influence over a junta's actions than its titular leader, a situation that prevailed in 1952 in Egypt when the "free officers" overthrew King Farouk and seized power under the titular leadership of General Muhammed Naguib while Colonel Gamal Abdel Nasser, later to become Egypt's president and a dominant figure in the Arab world for nearly 20 years, was the group's effective leader.

Negotiating the Leadership Position

There is no single road to leadership, no unique formula that you have to follow to become a leader. Indeed, it is probably safe to say that each leader follows a unique, singular road to gain a leadership position and that each institution searching for leadership engages in its own particular process. For example, my road as an "inside candidate" at Southern Methodist University without deanship experience was different from the road I had to take six years later as an "outside candidate" to become dean of the Fletcher School of Law and Diplomacy at Tufts University, a graduate school of international relations. Similarly, the two universities traveled different roads to find the leaders they were looking for in each case.

The various ways of gaining the power to lead seem endless. Some people, like the Egyptian colonels in 1952, seize leadership suddenly by force. Others, like King George VI, who unwillingly replaced his brother, King Edward VII, on the English throne when the latter abdicated to marry Wallace Simpson, have leadership thrust upon them. Still others, perhaps the majority, responding to their more or less strong personal ambitions, may gain leadership through a more or less careful plan, often involving the need to conduct an arduous campaign to gain the leadership position they desire. In all cases, regardless of a person's talents and determination, circumstances play an important role in allowing a person to successfully travel the road to leadership. Lyndon Johnson, a man of overwhelming personal ambition, steadfastly and single mindedly pursued political power throughout his life as he rose from poverty in the Texas Hill country to the White House.[3] But without the tragic assassination of President John F. Kennedy, Vice President Johnson would almost certainly never have gained the presidency in 1963. In my own case, the sudden resignation of my predecessor, the inability of the search committee to decide quickly on a replacement, and the unwillingness of the president's first choice for the job to assume responsibilities immediately were all important circumstances that enabled me to become dean at SMU.

Despite the endless variations in the roads taken, aspiring leaders hope that at the end the road chosen is a "leadership deal," an agreement between a potential leader and people having the authority to select him or her as leader. It is that deal that in the first instance gives the person chosen the power to lead. Like any other deal, the parties concerned must negotiate it either explicitly or implicitly. That agreement may be embodied in an elaborate written employment contract, for example, if you are chosen to head a multinational corporation, or tacit understanding as when you accept your neighbors' invitation to chair a community a task force to plan a town recreation area. In all cases, negotiation is fundamental to the process. No leader is magically anointed to assume a position of leadership. Leaders have to negotiate to gain their positions in groups, institutions and nations.

Formally, organizations and groups usually decide on a leader in one of two ways: by election or by appointment. In both cases, they have to

---

[3] See Robert Caro, *The Years of Lyndon Johnson: The Path to Power,* (New York: Alfred A. Knopf, 1982).

engage in a welter of negotiations in order to make that decision. The selection process is not as automatic as their constitutions and other governing documents might lead one to believe. For example, when a leader is elected by popular vote, the winning candidate will have conducted countless negotiations with various interest groups, from labor unions to religious organizations, in order to win their votes. Barak Obama, to be elected as the first African-American US president, had to negotiate a nation-wide coalition of minority groups, the young, and labor in order to win elections in both 2008 and 2012. Similarly, in parliamentary systems of government, like those of the United Kingdom, Israel, and many other countries, if no single political party is able to elect a majority of the members of parliament and thereby gain the authority to form a government, leaders of the dominant political party must negotiate a governing coalition with other parties so as to attain a necessary majority to govern and enable its own leader to assume the position of prime minister. Coalition building is a vital skill for both successfully traveling the road to leadership and, as we shall see, carrying out a leader's many tasks.

Many important leadership jobs are not decided by election but instead by appointment of a governing board, inner elite, or other group with authority to decide. In order to arrive at a decision on a leader and to make a leadership deal, the members of that governing board or committee will have engaged in a series of intense negotiations of four basic types: (1) among themselves, (2) with the institutions and groups to whom they are responsible, (3) with important interest groups, and (4) with potential leadership candidates. For example, in the search for a corporate CEO, university president, director-general of an international organization, or as in my case a law school dean, the members of the committee or group charged with finding a leader will negotiate among themselves to reach agreement on the type of leader needed by their organization and the specific candidates who meets their requirements, with the board of directors or other governing body on their recommendations, with interested parties such as senior executives and external constituents, and finally with the chosen candidate on the terms of his or her appointment. Many organizations seek outside assistance in that process from executive search firms and management consultants. While these organizations may provide valuable assistance in identifying and evaluating leadership candidates, their presence also introduces the prospect of additional negotiations and therefore heightened complexity in traveling the road to leadership.

The Drivers of Leadership Deal Negotiations

Like any negotiation, the negotiation of leadership deals is driven by the interests of the concerned participants: that is, the groups or organizations trying to find a leader and the people seeking to become their leaders. The participants in those negotiations have decided to engage in discussions because they believe that an agreement on a particular leader will advance their respective interests. To understand the process of negotiating leadership, one therefore must first understand the interests at stake, the interests that drive these negotiations. Let's look first at the nature of the organization's interests in seeking a leader and then consider the interests of people aspiring to leadership positions.

Organizational Needs for Leadership

Despite utopian speculation about the wonders of "leaderless organizations," few groups actually take the idea seriously and in fact no organization of any significance seems to be able to exist without a leader for any appreciable length of time. Leadership is the indispensable ingredient for effective organizational action. The founding documents of all nations and organizations formally recognize that fact by requiring the designation of a leader endowed with an array of powers. Informal leadership can also be seen in groups created to achieve a particular goal, like suburban neighbors in the United States who meet to pressure their town council to build a new park or farmers in a developing country who unite to demand that the government repair the local irrigation system. Although such groups may begin with no formal leader, inevitably, if the group is to achieve its goals, a leader emerges. That person may not have a leadership title but he or she will exercise leadership functions with the group's agreement. A group's failure to agree on a leader usually means that it cannot take effective action and will eventually disintegrate, just as the leaderless "Occupy Wall Street" movement did in 2011. Indeed, one important conclusion that may be drawn from such experiences is that leadership is the indispensable ingredient for effective group action and that without leadership the group will not only fail to achieve its objectives but may eventually disappear from the scene. As a result, the longer an institution is without a leader, the more pressure is felt by those responsible for finding a leader to fill the position as soon as possible.

The members of all organizations, large and small, formal and informal, usually believe that the group cannot achieve its goals effectively without a leader to guide its activities. Thus whenever a leadership position is unoccupied or about to become vacant because of death, resignation, or impending elections, groups, institutions, and nations expend considerable resources in seeking to find and designate another person to fill that role. Moreover, they often commit considerable resources in planning for the eventuality of a leader's departure and the arrival of a successor, an exercise usually called "succession planning."

The importance of leadership is seen at all levels of human organization, from international relations among states to community actions among neighbors. For example, although states are legally sovereign and equal, an important theory of international relations holds that that international regimes, which are agreed-upon systems for managing various matters of common concern, such as international trade, climate change, and nuclear nonproliferation, require the existence of a "hegemon," a country that, in the words of two scholars, "is powerful enough to maintain the essential rules governing interstate relations and willing to do so."[4] A hegemon is, of course, a leader. According to this view, often referred to as the theory of hegemonic stability, a regime cannot exist without a hegemon.[5] A hegemon, like any leader, not only maintains the organizational rules in order to preserve the regime for the benefit of its members but also because doing so advances the leader's own interests.

All organizations and social groups, like regimes, have rules that need to be enforced to preserve the organization and allow it to attain its objectives. Those rules may be found not only in written laws, regulations, and internal policy statements but also in a group's unwritten customs and traditions. The aim of those rules is to regulate and control the behavior of the organization's members. Human behavior is fundamentally indeterminate and unpredictable. Without rules and other forms of social restraint, behavior will be driven by individual perceptions of their self-interest. Such individualist behavior, if not regulated and restrained, may impede the attainment of group or organizational goals and objectives. It is the leader's job, whether as a corporate CEO, a social club chair, or an international hegemon, to find ways to cause followers to act in the best interests of the group, one of which

---

[4] Robert O. Keohane and Joseph S. Nye, *Power and Interdependence: World Politics in Transition* 44 (1977).
[5] Robert O. Keohane, *After Hegemony: Cooperation and Discord in the World of Political Economy* 32–39 (1984).

is to respect the organization's rules. A leader therefore is a behavior regulator.

In any negotiation, it is essential for each party to understand precisely the nature of the interests they are trying to satisfy. Groups in search of a leader therefore need to decide on the qualities their leader must have to satisfy those organizational interests. That decision may be shaped by many factors, but three of the most important are: (1) their perceptions of what the organization needs in a leader; (2) their own personal interests in the organization; and (3) their expectations on how a future leader may affect those interests. With respect to the first, groups and organizations searching for a leader should always ask a basic and preliminary question: What does our organization or group in its present state need in a leader? Thus, a wise search committee will often spend time formulating an answer to this question before thinking about specific people to lead them. For example, a corporation that has endured a damaging corruption scandal may give priority to finding a new leader who has a reputation for integrity and the public relations skills to persuade the company's constituents that it has cleaned up its act. On the other hand, a company that believes it is losing its technological advantage may look for a new leader who has the scientific and technological knowledge and experience to rebuild the company's research and development capacity.

The people responsible for selecting a new leader also have their own interests that may influence their choice. For example, corporate directors on a search committee may consciously or unconsciously be influenced in their decision on a new CEO by their belief in the likelihood that a particular candidate will support their continued membership on the company's governing board. Similarly, in the search for a university president, a member of the philosophy department may not only want to advance the interests of the university as a whole but also to secure increased funding for humanities departments. On the other hand, an alumni representative on the same search committee may give priority to finding a president who will build the football team to give the school a national reputation, a quality that the alumnus assumes will increase the value of his university degree. In their meetings with search committees, candidates for leadership roles in such institutions need to understand both sets of interests if they hope to travel the road to leadership successfully and land a leadership position for themselves.

Whatever the selection process used by a group or institution, the choice of anyone to become its leader is always based on the *appearance* that the person chosen has the necessary abilities to do the job. Any decision on a new leader by an organization is of necessity based on appearances, not the realities of the candidate's actual performance in the job. That reality will eventually emerge when a candidate assumes the position of leader. The decision on a new leader is thus always an uncertain prediction, never a certainty, that the person chosen actually has what it takes to lead a particular institution at a specific period in its history. Unfortunately, despite detailed succession plans, elaborate search processes, and the assistance of high-priced executive recruitment firms, that prediction too often proves wrong. According to one estimate, one-third to one-half of new CEOs fail within their first 18 months on the job.[6]

The Interests and Conditions of Leadership Candidates

Candidates for leadership positions may pursue a variety of interests in negotiating a leadership deal, depending on the nature of the leadership position sought and the personal preferences of the individual in question. For some, the primary interests are the material benefits of the job—the high salary, stock options, expense accounts, and chauffeur-driven limousine. For others, the primary attraction is prestige and public recognition attached to leadership. For still others, their interests lie in the opportunity to serve their community, their colleagues, or to effect meaningful change in important institutions or policies.[7]

A candidate's interests alone, however, are not sufficient to allow him or her to engage in a leadership deal negotiation. Regardless of interests, three conditions must also exist simultaneously for that negotiation to take place: (1) **candidate will**; (2) **organizational opportunity**; and (3) **apparent ability**. Let's look at each one individually.

(1) Candidate Will. To become a leader, you must have a desire or at least a willingness to assume a specific leadership position. The will to lead may be a powerful, all-consuming driving force, like that of Lyndon Johnson, who sought political power all his life, or a reluctant acceptance, like that of King

---

[6] Dan Ciampa, "After the Handshake—Succession Doesn't End When a New CEO is Hired," *Harvard Business Review* 61, no. 63 (December 2016).

[7] David C. McClelland and David H. Burnham, "Power is the Great Motivator," *Harvard Business Review* 54, no. 2 (2000): pp. 100–110. Somewhat similarly, McClelland and Burnham, in their study on power identified three motivational groups among managers: (1) those who care about doing something better have a need for achievement; (2) those who value friendly relations with other people have a need for affiliation, and (3) those who care most about having an impact on other people have a need for power.

George VI, who assumed the English crown only when it was thrust upon him. No one can force you to become a leader against your will, but not everyone is ready and willing to accept a leadership position when it is offered. Regardless of the material benefits, many people avoid seeking leadership position for many reasons: for example, because it will divert them from activities that they consider more important, more lucrative, or simply more interesting. For example, shortly after I was appointed dean at SMU Law School, a senior member of the faculty told me that he would never accept the dean's job because he considered it "essentially custodial in nature." Then too, people may avoid certain leadership positions, like those attained through political elections, because they will require significant changes in lifestyle entailing unacceptable personal and family costs. In those situations, as part of the negotiation process, groups charged with finding a leader for their organization may try to overcome a candidate's initial resistance by engaging in a courtship of negotiation, often extending over a long period of time. Usually, the goal of that phase of the negotiation is to convince the candidate that his or her situation as their leader will be better than if that person stays in his or her current position. Sometimes such courtship succeeds in bringing new and effective leadership to the organization, and sometimes it fails. The difference in result often resides in the terms of the leadership deal that you make to land the leader you want.

The strength of your will to lead can affect your chances of becoming a leader. Followers usually seek leaders who want the job. In fact, for people and groups with the power to select a leader, a candidate's degree of "commitment" and "passion" to lead the organization is an important asset that they seek in a new leader. In general, however, that commitment and passion should be primarily to the organization or group that the leader will serve, not to the candidate's own career or personal advancement. Groups and institutions look for leaders who will first of all serve the group, rather than themselves.

(2) Organizational Opportunity. Opportunity, in the context of leadership selection, is a set of circumstances that makes it possible for a person to become a leader of a particular group, institution, or nation. That opportunity arises from the fact that the group concerned believes that it needs a leader. The need for a new leader may be sudden, for example, because of the death by heart attack of a corporate CEO rushing to a meeting or the assassination of a prime minister at a political rally, or foreseen, when a bank president reaches the mandatory retirement age or a state governor's term of office is ending and the date for gubernatorial elections approaches. Most established institutions have rules and "succession plans" to deal with the inevitability of leadership change. And when new organizations and groups form that have never had a leader, one of their first impulses is to find a person to lead them so that someone has responsibility for seeing that important organizational tasks, to be discussed in Part II of this book, necessary to achieve organizational purposes, are in fact accomplished

Leadership opportunity usually ignites leadership ambition. The fact that a leader has passed or is about to pass from the scene will inevitably prompt other people to seek to replace him. Thus, when a prime minister resigns suddenly because he or she has lost the confidence of the parliament or a company CEO announces a decision to retire, potential candidates, who would never have dared challenge them while in office, will suddenly and eagerly emerge to replace them. In my case, the fact that a few senior members of the faculty thought that I might make a good dean was enough to ignite a leadership ambition that I never thought I had.

(3) Apparent Ability. All leadership positions require the person who holds them to carry out certain tasks of leadership. For a person to gain that position, those responsible for designating the leader, whether they are the corporate board of directors or the voters in a gubernatorial state election, must believe that he or she has the abilities to do the job successfully. The selection of a leader is often a competitive process in which two or more people are vying for a leadership position. As a result, a candidate for leadership must not only demonstrate that he or she has the ability to lead but also that his or her abilities are superior to those of other candidates. Candidates for leadership positions may have to engage in negotiations to convince those with the authority to appoint or elect them of their abilities lead.

Ability, for the purposes of choosing a leader, is never a matter of technical competence alone, but also includes that person's goals, values, and intentions—vital matters in leading any organization or group. And in view of the need to build relationships to lead effectively, relationship building may become an important quality for selecting a leader, as it apparently was for the group of colleagues who had come to my office to inquire about my interest in becoming dean.

The selection of a leader is also a prediction about his or her eventual policies and decisions. History is filled with examples of leadership choices by corporate boards, voters, and other leader selectors that have proven to be based on faulty predictions of a leader's abilities. So CEOs are fired when their companies' stock prices fall and they "lose the confidence" of boards that hired them, as was the case of Carly Fiorina at Hewlett Packard, deans are asked to resign when faculties adopt resolutions of no confidence because of prolonged freezes on salary increases, and governors lose re-elections when they fail to convince the voters they have done a good job in office because of severe cuts in public services.

On the other hand, the accuracy of a leadership prediction grows with increased knowledge about the candidate concerned. Thus, candidates who have worked for the organization often provide a more solid basis of predicting their future performance as leaders than do candidates who have not. Angela Merkel, who would rise to become Chancellor in Germany and "the most powerful woman in Europe," began her journey on the road to leadership when, after the reunification of Germany, she offered to help out in the offices of the Christian Democratic Party, which she would eventually dominate. By demonstrating her abilities through valuable contributions to the party, she enabled its members to make an accurate prediction that she had the ability to lead them effectively, causing them to give her increasing responsibilities. The same dynamic occurs in less formal organizations, such a community groups and civic associations, where people who by their actions have shown that they have something of value to give the group are often turned to for leadership.

On their side of the leadership deal, candidates for leadership positions, as they approach a particular leadership job, also are making a prediction—that they have the talents to do the job, that they will find the personal and professional fulfillment they expect, and that they will be willing to meet over the long term the special personal and professional demands of the office they have assumed. In order to arrive at that determination, they often have to engage in negotiations with their families to support them in assuming leadership positions, reassuring them that the change in status entailed in becoming a leader will not place unacceptable strains on important personal family relationships. Sometimes, candidates, too, learn from their experience in a particular leadership job that they made wrong predictions about the nature of the position they assumed and that they must leave leadership for other professional or personal paths.

The Processes of Leadership Deal Negotiations

Like any negotiation, a leadership deal negotiation is a process—a progressive movement toward a particular end: the selection of a leader for a group or institution. And like other negotiations, it tends to proceed through three phases: (1) prenegotiation; (2) conceptualization; and (3) detail arrangement.

(1) **Prenegotiation**. In this first phase, the parties to a potential leadership deal determine whether they want to negotiate at all and, if so, what they will talk about and how, when, and where they will do it. In the search for leaders, most of the conversations between search committees and potential candidates fall into this domain. In my own case, all of my discussions with the search committee at SMU were prenegotiation, a phase which ends when both sides agree to negotiate, that is, to try to reach a deal. Prenegotiation ended for me when the SMU president invited me to meet in his office to discuss my appointment as dean of the law school.

(2) **Conceptualization**. In the second phase of the process, the parties seek to agree on a basic concept on which to build a deal. In this phase, those charged with finding a leader make a decision on a particular person as a future leader and begin a conversation with that person to secure his or her agreement to serve. The basic concept discussed in most leadership deal negotiations is whether and on what conditions the chosen candidate will take the job.

(3) **Detail arrangement**. Once a candidate and an organization have reached a basic agreement on a leader, the final phase in the process is devoted to working out the details and implications of that decision, for example, the specifics of the compensation and benefits to be paid to the chosen leader or the date when service will begin. At this stage, the parties often encounter the truth of the old saying "the devil is in the detail" when they discover, as President Zumberg did in his negotiations with his first choice for dean, that disagreements over details can prevent a leadership deal from being made. Once he had begun negotiations with me, a serious detail would be how much the university would increase the law school budget

The Rules of Leadership Selection

Institutions, organizations, and entire countries have both formal and informal rules that prescribe how people may become leaders; therefore, leadership deal negotiations largely take place within the framework of these rules. These rules, which are be found in the prevailing laws, the governing documents of the institution, or in the unwritten traditions of the organization, give legitimacy to the selection of a particular leader. Normally, these rules embody the values of the group or organization to be led. Failure to follow the prescribed rules will raise questions of legitimacy about the leader selected, the validity of his or her actions as leader, and ultimately the need to remove that person from leadership. Thus, throughout history, opponents of the illegitimate children of kings have challenged them as ineligible to succeed to the throne of their late father, and more recently, the so-called "birther movement" sought unsuccessfully to convince the American public that Barak Obama, whose father was Kenyan, was not a "natural born citizen of the United States" required by the Constitution and was therefore ineligible to hold the presidency, hoping thereby to render illegitimate the country's first democratically elected African-American president.

In no system are the rules of leadership selection automatic and self-executing. All systems leave scope for and may require negotiation in the selection of leaders. In this sense, they all entail negotiating leadership. The following case, which concerns the efforts of the Walt Disney Company, the giant media and recreation conglomerate, to negotiate a leadership deal for a new president, not only illustrates the importance of the rules but also the pitfalls that may occur in the process.

Traveling the Road to Magic Kingdom Leadership

In 1994, Frank Wells, the president and chief operating officer of the Walt Disney Company, died tragically in a helicopter crash. The leadership team of Wells and Michael Eisner, Disney's chairman and CEO, had brought the company remarkable success. Not only did Wells' death leave an enormous leadership vacuum in the company but it also had the effect of shredding Disney's CEO succession plan. Although Eisner himself at first temporarily assumed the position of president, along with his other responsibilities, within three months he suffered a heart attack and had to undergo a quadruple bypass operation. As a result, Eisner and the Disney board strongly felt the urgency of filling the office of company president.

Instead of forming a search committee as many other organizations would have done in a similar situation, Michael Eisner himself took over the task finding a new president for Disney without consulting the company's senior executives or its board of directors, except for the chairman of the board's compensation committee. Moreover, he approached the task with a single candidate in mind: Michael Ovitz, his friend of 25 years. Ovitz was founder of and owner of a 55 percent interest in Creative Artists Agency (CAA), the most successful talent agency in Hollywood, an organization with 550 employees and a client roster of 1400 of the most sought-after and successful actors, writers, directors, and musicians in Hollywood: a roster that was generating revenues of $150 million a year for CAA. Under Ovitz's leadership, CAA had revolutionized the movie industry by putting together packages of talent for specific projects and then negotiating on behalf of the clients in the package with movie studies, a device that considerably increased CAA's negotiating power and made Ovitz the most powerful and best paid talent agent talent in America.[8] Eisner believed that Ovitz's skills, experience, and industry relationships made him the ideal person to serve as Disney's president. In the summer of 1995, Eisner, having learned that the Music Corporation of America (MCA), a Disney competitor, was talking to Ovitz about joining its organization, began serious negotiations with Ovitz to bring him to Disney. Eisner's desire to thwart a competitor seems to have played a role in his determination to hire Ovitz.

At the time Eisner sought to recruit him, Ovitz's income from CAA was between $20 million and $25 million a year, a cash salary far in excess of what Disney had been paying Wells. Indeed, that amount was more than Eisner's own cash salary and that of any CEO in the United States. In negotiating a leadership deal with any potential candidate, a constant challenge is to assure the candidate that his or her situation with the new organization will at least be as good as it is with his or her present employer. Thus, since Ovitz would be selling his interest in CAA and losing his highly lucrative annual salary, the challenge for Eisner and Disney was two-fold: (1) to provide compensation at least equivalent to what Ovitz had been earning at CAA and (2) protect him against the "down-side risk" of early dismissal from Disney.

In order to meet both concerns and convince Ovitz to join Disney as its president, Eisner, in consultation with the chair of the Disney board's compensation committee, agreed to offer Ovitz a five-year contract, renewable for an additional two years, with a base cash salary of $1 million per year but guaranteed Disney stock options that would raise his annual compensation in cash and stock options to $24.1 million a year for the five-year period. The contract also included a no-fault termination clause that guaranteed Ovitz rich payments if he should be fired without cause before the end of five years. The contractual provision was a form of "leadership loss insurance," an arrangement often found in leadership deals. In my own case, when I was negotiating to become dean of the Fletcher School, I also insisted on being

---

[8] For an example of Ovitz's role in helping to arrange major corporate transactions, see Jeswald W. Salacuse, *The Global Negotiator: Making, Managing, and Mending Deals Around the World in the Twenty-First Century* (2003): pp. 58–60.

appointed as a tenured professor of law, a status I had held at SMU, although I was told that none of my predecessor deans at the Fletcher School had held a similar rank. But of course, none of them had ever held a full-time university teaching post. In any event, I submitted to the usual process at Tufts for deciding on tenure, was granted tenure as a full professor, and viewed that appointment as a form of "leadership loss insurance" that would provide me with full-time employment in the event that I failed as dean of the School. Satisfied with his own leadership loss insurance and level of compensation, Michael Ovitz agreed to the leadership deal at Disney, and Eisner emerged from negotiations pleased with the deal they had made. The stock market was also pleased. When the deal was publicly announced, the price of Disney stock rose 4.4 percent, increasing the company's market value by $1 billion. Inside Disney, the reaction to Ovitz's potential appointment was quite different. Senior Disney executives both overtly and covertly rejected his leadership. When Eisner told the company's two most senior executives, its chief financial officer and its general counsel and executive vice president, of his intention to appoint Ovitz as president, both men flatly refused to report to Ovitz and made clear to Eisner they opposed Ovitz's appointment as president of the company, believing that he was a "bad fit" for Disney and would disrupt harmonious working relationships within executive ranks. Despite internal opposition, Eisner, after informing members of the board individually of his decision to hire Ovitz, presented the Ovitz leadership deal to a meeting on September 26, 1995. The board unanimously approved the deal.

In fact, Ovitz did not turn out to be a good fit at Disney. His presence in the company created so much internal dissension and opposition by other executives that Eisner ultimately decided to dismiss him in December 1996 after only 14 months, an action that triggered the no-fault termination clause in his employment contract and payment of severance compensation of $38 million in cash and 3 million Disney stock options worth approximately $100 million. What Eisner and the market had at first considered a good deal ultimately became a negotiator's "winner's curse," the feeling you have when you realize that you have paid too much for what you actually got.

The enormous size of the payments to Ovitz and the shortness of his tenure at Disney prompted a shareholder suit in June 1997 in the Delaware courts against the company's board, Ovitz, and Eisner, claiming that the payments to Ovitz violated the directors' fiduciary duty to the company and were a waste of corporate assets. The matter was not finally settled until 10 years later when the Delaware Supreme Court in a lengthy decision in 2006 ruled that the directors had neither breached their fiduciary duty to the corporate nor wasted corporate assets.[9] It therefore dismissed the case. The lower court, the Delaware Court of Chancery, had come to the same conclusion but stated that Eisner's conduct fell "far short of what shareholders expect and demand from those entrusted with a fiduciary position…"[10]

Negotiating Lessons from the Magic Kingdom

The Eisner–Ovitz case offers several lessons about negotiating leadership deals, lessons that you should bear in mind whether you are seeking a multinational company CEO or the head of a local charity.

First, Curb Your Enthusiasm

Your desire and enthusiasm to land a specific individual, particularly one with charisma or a high public profile, can distort your evaluation of the value that the person will actually bring to your organization as a leader. Scholars have found that charismatic candidates often fail in leadership roles and that because their number is limited they are able to demand higher compensation than equally qualified candidates who do not have that sought after quality.[11] Eisner's negotiation with Ovitz and its aftermath appear to support this conclusion.

Second, Know What Your Organization Really Needs

In searching for a leader, it is crucial to make a hard-headed evaluation of the needs of the organization, the precise nature of the role that such a person is to play, and whether the individual has the talents and expertise to fill that role and meet organizational needs. In most cases, high among the talents needed to lead an organization is the ability to forge effective working relationships with its members and cultivate their willingness to accept, let alone support, the candidate. It does not appear that Eisner made that

---

[9] *In Re the Walt Disney Company Derivative Litigation*, 906 A 2d 27 (Del. Supreme Court, 2006).

[10] *In Re the Walt Disney Company Derivative Litigation*, 907 A 2d 693 (Del. Ch., 2005).

[11] Rakesh Khurana, *Searching for the Corporate Savior. The Irrational Quest for Charismatic CEOs* (Princeton, NJ: Princeton University Press, 2004).

kind of functional analysis when he began his courtship of Ovitz. He seems to have been driven more by his friendship with Ovitz and by Ovitz's reputation in the entertainment industry than by an objective evaluation of how Ovitz would meet Disney's needs. So at the outset of the search for the leader of an organization, always ask first: What do we need? Not: Whom should we get? It appears that Eisner never asked that important first question.

Third, Create a Search Committee

The search for a new leader should not be entrusted to a single person, but should actively involve sufficient numbers of representatives of the organization's members who can bring appropriate balanced judgment and expertise in deciding on a candidate that meets its needs and the price it should pay. Eisner, on the other hand, conducted the leadership deal negotiation virtually alone and involved the company's board and executives only once the deal was effectively a *fait accompli*. An appropriately structured search committee[12] to find Disney's new president might have helped him avoid the costly mistake he made in negotiating a leadership deal with Ovitz. Equally important, since Wells had been designated as Eisner's eventual successor, the board, by leaving the search for his replacement entirely in the hands of Eisner, was in effect allowing the company's current leader to choose his successor. That approach has serious risks for the organization since leaders in searching for their own successors may be driven less by concern for the future welfare of their organizations than by their own self-interest in prolonging their tenure as leaders, protecting their legacy, and continuing to exert influence within their organizations through hand-picked, pliable successors.

Fourth, Develop Options

Just as the SMU president did, the search committee should be instructed to identify more than one suitable leadership candidate so that the person or body making the leadership appointment has in reserve a good second choice, that is, a good BATNA, in the event that negotiations with the first choice fail. Eisner did not try to identify external or internal candidates

---

[12] Morten Nielson and Keith Meyer, "Building Your CEO Search Committee," *The Corporate Board* 22–27 (May–June 2013).

other than Ovitz who might serve as Disney's president. As a result, his only BATNA was to assume the presidency himself, not a great option for a man recovering from quadruple heart surgery. The lack of an acceptable BATNA considerably reduced his bargaining power with Ovitz and greatly diminished Eisner's ability to evaluate in an objective way Ovitz's potential value to Disney as president. On the other hand, the fact that SMU's president had an acceptable BATNA allowed him to avoid what he considered unacceptable costs, allowing the law school to be without a permanent dean for another year and a half.

Finally, Pave the Way for the New Leader

Eisner seemed to have assumed that the Disney organization would accept Ovitz, without exploring the truth of that crucial assumption. Broader consultation with the board and other Disney executives might have allowed Eisner to avoid the winner's curse that his deal with Ovitz engendered. An organization's members do not always readily accept the leaders chosen for them. Eisner was aware that his two top executives opposed Ovitz's appointment yet he seemed to have done little to try to convince them to accept him. In most cases, the selection of an external candidate to lead an organization necessities careful planning to pave the way for the entry of that person into the organization,[13] a process that may require yet another kind of leadership negotiation,—a negotiation about leadership roles, the subject of the next chapter.

---

[13] "Inside One CEO's Transition," *Harvard Business Review* (December 2016): pp. 67–68.

3

Negotiating Leadership Roles

The Second Leadership Deal

Successfully traveling the road to leadership not only requires you to negotiate a deal that gives you a leadership position, but it also demands that you negotiate a second leadership deal: a deal that gives you the leadership *role* you want to play. Leadership is not just a matter of *position;* it is also about a *role*, the diverse set of actions and functions that a leader actually takes to lead an organization or group. Your role concerns what you really do in the organization. The first leadership deal, the one about position, is usually the product of your negotiation with the people who have the authority to hire you and grant you a leadership position. The second is also the product of negotiations, albeit a much more complex and lengthy negotiation that must continually go on between you and the people you are supposed to lead. To travel the road to leadership successfully, you need to succeed at both negotiations.

Michael Ovitz was very successful in negotiating the deal that landed him the position of Disney's president with extremely lucrative compensation, but he failed in negotiating the role that he wanted to play as president of Disney. While Ovitz clearly knew that his position at Disney was president, he also believed, based on conversations with Michael Eisner, that his role as president would be that of co-leader of the entire Disney Company, a role he would play on equal terms with Eisner. Eisner, however, did not view Ovitz's role in that light and clearly neither did the other senior executives of the company. In fact, senior management at Disney strongly opposed and

© The Author(s) 2017
J.W. Salacuse, *Real Leaders Negotiate!*,
DOI 10.1057/978-1-137-59115-9_3

rejected Ovitz's conception of this role, thus creating a debilitating conflict within the Disney organization. To resolve that role conflict and return the organization to stability, Michael Eisner, the Disney chairman and CEO, fired Ovitz, an action that cost the company over $130 million dollars in addition to millions of dollars in legal fees incurred over 10 years of litigation. In this chapter, we will examine the challenges that people chosen to lead face in negotiating their leadership roles.

A Theory of Roles

To understand the process of negotiating leadership roles, we can seek guidance in "role theory," a body of learning developed by social scientists.[1] Drawing on the theatrical metaphor, role theory is based on the assumption that people behave in particular ways depending on their social roles just as actors in a play act in accordance with the parts they are given. Whereas theatrical roles are created by playwrights, social roles are determined by expectations, the strong beliefs that something will or should happen in a particular way. In the realm of leadership, the expectations of three groups are particularly important in shaping a leader's role: the expectations of those who have chosen or elected the leader; the expectations of those who are supposed to follow the leader; and the leader's own expectations about his or her leadership role. The negotiation of a leader's role is driven by the interplay of expectations among these three groups.

Leadership roles are not stagnant; they change over time, even though the leadership position may appear stable. For example, the position of the US president in constitutional terms seems to have changed relatively little in the more than 200 years of the republic's history, but the actual role played by US presidents within that position has undergone dramatic variations. Thus, Franklin Delano Roosevelt played a vastly different role as president from that of his predecessor, Herbert Hoover, in order to meet the unprecedented challenges of the Great Depression and World War II, events that generated new expectations in the electorate, the people following Roosevelt, and within FDR himself. Similarly, in the corporate world, David Packard, co-founder in 1939 with Bill Hewlett of Hewlett-Packard, one of the early great US technology companies, redefined the role of the company CEO by

---

[1] J. B. Biddle, "Recent Developments in Role Theory," *Annual Review of Sociology* 12 (1986): pp. 67–92.

introducing a management system that involved walking among the employees, maintaining a highly visible presence in the workplace, and fostering a policy of openness with workers. Packard's role as CEO sharply contrasted with the role conceptions of many corporate leaders of the past who believed that management and the workforce were breeds apart and should have little to do with each other.[2]

In order to analyze variations in social roles, role theory differentiates among *role prescription*, which is the expectation of external actors about how the role should be carried out, *role performance*, which relates to the role player's actual behavior in that role, and *role conceptions*, which concern the actor's own perceptions of his or her appropriate behavior in the role.[3] Thus, once in office, an individual having negotiated a deal to hold a particular leadership position may encounter different conceptions from various people about how to carry out the role of leader. The people to be led may have one or more ideas, the authority that selected him or her as leader may have another, and the leader may have yet a third. For example, when a new leader takes over a troubled corporation: the shareholders will usually expect the CEO to work exclusively on raising the share price and increasing dividends; the board of directors, while hoping for the same things, will expect protection of their positions and compensation as directors; the company employees will expect the CEO to preserve their jobs and increase compensation; and the new CEO will expect the loyalty and support of all, not only to make the changes necessary to enable the company prosper but also so that he or she can continue to hold onto leadership of the corporation.

Difference in such prescriptions and conceptions can cause significant role conflicts within organizations, conflicts whose resolution will require negotiations among the interested parties. Leaders' inability to resolve such conflict can seriously impair the functioning of the organization and in extreme situations ultimately cause the resignation or removal of the leader, a situation that prevailed at Disney during Michael Ovitz's 14-month tenure. Too often, leaders assume that their job descriptions, their titles, and the briefings and instructions they received from the people who selected them explain what they are entitled to do as leaders. In reality, their actions are determined by the leadership role that they negotiate after they take office. The participants in that negotiation may include not only those who appoint

---

[2] *The Capstone Encyclopedia of Business* 341 (Oxford: Capstone Publishing, 2003).
[3] J. B. Biddle, "Recent Developments in Role Theory," *Annual Review of Sociology* 12 (1986): pp. 67–92.

the leaders but also those whom they are supposed to lead. The various individuals and groups holding such expectations about the leader's role are also the leader's *constituents*—people whose support or at least lack of opposition is important if the leader is to achieve leadership goals and in the end hold on to the position of leader. The process of mediating among the expectations of diverse constituents often resembles a multilateral negotiation.

One important way for a leader to succeed in role negotiations is to find ways of managing or changing the expectations of important constituencies about what a leader does and should do. Often changing times and circumstances assist a leader in changing those expectations. Thus, one of the reasons Franklin Roosevelt was such an effective president was his ability to change the expectations of vast numbers of Americans so that they came to accept and indeed demand that he play the role of an activist president in confronting national economic and social problems. To wage a campaign to change national expectations of the president's role, Roosevelt skillfully used the country's new radio networks to communicate his ideas through his famous "fireside chats" directly into the homes of millions of people. The broadcasts had the effect of creating a sense of national identity, indeed an "imagined community," which fostered the development of an intimate relationship between the president and the public.[4] This technique mobilized mass public support for his New Deal policies and at the same time created new expectations about the role of the US president.

When we think of great theatrical performances, we usually assume that the end product is due to the talents of the actors alone. Thus, we tend to think that the memorable presentations of Hamlet by the great English actors John Gielgud and Lawrence Olivier, while strikingly different, were uniquely the result of their remarkable, though differing, talents. On closer examination of the processes that goes into creating great theatrical productions, one may see that the roles finally presented by Olivier and Gielgud were the result of a set of explicit and implicit negotiations among the star, the director, the producer, Shakespeare through his script, the other actors in the production, and sometimes even the audience. Similarly, like an actor who has just landed a part in a play or movie, your role is not ready-made in your job description or title any more than the actor's role is prefabricated in the script. You will have to shape that role to meet your own expectations and those of the various people you lead, a

---

[4] "Franklin Roosevelt and the Fireside Chats," *Journal of Communication* 49 (1999): pp. 80–101.

process that often requires intense negotiation. I learned this lesson several years ago when I became dean of the Fletcher School at Tufts University.

A Case of Academic Role Negotiation

I left SMU in 1986 to take up the deanship of the Fletcher School of Law and Diplomacy, a graduate school of international relations at Tufts University in Medford, Massachusetts, just outside of Boston. The Fletcher School is not a traditional law school but a multidisciplinary institution whose faculty consists of experts from many fields, including an exciting mix of economists, political scientists, regional specialists, and lawyers. When I assumed the leadership of SMU law school, I knew the culture of the institution and the personalities of the faculty well because I had been teaching there for two years at the time of my appointment as dean. The Fletcher School presented me with a very different situation. I was an outsider who did not know the school's culture, had not previously taught there, and had formed no relationships with individual faculty members. Equally important, the faculty and the staff did not know me. My knowledge of the place was based on two, short, site visits, a few meetings with faculty, students, and the search committee, my reading of various reports and documents, and briefings from the university president, its provost, and the school's acting dean.

During one of those visits, I met with a small group of students and asked them if they had any concerns about the school. They replied that they were worried that the Fletcher School's current reality did not live up to its reputation. I heard similar concerns from individual professors at the school. When I raised this issue with the university president, Jean Mayer, and the provost, Sol Gittleman, they readily agreed. "The Fletcher School," Gittleman said in his usual colorful style, "is living on its hump."[5] Both felt that the institution was relying on its past accomplishments, instead of building for the future, and that significant change had to take place. "The reason we are bringing you here," Gittleman told me when I accepted the job, "is to build." He wasn't referring to bricks and mortar but to the

---

[5] Gittleman would later repeat this statement in his excellent book about the transformation of Tufts University. Sol Gittleman. *The Entrepreneurial University: The Transformation of Tufts University, 1976–2002* (Medford, MA: Tufts 2004), p. 228.

essential intellectual capital of a university—its faculty. He had made his expectations of my role as dean exceedingly clear.

Previous deans at the Fletcher School had been distinguished former U.S. ambassadors without experience as university faculty members or leaders of academic institutions. As a result, they had tended to focus on the external dimensions of the dean's job and had left the academic matters of managing and developing the faculty and curriculum in the hands of an "academic dean," usually a senior faculty member appointed by the dean to handle such issues. Thus my predecessors had a distinct role conception of the dean's leadership job and had through their actions over the years set a pattern for the dean's role that the faculty, students, and the alumni had come to accept. Indeed, Tufts University's announcement of my appointment as dean raised concern among certain alumni about president Mayer's failure to select a former ambassador or other "member of the foreign policy community." Both Mayer and Gittleman received telephone calls questioning my appointment. The president therefore asked me to fly to Washington to attend the next meeting of the School's Board of Visitors, a body that included several influential alumni, to take place three months before I formally assumed the position of dean. The purpose of the trip was, of course, to begin to change alumni expectations about where a Fletcher dean should come from and how he or she should approach the deanship job.

My own conception of the dean's role at Fletcher differed from that of my predecessors. I believed that if I was to help the school rebuild, as the president and provost had urged, I would as dean have to be deeply involved in all matters relating to the faculty, particularly hiring and promotion, and the development of a curriculum in international relations that would meet the needs of the international professionals we were educating to work in the twenty-first century. An important step in building a strengthened faculty, I believed, was for the dean to actively participate in decisions about the hiring and promotion of the school's teachers and scholars. Having been a dean at a law school for six years and having served on and chaired various national peer review bodies like the Council for International Exchange of Scholars, which decided on Fulbright grants to professors for teaching and research abroad, I believed that I had the knowledge and experience to make similar academic judgments at Fletcher School in my role as its dean.

At the Fletcher School, like virtually all university institutions, the dean had final authority within the school regarding promotions and tenure of faculty members. In my second year at school, my power to actually use that authority in my role as dean was tested in two cases.

At the time of my appointment as dean, the Fletcher School, unlike many other university schools in the United States, had no standing tenure and promotion committee of senior scholars, appointed by the dean, to review and make recommendations on the renewal of faculty contractual appointments and the award of permanent tenured professorial positions. Instead, for each such case, a separate, small ad hoc committee would be created to make a recommendation on that particular case, a process that I felt was dubious since the ad hoc committee, unlike a standing committee, could not acquire the experience and institutional memory to develop and apply a common set of standards applicable to all candidates on an equal basis. Moreover, the use of ad hoc committees could lead to the creation of "sweetheart committees" whose membership was chosen in order to favor (or disfavor) the particular candidate concerned.

The first of the two cases I faced involved a decision on tenure for a young economist who had been teaching at the school for nearly 10 years. He was well liked by students and faculty and was considered a strong teacher. Although the ad hoc committee recommended that he be granted tenure, which would mean a life-long appointment at the school, I considered that his record of publications, which included no books and only a few articles in secondary journals, was too weak to justify his continuation at the school on a permanent basis. In order to build a strong faculty, I felt it was vital to affirm the importance of research competence and a commitment to scholarship in the selection and promotion of individual faculty members. I therefore decided to deny the request for tenure. Although a few of my colleagues asked questions about my decision, it was generally accepted without opposition by faculty, and the young economist left the school the following year at the end of his contract. The second case, however, provoked a storm.

That case involved the renewal of the contract of a young political science instructor who was the protégé and former student of a senior faculty member who was a somewhat somber, some would say sinister, individual, who one female professor told me she was afraid of. Born and trained in Europe, he had built his own independent academic fiefdom within the school over his years at Fletcher and resisted all efforts at cooperation with other parts of the institution. As a former academic dean described this professor to me, "He's never grateful for what you do for him. Every day, he wipes the slate clean."

Prior to my arrival as dean, the senior professor had managed to secure a three-year teaching appointment for his former student without a national, publicized search, a clear departure from the usual hiring practices at the school and most other academic institutions. Since that contract was to expire within a year, a process needed to be set in motion to determine whether the young's man's appointment should be renewed. Although the senior professor struggled mightily to secure the appointment of a review committee consisting only of his close associates in order to achieve a favorable decision, I insisted on including the school's academic dean, a woman of high academic standards, on the ad hoc group carrying out the review. Ultimately, the committee, by a divided vote, issued a report recommending renewal but with a strong dissent by the academic dean. After studying the entire case and the young man's publications, I decided that the contract should not be renewed and therefore informed the candidate that his appointment at the school would end at the completion of his contract.

The senior professor immediately launched a campaign against the decision and against me personally. That campaign became in effect a protracted negotiation about my role as dean of the Fletcher School. He did not think a dean's role should include close involvement in faculty appointments, whereas I did. In support of that position, he pointed to precedent set by previous Fletcher School deans who had left such academic matters to their academic deans. His campaign took place both within and outside the school. As a first step, he rushed to my office to protest my decision about his protégé, demanding that I reverse it and give the young man a new three-year contract. At the end of the stormy meeting, he left angrily, assuring me ominously that he was keeping "a detailed dossier" on my activities at the school.

His next step was to write a letter of protest to the chairman of the school's Board of Visitors, Charles Francis Adams, former CEO and chairman of Raytheon and a long-time pillar of the Boston business community. The function of the Board of Visitors, consisting of leading alumni and other influential people in international business and relations, was to advise the dean on matters relating to the school and to assist in fundraising. At our next regular luncheon meeting, Adams, who had long experience serving on governing boards at Harvard and other universities, asked me what the issue was about. When I explained, he dismissed the matter as "just a tenure case," indicating it was not an issue meriting his or the Board of Visitors' attention. Tenure was a matter for the dean, not for the Board of Visitors.

Receiving no answer to his letter, the senior professor persuaded a colleague at the school to raise the matter with Adams personally at a meeting both were scheduled to attend. On approaching Adams, the colleague asked, "Charles, may I talk to you about a tenure case at the School." With all the authority gained as an international business leader, scion of a founding family of the Republic, and the direct descendant of two U.S. presidents, Adams replied pre-emptively, "No, Bob, you may not."

Inside the school, the campaign against the decision became more serious. While the faculty generally supported my decision, the senior professor used his teaching and research assistants to spread concern among the students that I had acted unfairly, arbitrarily, and without authority in not renewing the contract of the young teacher. The thrust of his argument was that I had exceeded my role as dean. These rumors began to have effect among the students, some of whom were becoming agitated about the case to the point that the associate dean in charge of student affairs came to my office and said that we needed to do something to calm the situation. We decided to hold an open meeting for students at which I would explain the decision and respond to any questions they might have.

A few days later, in the late afternoon of a bright October day, I entered the scheduled meeting room and was surprised to find more than 100 students waiting for me, as well as a few members of the faculty, including the senior professor who had instigated student concern. After explaining the nature, purpose and process of faculty contract renewals and the specific actions taken in the case of the young political scientist, I opened the floor to questions from students. I recognized the first few questioners as student assistants of the senior professor, guessing that he had primed them for the session. I answered each and every question as patently and as completely as I could. The students appeared satisfied with my answers. Within an hour, questioning waned and the students themselves began to drift away from the meeting.

At this point, the senior professor, apparently dissatisfied with the student reaction, jumped to his feet and took an active part in the debate, an action that some students viewed negatively since the declared purpose of the meeting was to address student questions, not to provide a forum for faculty. The main thrust of his argument was that I had no authority to oppose a teaching appointment desired by certain faculty members. In short, that I had exceeded my role as dean. At one point, in response to his objections to my actions, I said, "But that is what deans do. It is a difficult part of the job, but that is what we are supposed to do." The students, all of whom had at least one university degree, nodded and chuckled sympathetically. At that point, I sensed that any student opposition to my decision in the case had evaporated. The students began to leave the meeting, but the senior faculty member refused to give up the floor. Finally, with only a few people left in the room, a sympathetic colleague, whom I shall always remember with fondness, rose to his feet and said, "Mr. Dean, you have been answering question patiently for more than two hours. Since I think you have answered all questions, I move the meeting be adjourned." With no opposition, I closed the meeting, satisfied that my role as chief academic officer with final authority over faculty appointments was established.

A few months later, the senior professor resigned from Tufts and secured a contract to teach at another university. More important, during the next eight years of my tenure the School hired a superb group of professors, established a standing tenure and promotion committee governed by rigorous academic standards, completely revised the curriculum to meet the demands of the post-Cold War era, and launched several new important programs, including those in environmental studies and negotiation and conflict resolution. When I resigned the Fletcher deanship in late 1994, approximately 70 percent of the School's faculty had been hired during my tenure. The rebuilding job was done.[6]

Lessons for Negotiating Leadership Roles

As you undertake the leadership of an organization, your plans should not only take account of the powers and privilege of your position but equally important the nature of the leadership role that you will play. My own leadership experience at the Fletcher School and other organizations, as well as my research, suggests a few additional lessons that other leaders, particularly those who are newly appointed to their positions, should bear in mind as they think about their roles.

First, do not assume that your role as leader—that is, the specific functions and tasks you will actually carry out—flow automatically from the position to which you have been appointed or elected. You will have to negotiate that role with a variety of constituents within and outside the organization.

Second, in undertaking to negotiate your role as leader, remember that you are *not* writing on a clean slate like a deal maker planning a new venture. In most cases, you will be negotiating against a background of precedent made by your predecessors, precedent that has created certain expectations in the people you are supposed to lead about how you should perform your leadership role. If those expectations obstruct what you hope to achieve as leader, you will need to understand them and develop a strategy to change

---

[6] For a detailed description of the transformation of the Fletcher School during that period, see Gittleman, supra, pp. 94–97.

them. When Carly Fiorina arrived at Hewlett-Packard and began to intro-duce significant changes in the management of the corporation, she was opposed by insiders who lamented the loss of "the HP way," the manage-ment methods and culture introduced by its founders, but which Fiorina saw as a major reason for the company's mediocre performance.[7]

Third, as you plan your role negotiation campaign, you need to identify the various constituents that you will need to address and to determine who supports you and who needs to be persuaded to give you their support. Remember, every leader needs the support of some constituents to do the jobs of leadership and even to stay in office. In my case, I had to address and gain the support of four important constituents to shape my leadership role at Tufts University: senior university leaders, especially the president and the provost; the Fletcher School faculty; the Fletcher student body; and impor-tant external supporters, particularly the School's Board of Visitors and its chairman, Charles Francis Adams. On the other hand, Michael Ovitz, while he may have felt that the stock market, because of the jump in the Disney share price at the announcement of his appointment as president, strongly supported him, seemed to have no internal supporting constituents, except Eisner, once he actually tried to do the job—a situation that ultimately led to his dismissal.

Fourth, negotiating your leadership role is not a one-time exercise in deal making. You don't close the deal on your leadership role once and for all. It is a continuing negotiation with the various constituents whose support you need to do the job and that you must constantly bear in mind as you go about the tasks of leadership. Your leadership role is very much connected to your relationship with the people you lead. That relationship needs to be tended and cultivated the way a country's diplomatic corps manages its relationship with other nations. In this connection, it is well to remember the admonition of the distinguished eighteenth century diplomat Francois de Callières, who wrote one of the first practical manuals of modern diplomacy stressing "the necessity of continual negotiation,"[8] a novel idea at the time that has become a basic tenet of modern diplomacy.

Fifth and finally, the nature and scope of your leadership role may change over time, either because of changes in external circumstances or because of your own leadership actions. For example, a CEO who has made a series of

---

[7] Carly Fiorina, *Tough Choices: A Memoir* 183 (New York: Portfolio 2007).

[8] François de Callière, *On the Manner of Negotiating with Princes* 6 (New York: Houghton Mifflin, 2001).

bad investments for his company may cause that corporation's board of directors to put in place various controls to limit his or her role in exploring new investments in the future. On the other hand, if you are chairing a community task force to create new economic opportunities for the town, the group may require at the beginning of your tenure that you include the executive committee in any of your meetings with the mayor but ease that restriction as they develop confidence and trust in your leadership.

Part II

Leadership Action: Negotiating the Leadership Road

4

The Seven Tasks of Leadership

Now that you have won that leadership position you wanted and received congratulations from friends and admirers, it's time for a lesson in humility. As you revel in the luxury of the corporate CEO's private jet, the foundation head's limo, or the university president's sumptuous office, you need to ask yourself two fundamental questions: Why should the people I am supposed to lead follow me? And what am I supposed to give this organization to help it succeed? If the only answers you can come up with to those two questions are "my charisma" or "my vision," you are in trouble.

The work of leaders rarely includes doing the tasks that their organizations are designed to accomplish. CEOs don't actually make the products their corporations sell. University presidents rarely teach students. Senior hospital administrators never treat patients. And generals hardly ever "fight" the enemy, at least in the sense that the ordinary soldier understands that word. So what is it that leaders really do?

Most discussions of leadership look at the subject from the leader's perspective, from the view point of individuals who are supposed to provide organizations with this elusive but supposedly essential quality. So scholars of leadership tell us what leaders do and how they do it, and leaders themselves in their memoirs recount their triumphs and failures. They are looking at leadership from the supply side. While an understanding of leadership from the leader's perspective is undoubtedly illuminating, it is equally important to examine leadership from the follower's point of view, that is, from the "demand side." Indeed, the follower's

© The Author(s) 2017
J.W. Salacuse, *Real Leaders Negotiate!*,
DOI 10.1057/978-1-137-59115-9_4

perspective may even be more important since the whole purpose of leadership is to serve the organization, not the leader.

Demand-Side Leadership

So what is it that organizations need from their leaders? It is often said that people in organizations want and need to be led.[1] But what exactly do organizations and institutions, employees and associates expect, want, and need from their leaders? When a corporate vice president says that his company needs "better leadership," what exactly does he mean? When a professor complains of her university's "poor leadership," what precisely is she concerned about? When a museum trustee calls for more "effective museum leadership," what is it that she is seeking? As consumers of leadership, what is it that all of these people feel they need but are not getting?

One way to try to answer this question is to look at the tasks and functions that followers expect of their leaders. A review of what leaders do or are expected to do by their followers reveals that there are seven basic tasks that leaders must accomplish every day.

The first task is **direction**. Every organization, large and small, looks to its leader to articulate and help establish the goals of the organization. That does not mean that the leader simply declares his or her vision for the organization and then orders its members to follow it. The process of goal setting in a complex organization with a diverse group of followers and constituents is usually complicated, lengthy, and elaborate. As we will see in the next chapter, Goldman Sachs needed nearly a decade of discussions among its partners to decide to convert itself from a partnership to a publicly traded international corporation. Mere articulation of the vision is not enough. Leaders must also convince their followers to accept it. Indeed, their principal function may be to orchestrate a process whereby the followers can participate in defining and shaping the vision which is to guide the organization's future development. Negotiation is an important instrument to carry out that process.

Organizations not only demand that leaders point the way but, like shepherds directing their flock, they also need to oversee the organization's movement in that direction. Many failures of corporate governance, such as

---

[1] See, e.g., Robert H. Rosen with Paul Brown, *Leading People: The Eight Proven Principles for Success in Business* (New York: Penguin Books, 1996), p. 7.

the collapse of Enron in 2001 and the sub-prime mortgage crisis of 2007, which led to financial loss, civil suits, and even criminal charges, have been the result of failed oversight by corporate leaders. Effective performance of the task of direction includes oversight to ensure that the organization avoids the legal, ethical, and financial traps that lie in wait for an organization that is moving forward, especially when it is moving onto terrain that it has never traversed before.

The second everyday leadership skill is **integration**. All organizations require their leaders to bring together diverse people, each with individual wills, differing interests, and varied backgrounds, to work for the common interests of the organization. All leaders seek in varying degrees to integrate the people they lead into a single organization, team, or community. Many people, driven by their individual interests, resist efforts at integration, a fact that requires the application of innovative approaches to the process, including creative problem-solving negotiation.

The third leadership challenge is **conflict management**. All organizations consist of people with different interests, a factor that invariably results in conflict among members. Individuals in the same organization may struggle over turf, resources, responsibilities, and policies. Indeed, most organizations, no matter how harmonious they appear on the surface, are rife with conflict. When an organization's members are unable to resolve their disputes, they usually look to their leaders to settle the matter. Leaders normally do so in one of two ways: by arbitration, in which they impose a solution; or by or by mediation, a process in which they, like Jimmy Carter at Camp David or George Mitchell in Northern Ireland, help the contending parties reach a negotiated settlement of their disagreement.

Education is the fourth everyday leadership task. Leaders educate, coach, guide, and advise the people they lead. Through that process, leaders give the necessary knowledge and skills that empower the people they lead to carry out the jobs of the organization. The traditional view is that leaders give orders to get things done in organizations. In fact, many modern leaders achieve their goals through advice and counsel. Generally speaking, the more decentralized the organization and the more educated its members, the more important advice and education become as a tool of leadership. This is especially true when leading highly educated professionals such as investment bankers, medical doctors, or lawyers, people who are often loath to seek help and quick to reject attempts to educate them. As a result, finding an education process that such individuals will accept is often a matter of negotiation.

The fifth daily skill of leadership is **motivation**. People you lead will look to you to motivate them, encourage them, and strengthen them to do the right thing for the organization. But in order to find the right incentives that will move people in productive ways, leaders may have to engage in a process of negotiation with them. For example, to retain a valued employee who is considering taking a job with another organization, a leader will have to probe to understand what interests are driving that employee and how the organization can satisfy those interests to avoid a departure.

Representation is the sixth daily leadership task. Leaders are constantly representing the organizations they lead, whether they are negotiating a labor contract or attending a reception given by a customer, persuading the company's board of directors to improve the bonus system, or seeking to arrange a merger with another corporation. In these situations, leaders are not negotiating for themselves. Instead, they are negotiating on behalf of the organizations they lead. In short, they are negotiating as agents. As a result, they are always concerned that the representations they make and the deals that they strike will be approved by the organizations and groups they represent. Their leadership roles usually give them a mandate to represent the organization. In order to negotiate on behalf of their organizations, leaders need a *mandate*, that is, an authorization—general or specific, formal or informal—from the organization or group on whose behalf they are empowered to act. They also need some means of assuring the people with whom they are dealing that they are indeed acting for their organizations and not just for themselves. For example, if you, as CEO, are engaged in merger negotiations, you will want some assurance that your organization will approve the agreements you negotiate. Second, the existence of a mandate gives you assurance that you will be able to induce your board of directors to approve the deals you make.

And finally, the seventh daily skill of leadership is **trust creation** or, more specifically, earning the trust of the people led. Creating trust is a vital skill, for without it leaders will find it difficult, if not impossible, to direct, integrate, resolve conflicts among, educate, motivate, or represent the people in their organizations. In short, without trust, a leader cannot lead effectively. Creating and maintaining the trust of an organization's members, who are often skeptical of new initiatives, raises special challenges for its leader. Negotiation is an important tool of trust building.

These seven tasks, while conceptually separate, are interrelated in practice. Helping an organization find an agreed-upon direction may also facilitate its integration, since a common goal gives a sense of unity to its members. Similarly, arriving at a common agreement on organizational direction may first require a leader to engage in extensive education of its members about the threats and opportunities that face the organization. All good leaders perform each of these tasks every day. No leader has the luxury of focusing on one to the exclusion of all others. Leaders must multitask constantly. If they don't, they may not stay leaders for long. Figure 4.1 illustrates the inter-connections among the seven tasks of leadership.

Few leaders do all seven tasks equally well. Some leaders perform certain of these tasks more effectively than others because of differences in natural abilities or personal preferences.

An outgoing, gregarious managing partner of a consulting or law firm may spend more time on and be more effective in representing the firm to various outside constituencies than in mediating the internal conflicts among part-ners that are paralyzing the firm and keeping it from adopting a new strategic direction. While resolving internal conflicts should be a matter of priority at this particular moment in the history of the firm, the managing partner without the ability or the desire to engage in conflict resolution may find more satisfying, not to say easier, ways to exercise leadership by spending time out of the office working on what he considers "essential matters" of representation. In my own experience in teaching corporate training pro-grams, I have found that the task that participants were least drawn to among the seven has consistently been education, while at the same time acknowl-edging its crucial importance for the future of their companies. The reason for this reluctance seems to be that the corporate executives generally felt least prepared to deal meaningfully with the educational challenges of their organizations. Few MBA programs, for example, explicitly teach their stu-dents, once they are in the workplace, how to educate their subordinates.

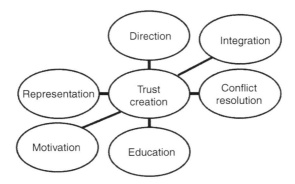

Fig. 4.1 Seven daily tasks of leadership

When followers complain of poor leadership, they may be referring to a leader's performance on different tasks. A corporate vice president may feel that the CEO is not giving strong leadership because he is not articulating a vision—*a direction*—that will allow the company to face the challenge of changing technology. On the other hand, a professor, complaining of a university president's poor leadership, may mean that the president is not doing enough to *motivate* and support the faculty in their work. And a museum board member lamenting the ineffective leadership of the museum's executive director may really be criticizing the director's failure to *represent* the museum powerfully to the community and thus raise the funds necessary for the museum's development.

For both leaders and followers, it is therefore essential to understand the individual tasks of leadership in all their complexity so leaders may deliver this vital commodity more effectively and followers may better evaluate and use what is being delivered. As will be seen in the following chapters, the fundamental technique used to deliver all seven of these vital tasks of leadership is negotiation. As a result, rather than focusing their efforts on being "visionary leaders" or "charismatic leaders," it may be far better for leaders to become skilled at being "negotiating leaders." One example they might seek to follow in this regard is Warren Buffett.

Warren Buffett: A Negotiating Leader

In December 1990 and February 1991, a team of bond traders at Salomon Brothers, then the fifth largest financial firm in the United States, submitted unauthorized bids in the name of clients in a deliberate violation of U.S. Treasury Department rules governing auctions of U.S. government securities. Through this stratagem, the Salomon Brothers bond traders circumvented a recent Treasury rule limiting any firm's bid on and award of five-year government notes to no more than 35 percent of the issue, a rule intended to prevent no single company from cornering the market in U.S. treasury securities. Within Salomon Brothers, the team, consisting of two managing directors, six traders, and 12 support personnel, were viewed as an important contributor to the firm's profits. At the time, Salomon Brothers was led by its chairman and CEO John H. Gutfreund, known as the "king of Wall Street," a brilliant and innovative financial player who had transformed the company into one of the world's largest securities traders and a leading dealer in U.S. government bonds.

It appears that as early as April 1991, the offending bond traders' supervisors and Gutfreund had learned of the traders' activities but had done nothing about it and did not even inform the Salomon board of directors. In August 1991, word of the bond traders' ploy leaked to the press, the financial community, and the public despite management attempts to cover it up. In response, the Securities and Exchange Commission (SEC), the U.S. Treasury Department, the Justice Department, the Federal Reserve Bank, the Federal Bureau of Investigation, and the Manhattan district attorney all launched criminal investigations. In addition, Congress was preparing to hold hearings on the matter. Even worse, the Treasury Department decided to ban Salomon Brothers from participating in Treasury auctions in the future, an action that would end a profitable line of business, cause the loss of important customers, prompt the flight of vital short-term creditors, and seriously—perhaps mortally—damage the company's reputation. Salomon Brothers, it seemed, was about to go down the tubes.

With the firm's future clearly in jeopardy, the legendary investor Warren Buffett, a member of Salomon Brothers board of directors and whose firm, Berkshire Hathaway, was the company's largest single shareholder with some $700 million at risk, took over as interim company chairman on Sunday, August 18, 1991, when Gutfreund and other top executives were forced to resign under pressure. At the same meeting, the board designated Deryck Maughan, a British national and Salomon's co-head of investment banking, as the operating head of the firm.

Consider the nature and magnitude of the leadership tasks that Buffett and Maughan faced as the new leadership team at Salomon Brothers. In general, they had to successfully achieve all seven of the basic tasks of leadership by: (1) finding a new direction for the firm that would lead to its rehabilitation; (2) holding together—that is, integrating—its staff, primarily to persuade its top employees to remain with the firm at a time when all their careers seemed in jeopardy; (3) negotiating a host of conflicts with regulators, prosecutors, and creditors, to name just a few; (4) motivating a demoralized staff that felt threatened and embarrassed by the scandal; (5) planning and executing the re-education of the firm in a way that would change its culture and prevent a repetition of the regulatory violations that threatened its existence; (6) representing the firm to the government, regulators, creditors, clients, and the public in a way that would convince them that a new Salomon Brothers was emerging from the crisis and that its errors and illegalities were behind it; and finally and probably most important, (7) regaining the trust of the firm's numerous vital constituencies in a business that is crucially dependent on trust. To complicate matters, many of these actions had to take place under acute time constraints

Leading Salomon Brothers out of the crisis was particularly complex and difficult because of the number of vital constituents that Buffett and Maughan had to negotiate with and the diversity of their interests. They included the U.S. Treasury Department, the New York Federal Reserve Bank, the Securities and Exchange Commission, the U.S. Department of Justice, the New York District Attorney, various foreign governments and regulators in countries where Salomon Brothers had operations, the firm's employees, the firm's creditors who were withdrawing their short-term financing, the firm's clients who were seeking to move their business to other firms, the credit rating agencies that had downgraded Salomon Brothers' securities, the financial press, Congress and the general public, to name just a few. The successful completion of these tasks would, in effect, require Buffett to undertake a negotiation campaign. As in pursuing any campaign, a crucial question that Buffett as a negotiator had to decide was: Where should I start?

When Buffet learned that Sunday, which he later described as "the most important day of my life,"[2] that the US Treasury Department was preparing to issue a press release banning Salomon Brothers' participation in future government securities auctions, he knew that somehow he had to persuade the Treasury to reverse that ban. As Maughan said at the time, "When your home government throws you out of the home market for government securities, you know you are in trouble."[3] The damage done by such a ban was not just the loss of income to the firm from that line of business, but its signal to all the world's financial markets that Salomon Brothers was not to be trusted. For that reason, Buffett believed his failure to negotiate a reversal of the ban would mean the ultimate demise of the firm.

Despite his wealth and influence, Buffett, like anyone contemplating a negotiation with the government, faced a major challenge in figuring out how to move a massive government organization to take action in his favor. A first step in the process was to find the right governmental unit and, within it, the right person or people to talk to about his problem. That unit and the people within it not only had to have the power to change the government's position but also be willing to talk to Buffett. Moreover, that conversation

---

[2] Carol J. Loomis, "Warren Buffett's Wild Ride at Salomon: A Harrowing Bizarre Tale of Misdeeds and Mistakes that Pushed Salomon to the Brink and Produced the 'Most Important Day' in Warren Buffett's Life," *Fortune*, October 27, 1997, p. 114.

[3] Harvard Business School, *Salomon Brothers* (HBS case study, no. 9-305-019, rev. May 5, 2005).

had to happen quickly, preferably that very Sunday afternoon, before word of the ban began filtering into foreign markets, which were scheduled to open within a few hours.

Buffett chose to contact Nicholas Brady, U.S. Secretary of the Treasury, in an effort to lift the ban. Through a series of telephone calls that afternoon, which also involved Gerald Corrigan, president of the New York Federal Reserve Bank, Buffett succeeded in negotiating an agreement with Brady and the Fed that allowed Salomon Brothers to continue to participate in U.S. Treasury auctions for its own account, though not for the account of customers. His approach in those negotiations was to stress that the continuation prohibition would mean the bankruptcy of Salomon Brothers, which in turn would have disastrous consequences worldwide and have a domino effect on international finance. Thus Buffet's negotiating tactic was to emphasize that his BATNA, that is, his best alternative to securing a modification of the ban from Brady, would not only have negative consequences for Salomon Brothers but also for the U.S. government and by implication for Brady professionally since he had responsibility for managing the country's financial system. Later that day, Brady announced the change in the Treasury's position on the ban, stating that he looked forward to a constructive relationship with Salomon Brothers' new chairman. Buffett's successful negotiation with the U.S. government was an important first step in ultimately saving the firm.[4]

Over the next 14 months, Buffet, with the assistance of Maughan, would conduct or oversee a series of negotiations with the diverse constituencies of Salomon Brothers and in the end save the firm. Throughout that process, his fundamental strategy was full candor, transparency, and a willingness to apologize for the firm's errors. He set the tone at his first press conference on that fateful Sunday when he became the firm's chairman: "My job is to clean up the sins of the past and to capitalize on the enormous attributes that this firm has…Salomon Brothers has to earn back its integrity." This approach contrasted sharply with that of his predecessor chairman John Gutfreund, who was considered hard-edged, arrogant, closed, and unapologetic. "No apologies to anyone for anything," he is quoted as saying at the time of the crisis. "Apologies are bull–."[5]

---

[4] Harvard Business School, *Salomon Brothers* (HBS case study, no. 9-305-019, rev. May 5, 2005). See also Loomis, "Buffett's Wild Ride."

[5] Linda Grant, "Taming the Bond Buccaneers at Salomon Brothers," *Los Angeles Times Magazine*, February 16, 1992, p. 22.

Warren Buffet's effectiveness as a negotiating leader enabled him to save the firm and eventually allowed it to return to profitability and to its place as a respected financial institution. His final negotiation success was the settlement reached with the U.S. Department of Justice in May 1992 and approved by the Treasury Department, the Federal Reserve Bank, and the Securities and Exchange Commission. Although the firm would have to pay the government $290 million of which $100 million was to create a fund to pay private damage claims, the U.S. Department of Justice announced that it would not bring criminal charges against Salomon Brothers. The U.S. Attorney for the Southern District of New York stated that the firm's cooperation in its investigation was "virtually unprecedented". Both the press and the financial industry saw this result as a success for both Buffett and Salomon Brothers.

Shortly afterwards, Buffet resigned as interim chairman of Salomon Brothers and returned home to Omaha, Nebraska, and Deryck Maughan became chairman and CEO of the company. In 1997, Travelers Group would buy the firm for $9 billion of which approximately $1.7 would go to Berkshire Hathaway for its investment in the firm.

Looking back on Buffett's crucial role as a negotiating leader of Solomon Brothers, Deryck Maughan summed up the experience succinctly: "No Warren, no firm." [6] It was not Buffett's charisma or commanding presence —two things that no one has ever accused him of having—that saved the firm from bankruptcy. It was his skill and effectiveness as a negotiating leader.

---

[6] Seth Faison, Jr., "Salomon's Renovation Enters a New Phase," *The New York Times*, February 11, 1992, p. D1.

5

Negotiating Direction

Organizations are not composed of robots controlled from a command center. Organizations consist of individuals—each with separate wills and sets of interests. If all those individuals were to exercise their own wills and pursue their own interests independently and without regard to others, the organization would not be likely to achieve the goals for which it was established in the first place. Indeed, chaos would almost certainly result. For those wills and interests to be harnessed for the benefit of the group or organization, the organization needs a sense of direction—a sense of direction that its members have accepted and agreed to work toward.

Organizations look to their leaders to help determine that sense of direction and then ensure that their members move towards it. In this regard, the leader of any organization faces three fundamental, interrelated questions:

(1) How do I help my organization determine that sense of direction?
(2) How do I lead my organization's members as a whole to adopt that indicated direction as a goal and work to achieve it enthusiastically?
(3) How do I keep the organization moving purposefully in that direction over time yet make necessary adjustments as the unexpected arises?

Direction, the first daily task of leadership, thus has three basic dimensions: direction determination, direction commitment, and direction oversight and adjustment. In order to carry out each one, real leaders need to negotiate.

© The Author(s) 2017
J.W. Salacuse, *Real Leaders Negotiate!*,
DOI 10.1057/978-1-137-59115-9_5

Direction Determination: Negotiating the Vision

If every organization or group needs an agreed-upon direction towards which to move in order to achieve its goals, one may ask a fundamental question: Where does this sense of organizational direction come from? Books on management and leadership stress the importance of the leader's *vision* in determining an organization's direction. Leaders exert their leadership, they tell us, by giving their organizations a "strategic vision," a picture of a new and better future. Martin Luther King was a visionary leader who galvanized the civil rights movement in the United States by eloquently painting a picture of a future in which people would be judged "not by the color of their skin but by the content of their character."

Organizations, large and small, look to their leaders to establish an organizational vision. Popular commentary on corporate leadership presupposes that a company's vision comes from its CEO, that, without a strong CEO, the company has no vision, and that a new CEO arrives on the scene to find a visionary *tabula rasa* within the organization. Of course, that's not the case. In any organization, members throughout its structure have ideas, thoughts, images, and, yes, visions of what they would like their organization to be. For example, some members of a law firm may have a vision of their organization "as a boutique operation specializing in what it has done for the last half century," while others may view its future as a "full-service global firm with offices in major capitals." Within an investment bank, some partners may have a vision for their firm as a publicly held financial services institution, while others may view its preferred future as specializing in investment banking without external shareholders but with close personal relationships with clients.

In most organizations and groups, members are likely to have quite distinct organizational visions. Moreover, in addition to their diversity of views about the future, followers strongly hold onto their visions and will not allow a leader, no matter how charismatic, to replace them easily with his or her own vision. Thus instead of being the organization's lone visionary, a leader may find the visionary field quite crowded indeed.

None of this is to belittle the importance of a vision in determining the strategic direction of an organization or the leader's role in shaping and articulating it. It is only to underscore that in leading other people, you are more likely to find a situation of *competing visions* among them rather than a group of befuddled individuals who are not quite sure of what to do and are only looking for the right leader to arrive on the scene and point the way in an eloquent fashion. For leaders of most organizations, the challenge of determining a direction for the group lies especially in forging a single vision out of the multiplicity of visions held by its members. Instead of handing down a vision for the organization from on high like a prophet, the process of articulating a vision in such an environment is one of negotiation. The most important action that a leader can take—an action that usually only the leader has the legitimacy to take—is to take the initiative in initiating the process that will result in the determination of a new direction for the organization.

Like a skilled diplomat in an international setting, the effective leader, whether heading an investment bank, museum board, or research institute, creates a common vision for the organization by building a coalition among its members who support that vision. Leaders need to be visionary diplomats rather than visionary prophets. Building a coalition in support of a vision for the organization demands intense one-on-one leadership through the effective use of negotiation and conversation. It is an extremely labor intensive process, requiring the leader to connect and interact with all the key players. For example, to resolve the long-standing conflict between the United Nations and the United States over the nonpayment of its UN dues, Richard Holbrooke, then U.S. Ambassador to the United Nations, met individually in one-on-one sessions with representatives from nearly 150 countries and scores of senators and congressional representatives in order to forge a coalition in support of a deal that led to a reduction in the U.S. dues rate in return for payment by the United States of dues in arrears.[1]

In my own experience as the leader of two graduate schools, while I had strong ideas about the directions that both institutions should take, for me to have tried to legislate a vision for each one using my powers as dean would have been considered illegitimate by the faculty and would have ultimately been rejected. On the other hand, the faculty and staff of both institutions-not only considered it totally appropriate to start a process of determining a direction forthe two schools but many strongly approved, so that is what I did. At both SMU Law School and the Fletcher School during my first year as dean, I engaged the faculty in writing a five-year strategic plan with two-day retreats at sites away from campus to brain storm and forge a consensus about the desired direction for each institution.

---

[1] James Taub, "Holbrooke in Turtle Bay," in Derek Chollet and Samantha Powers (eds). *The Unquiet American: Richard Holbrooke in the World* 240–262 (2011).

Direction Commitment: Negotiating to Stay the Course

Having determined a direction for the organization and built the necessary supporting coalition, the leader must next secure genuine commitment from the organization's members to work toward achieving the vision. It is naïve to assume that people in the organization will be committed to its goals for the sake of loyalty. People become committed to visions primarily because they perceive it is in their interests to do so, and secondarily because of the rewarding relationships they may have with others in the organization, including the leader.

In this regard, leaders should recall the warning of Niccolò Machiavelli, still one of the world's foremost leadership thinkers, about the challenges of establishing new directions:

> And let it be noted that there is no more delicate matter to take in hand, nor more dangerous to conduct, nor more doubtful of success, than to set up as a leader in the introduction of changes. For he who innovates will have for his enemies all those who are well off under the existing order of things, and only lukewarm supporters in those who might be better off under the new.[2]

Modern psychological research has confirmed Machiavelli's insight of 600 years ago: Fear of loss, which psychologists call "risk aversion," is a more powerful factor in human behavior than the drive for gain.[3] This is especially true for elites, a risk-averse bunch, who often feel that they have a lot to lose by any change in direction.

Experienced diplomats know that countries, even though they have agreed to join or at least not oppose a coalition, play a variety of roles with varying degrees of commitment to the coalition's goal. Some are enthusiastic *partisans*. Some are cautious *joiners*. Some are *cruisers*, just along for the ride, ready to jump off the coalition when it encounters difficulties. Some are *neutrals* who don't oppose the coalition but at the same time don't work to achieve its goals. And of course some are *spoilers*, who while not expressing overt opposition to the visionary coalition, nonetheless won't miss an opportunity to weaken or destroy

---

[2] *The Prince* (translated by N. H. Thomson; New York: Dover Publications, 1992), p. 13.

[3] See for example, Amos Tversky and Daniel Kahneman, "Loss Aversion in Riskless Choice: A Reference-Dependent Model," *The Quarterly Journal of Economics* 106 (1991): pp.1039–1061.

it.[4] In organizations, people who have in one way or other indicated their support for the direction—the vision—that the leader has negotiated with them also play the same assortment of roles as do countries in coalitions. Agreement to a vision does not necessarily mean strong commitment to it. As a result, a leader, often using one-on-one negotiations, must make a hard-headed assessment of the degree of genuine commitment that each follower may have to pursuing the new direction seemingly agreed upon. Beware of becoming so intoxicated by your own vision for the organization and the sense of your own charisma and authority that you fail to see clearly the reservations and hesitations that members of your organization may have about pursuing that vision enthusiastically. When an organization member says, "Yes, but..." to the vision, too often enthusiastic leaders seize on the "yes" but miss the "but."

Sometimes members of your organization will state their reservations and hesitations openly; sometimes they may not. In the latter case, you need to look for tell-tale signs indicating less than genuine commitment. For example, is a member who normally participates actively in meetings curiously silent about new directions and visions for the organization? Has another member declined to join task forces or committees working on the new vision or, if he or she has accepted membership, has that person frequently missed its meetings? Does the normally enthusiastic, sprightly, free-wheeling conversationalist become uncharacteristically reserved when the subject of the organization's new vision and direction arises? A first step in commitment strengthening is to understand why the people you are hoping to lead in a new direction have hesitations or reservations. That understanding will help you develop an approach to easing those concerns, thereby hopefully strengthening commitment to the new direction.

Even though an organization may have adopted a new direction by a unanimous vote, an experienced leader learns to recognize and interpret these signs to mean that some one-on-one negotiations with these people will be required in order to strengthen their commitment to the strategic decision that the organization has taken. One technique that U.S. presidents have used to establish the commitment of cabinet members to decisions that may have been adopted by acclamation or even unanimous vote is to go around the table and ask each member to publicly declare, in

---

[4] For a conceptual discussion of coalition building and the various roles parties may play in a coalition, see Christophe DuPont, "Negotiation as Coalition Building," *International Negotiation* 1 (1996): pp. 47–64.

front of all the other members, that he or she supports a potentially contentious decision, such as going to war.

Negotiating Oversight and Adjustment

An organization not only expects its leaders to help its members determine and then commit to a direction, but also to ensure that the organization actually moves in the direction it has adopted. The process of direction oversight is crucial to an organization's success. Understand that no strategic plan can predict the future with absolute accuracy. While pressing forward with determination to move the organization in a desired direction, you must also be ready to recognize and deal with the unexpected, perhaps to slow down movement toward, halt progress completely, or veer away from the direction that the organization had previously adopted.

Determining, securing commitment to, and overseeing progress toward a direction for an organization is thus a basic yet complex task of leadership, one that requires the effective use of negotiation. A case in point occurred when Goldman Sachs, the great Wall Street investment bank, made a strategic decision to adopt a new direction in 1998.

Negotiating a Vision for Goldman Sachs

Goldman Sachs is one of the most successful investment bank in the world. Founded in New York City in 1869 by Marcus Goldman, a German immigrant who set up shop as a broker of commercial IOUs in lower Manhattan, the firm would grow to become an international financial powerhouse. By the end of the twentieth century, Goldman Sachs had masterminded some the major deals of the century, including the Ford Motor Company's initial public offering (IPO) in 1956, the privatization of British Petroleum in 1987, General Electric's acquisition of RCA in 1986, the $13 billion privatization of Deutche Telecom (the largest IPO ever undertaken) in 1996, and the $38 billion merger of Daimler Benz and Chrysler Corporation in 1998, the largest industrial merger up to that point. Its success has been attributed to three consistent factors over the years: its leadership, its people, and its culture.[5] To a significant extent, its

---

[5] Lisa Endlich, *Goldman Sachs: The Culture of Success* (New York: Simon & Schuster, 2000), p. vii.

singular culture and its ability to attract excellent people were dependent on the special structure that it maintained throughout the twentieth century—a private partnership.

In 1986, 80 percent of the capital of this $38 billion business was owned by its 104 active partners, with the remaining 20 percent held by retired partners. The partnership structure gave the firm several distinct advantages over the years. First, the fact that it was private meant that it did not have to respond to the vicissitudes of the stock market but instead could undertake long-term, profitable strategies that the shareholders of publicly traded firms would not have tolerated. As one of its partners was fond of saying, "Greedy, but long-term greedy."

Second, as a private firm, it was not subject to the reporting requirements of publicly held corporations and this fostered a culture of confidentiality that not only served the partners but their clients as well. Goldman Sachs developed a strong client-oriented culture that resulted in enduring and extremely lucrative business relationships.

Third, since the net worth of the partners was to a large extent based on their ownership interest in the firm, and since its growth depended on firm profitability, the partnership structure fostered a culture of team work among the partners, a factor that was an important reason for the firm's financial success. It also engendered a high degree of trust and commitment among the partners to the all-consuming task of the partnership business.

Fourth, the prospect of becoming a partner at Goldman Sachs was a key factor in the firm's being able to hire, retain, and motivate some of the best and brightest financial talent in the world. Not only would a partnership result in considerable wealth to a recipient, but a Goldman Sachs partnership came to have a special cachet on Wall Street, a cachet that meant its recipient was among the elite of the financial world. As a result, Goldman Sachs partners included some of the smartest, most talented, richest, and most powerful people on Wall Street.

But if the partnership structure had served the firm well for nearly 130 years, by the 1980s it also began to reveal some disadvantages. First, it rendered the firm's capital base unstable. Whenever partners withdrew or retired from the firm, they took their share of the capital with them. Second, a partnership meant that the growth of the firm's capital depended largely on retained earnings. The partnership structure prevented it from raising large amounts of capital from the stock market in order to take advantage of new business opportunities that were emerging as a result of globalization. Third and perhaps most constraining of all, being a partnership meant that Goldman Sachs, unlike all of its competitors, which had one by one become publicly held corporations, could not make acquisitions through the issuance of stock and thus could not grow rapidly.

Moreover, because of the partnership structure, the partners, unlike shareholders, were personally liable for all of the firm's obligations, a factor that came to be of increasing concern as mammoth law suits struck the financial industry with growing frequency. And finally, an initial public offering would result in considerable personal enrichment for the Goldman Sachs partners, particularly the more senior partners, whose capital accounts had grown as a result of the firm's accumulated profits.

Goldman Searches for a New Direction

Because of these factors, the leadership of Goldman Sachs, beginning in the 1960s, considered from time to time the possibility of converting the firm to a corporation and making an IPO of its shares. Finally, in 1986, the firm's nine-person management committee formally recommended to the 95 other partners that Goldman Sachs make this fundamental strategic change. The management committee, which included Robert Rubin, soon to be co-vice chairman of Goldman Sachs and later U.S. Secretary of the Treasury during the Clinton administration, was in effect presenting a new vision for the firm, setting a new direction to enable the firm to attain the goal of becoming the pre-eminent investment bank in a rapidly globalizing world.

Over a weekend in December 1986, all of the partners, slightly more than 100 in number, met to consider this vital proposed change in direction. Prior to the meeting, Rubin and his colleagues on the management committee had sought to lobby key senior partners in support of the proposal to go public. In competing organizations that had already taken a similar decision, the leadership had faced the members with a *fait accompli* and had merely asked them to give formal approval. That approach was rejected at Goldman Sachs. For one thing, it would have violated the engrained culture of teamwork and collegiality that had been so assiduously developed over the years. For another, it might have prompted key partners to leave the firm, depriving it of vital capital and talents and thus rendering Goldman even less able to compete in the new, dawning financial world.

For two days, the partners debated the proposal, often with high emotion. Opposition to the idea of an IPO was strong, perhaps stronger than the management committee had anticipated. At the end of two days, without a formal vote being taken, the committee and the other partners saw clearly that there was no consensus for going public, and so the meeting was ended with no decision, which meant that Goldman Sachs would remain a partnership.

Various reasons have been advanced for the failure of the firm's leadership to arrive at an agreement on a new direction in 1986. First, the formal proposal was not well prepared. The partnership included some of the most financially astute people in the world and they quickly applied their talents to challenging much of the financial analysis that underpinned the proposal. Second, a shift from the traditional culture of Goldman Sachs—characterized by teamwork, privacy, and solidarity, a culture that they all valued highly—to the unknown of a publicly traded corporation was just not one that the partners were psychologically prepared to make, despite the fact that an IPO would make many partners much richer than they already were.

While some partners believed that a publicly traded structure would have net advantages and some believed it to be a net loss, all partners regretted the change of culture that a public offering would entail. In addition, the firm had taken in an unusually large group of 37 new partners in 1986. Having had no time to accumulate equity in the first year, they stood to gain little from an IPO, and they therefore uniformly opposed it. An IPO was simply not in their interest. And finally, although the management committee had put forward the proposal for an IPO to the group, it did not aggressively push to secure its adoption with the other partners. Rather, the committee advanced the idea, listened to what the partners had to say, and in the face of strong opposition, ultimately withdrew.

On the one hand, the 1986 meeting could be seen as a rejection of the proposed new direction by the firm's leadership. On the other hand, all the partners left the meeting knowing that the issue was far from dead and that the conversation about the firm's future had really just begun. At the same time, in retrospect, the partners seemed to have adopted the vision of Rubin and the other management committee members that Goldman Sachs's basic goal was to become a "world-class financial organization."

Goldman Continues the Search for a New Direction

Ten years later, with the firm now under the leadership of Jon Corzine, who would within a short time be elected to the U.S. Senate from New Jersey and later that state's governor, the Goldman Sachs partners once again considered a proposal to become a publicly traded corporation and abandon its traditional partnership structure. In the interim, as discussion continued among the partners, the firm had instituted a variety of internal changes and raised capital from outside through private placements. The firm also encountered various problems, one of which was the fact that increasing numbers of partners were withdrawing from the firm and taking their capital with them. To counter this threat, Corzine and the firm leadership believed that an IPO would stabilize the firm's capital and allow it to retain its talent, Goldman Sachs' primary asset. So as not to repeat one of the mistakes of the 1986 meeting, prior to the 1996 partners meeting, a special committee was appointed to prepare in great detail a complete proposal for an IPO.

The world of finance had changed significantly during the preceding decade. Goldman Sachs had grown in size and scope but its members realized that it still had to grow even more through the process of acquisitions if it was to attain its goal of becoming a world-class financial firm. Potential objections to an IPO were anticipated and arguments made to counter them. In addition, Corzine and the leadership engaged in extensive "pre-selling" with other partners before the meeting took place. Once again, an all weekend meeting took place among the partners to consider the future of the firm through extensive discussions. By Sunday, it had become clear to Corzine and the executive committee that the partners did not want to sell the firm, so they withdrew the IPO proposal from consideration. Their reasons were the same as those advanced in 1986, but in addition due to the existing state of the stock market the partners probably also concluded that the premium to be gained from an IPO was not worth the cost of losing their valued firm culture.

The 1996 meeting was not, however, a total defeat. First, it served to further educate the partners about all the implications of an IPO. As a result, discussions about the firm's future directions would continue after the meeting. Second, and perhaps more important, the partners authorized Corzine and the executive committee to take a variety of measures to alter the firm's structure, all of which would facilitate an eventual IPO. Thus, the firm was converted from a partnership to a limited liability company and it ceased to use the term "partner" to designate its members. Henceforth all partners as well as hundreds of the firm's other highest executives would be designated managing directors, who would have all the rights and privileges of partners except that they owned no equity in the firm. Moreover partnership rules on withdrawal of capital were changed to give increased stability to the firm's capital base. It was also understood that in the future the firm would periodically revisit the question of whether to go public.

In 1998—just two years later—the leadership decided it was time to reconsider the issue of going public. Two powerful intervening forces prompted this decision. First, the stock market had experienced spectacular growth, causing the firm to be worth much more than in 1996 and potentially enabling individual partners to reap significant financial rewards from an IPO. Second, and even more important for the future of Goldman Sachs, many of the firm's principal competitors had rapidly grown into global giants through mergers and acquisitions, primarily by issuing stock. Goldman Sachs, because of its structure, had been unable to grow in the same manner. The size, breadth, and global reach of these new financial institutions, it was feared, would put Goldman Sachs at a competitive disadvantage that would only increase over time.

In response, the management committee established a subcommittee to review the firm's strategy in this new and rapidly changing business environment. The subcommittee's goal was not to recommend whether to go public, but rather to propose a business strategy that the firm should adopt. "Structure follows strategy" was the group's watchword, and this was made clear to all of the Goldman partners. The subcommittee was to look forward 10 years and decide what kind of a firm Goldman Sachs was to become at the end of that time. As it undertook this study, it realized that the firm's most important strategic issue was how fast to grow. Ultimately, the committee recommended a program of aggressive growth, doubling the number of people engaged in the client-service portion of the business in just five years.

Having set out that strategic goal, it then outlined the various ways in which the firm might attain this goal, one of which was by going public. Its recommendations were then presented to all the partners, and the firm scheduled yet another partnership meeting to consider them. During the intervening period, Corzine, now joined as co-chairman by Hank Paulson, who would later become U.S. Secretary of the Treasury during the administration of George W. Bush, engaged in one-on-one pre-negotiation conversations with nearly all of the firm's 190 partners.

In June 1998, for the third time in 12 years, all the partners of Goldman Sachs convened in a weekend retreat to consider the strategic proposal and the means to implement it. The session began with a general presentation of the proposal by Paulson. But rather than making a hard sell in favor of an IPO, Paulson very carefully discussed the pros and cons of the proposal, raising all the hard questions that the partners had to satisfy themselves about. His goal was not to sell an idea but to make his fellow partners think hard about what was in the best interests of the firm. After Paulson's presentation, the partners broke up into small working groups known as "echo tutorials," whose purpose was to give them a deeper understanding of the proposed strategic direction's implications. Informal conversation about the future continued among the partners over dinner in the evening.

The next day Corzine made a presentation about the question of the fairness of the proposal to go public and also read a letter from two distinguished former partners who opposed a change in structure. Thereafter, the floor was turned over to the partners for their views, and more than 100 partners would speak, expressing both approval and opposition to the idea of selling the firm to the public. Finally, on Saturday afternoon, the partners were given a ballot, asking which ownership structure they preferred and why. The meeting then adjourned and the executive committee convened to consider the views expressed by colleagues. The Goldman leadership had decided in advance that any new strategy had such momentous consequences for the firm that a mere majority of partners would not be enough to make the change. Instead, a supermajority would be needed.

Goldman Finally Negotiates a New Direction

The following Monday, the executive committee announced that it had been decided to sell the firm's shares to the public. After 13 years, numerous meetings, and virtually endless discussions, the leadership of Goldman Sachs was able through skillful negotiation to forge a concensus to adopt a significant new strategic direction for their venerable firm.[6] The public offering itself did not take place immediately. Right after the decision was made, the stock market experienced downward pressure and so the firm leadership exercising discretion and oversight deferred the IPO until May 1999.

Goldman's decision to go public did not just happen. The firm was led to make that decision through the efforts of its leaders. On the one hand, leaders like Robert Rubin, Hank Paulson, and Jon Corzine knew that the firm needed to seek a new strategic direction because of significant changes taking place in the world. On the other hand, they also realized that they themselves could not force that decision on the partners. Rather, over time, they had to negotiate agreement on a new vision for the firm and build a

---

[6] For an excellent history of Goldman Sachs and its decision to go public, see Lisa Endlich, *Goldman Sachs: The Culture of Success* (2000).

coalition among the partners to support it. In short, they had to play the role of visionary diplomats, rather than visionary prophets, if their organization was to make a vital change of direction.

You may ask: Did it have to take so long? Could other leaders have achieved the same result in less time? Would the prototypical, dynamic corporate CEO—a Jack Welch, a Louis Gerstner, or a Sandy Weill—have done a more effective job of leading Goldman Sachs to a new strategic vision than a Rubin or a Corzine? The answer to that question is: almost certainly not. The Goldman Sachs partners, by virtue of the fact that they owned the firm, had the power to say "no" to any proposal, to remove from leadership anyone who they felt threatened their interests, and to replace that person with someone who better served them. In the Goldman Sachs situation, it was not vision and charisma that would lead leaders, but an understanding of the partners' interests and an ability to convince them that a needed new direction advanced those interests. The strategic change at Goldman Sachs was an example of an interest-based negotiation of the highest order.

Basic Principles for Negotiating a Direction

Although the Goldman Sachs case is special, in many ways, it does illustrate some basic principles about the way leaders should negotiate a new direction for their organizations. Here are a few principles that should guide you.

(1) Determine a direction for an organization by structuring and conducting a campaign of negotiations and conversations

For Goldman Sachs, determining a new direction for the firm was the product of a protracted negotiation that took 13 years. For most organizations composed of leaders, finding a strategic direction is also the product of a conversation, really a negotiation, as Chapter 1 defined that process. The basic task of the leadership is to structure and conduct that negotiation, rather than to try to impose a new vision from the top. While few organizations will require 13 years to find their way as Goldman did, it is important to realize that conducting a negotiation about organizational direction can be time consuming and often frustrating.

(2) Develop a fair process for conducting the negotiation about direction

If you as the leader have a clear vision of the organization's future and a distinct sense of the best direction to follow, resist the temptation to try to impose it on your organization. As Machiavelli noted 600 years ago, the dangers for a leader in trying to impose a new order is that you will make enemies of those who benefited from the old order and gain only lukewarm support from those who stand to benefit from the new. In the end your enemies may prevent you from imposing your new order, and even if you overcome them they will remain opponents as you go about the process of implementing it. This does not mean, of course, that you abandon any hope of moving the organization in a more productive direction. Rather, it means that you need to find and develop a process that will enable the organization's members to participate in determining new directions. In the Goldman Sachs case, the firm worked out a definite process of meetings and consultations to help the partners negotiate a new strategic direction.

Leaders often become impatient with process. They want to get things done, to get the organization moving in the right direction as quickly as possible. Worrying about process, they think, merely delays the important tasks of leadership. Moreover, many leaders feel that becoming embroiled in process makes them look weak and indecisive and gives their opponents within the organization an opportunity to undermine them. But developing the right process for determining organizational direction is essential for several reasons.

First, as research has shown, people are more likely to accept and act on a decision if they believe it resulted from a fair process, even if they do not fully agree with that decision, than if that decision was imposed from above or resulted from an unfair process. Second, effective process will allow you to tap fully the resources of your organization. Many people within an organization have valuable ideas, experience, and knowledge that you can profitably use in determining the direction for your organization. Admit it: there are people in your organization who know a lot more than you do. Third, involving the members of your organization meaningfully in the process of negotiating direction is a concrete signal that you respect them and their ideas and is thus an important element in gaining their trust, an essential asset if you are to lead the organization effectively. And fourth, good process gives legitimacy to decisions on new directions.

No matter how much charisma you have, some members of an organization may remain opposed to the new direction, or at most offer very lukewarm support. However, they are less likely to be able to thwart or sabotage those new directions when decisions on directions have emerged from a fair process than if you had had handed them down by fiat like a Machiavellian prince. And finally, the existence of a fair process for direction setting may serve to place a check on the charismatic leader whose vision for the organization—for example rapid acquisition of unrelated businesses—is essentially self-serving as a means to increase an empire over which that leader hopes to rule.[7]

(3) Establish a fair process that includes the opportunity for followers' genuine participation and decisions based on acceptable principles and standards

The process by which Goldman Sachs arrived at a decision to adopt a new strategic direction was based first of all on the full participation of all the partners in the deliberations. All partners had the right to speak, and all were sincerely encouraged to do so. They exercised that right throughout the 13 years that the decision was under consideration. The goal of the conversation is not merely to determine a direction but to cause the members of the organization to adopt, believe in, and work enthusiastically toward the direction that is decided. Ownership of the decision by members of the group is a key to success. Ownership is much more likely to result if the members played a part in making the decision on direction than if the organization's leaders arrived at *their* desired result by manipulating, short-circuiting, or dominating the process.

(4) Once you have established a process, use it genuinely to help determine a direction for your organization

Sometimes leaders put in place a process of consultation and negotiation that is merely a charade, a means to justify what they wanted to do in the first place. An organization's people will quickly come to know when they are engaged in meaningless activity. Once they realize that they are involved in a

---

[7] See Yassin Sanher, "Character Not Charisma," *Journal of Leadership and Organizational Studies* 9, no. 4, (2003): pp. 47.

purely formal process that has little or no significance, they will also participate in a purely formal way, if at all.

During the Soviet era, Russian workers jokingly explained their less than diligent work habits by saying: "They pretend to pay us, so we pretend to work." Similarly, followers asked to participate in a process that will have no influence on the organization's direction are likely to say, referring to their leaders, "They pretend to have an interest in our ideas, so we pretend to tell them."

(5) One of a leader's primary functions is to frame and ask the right questions

Traditionally, leaders have seen their function as pointing the way, as indicating, if not formally *ordering,* a definite path for the organization to follow. In leading an organization, however, the most effective instrument is not an order but the right question. The leadership of Goldman Sachs, after two failed attempts to convince the partners to go public, reframed the question that they were to answer from "Should the firm go public?" to "What should be the firm's strategy in the radically changed financial environment at the end of the twentieth century?" This was a question that affected the vital interests of the firm and all its partners. It was a question that was designed to elicit the strong and positive participation of all. Once the firm had answered the basic questions by deciding to be a world-class financial firm, it then had to face the issue of how to find the resources to compete with much larger competitors. This question, in turn, led the partners to decide on going public. Effective negotiators know that *framing*—the particular way in which a situation is characterized—can orient people's thinking in either productive or unfruitful ways, and the frames that work best take into account the interests of those who are to be influenced.

(6) Discern patterns of deference

Within any group, some people are more influential than others. Among the Goldman Sachs partners, some had more influence on their colleagues than others. The effort of determining and adopting a direction for a group of leaders is similar to building a coalition in a diplomatic conference or a legislature. Some leaders, like some countries or some legislators, may be more influential in the process than others. Moreover, even if individual partners have little influence, they may enhance their clout by forming blocks or coalitions, as the 37 new Goldman partners did to considerable effect in the 1986 meeting. It is therefore important for a leader conducting a negotiation on direction, as one scholar has said, "to discern patterns of deference" among the members of the group to be led and then to mobilize those patterns to arrive at an agreement on strategic directions.[8]

While all leaders, such as the partners at Goldman Sachs or ambassadors at a conference, would reject the notion that they are subject to the authority of another leader, ambassador, or partner, they are nonetheless willing in many cases to "defer"—that is to be influenced by—the views and opinions of certain of their colleagues. The source of that deference among theoretically autonomous equals may be derived from many factors—a personal relationship, seniority, favors done in the past, or benefits expected in the future. The effective leader not only seeks to discern those patterns of deference but to understand their basis and then to use that information to achieve organizational goals.

(7) The process of effective direction setting is actually a multilateral negotiation

It is wise to see yourself as guiding that process and perhaps to take lessons from international diplomacy: (1) participants should be recognized as sovereign and equal with respect to the right to participate in the process; (2) the process should be governed by a set of rules that are known to all; and (3) the elements of the final result will be drawn from the ideas and thoughts of the participants in the process.

---

[8] Lance N. Antrim and James K. Sebenius, "Formal Individual Mediation and the Negotiators' Dilemma: Tommy Koh at the Law of the Sea Conference," in Bercovitch and Rubin, eds., *Mediation in International Relations: Multiple Approaches to Conflict Management* (New York: St Martin's Press, 1992), p. 124.

6

Negotiating Community

Early in my tenure as dean at SMU, a senior professor, in talking to me about a particularly difficult issue that had divided the faculty, suddenly said forcefully, "You've got to bring us together, to unify us." He clearly felt that in addition to the other dimensions of my job I had the task of integrating the faculty as an effective working organization. My job as dean, in addition to my other tasks, was to unite the group, to create a community from diverse and talented individuals who each held fiercely to their sense of independence. In short my job, like that of any leader, was to be a community developer.

The Leader as Community Developer

The word "community" comes from the Latin *communitas*, which means common ownership or things held in common. For a leader the task of community development within a group, organization or nation is to unite a group of independent, autonomous human beings, however large, each with diverse interests and goals, by making them believe that they are connected to one another because they have a common "ownership" in the group, organization, or nation led by its leader. There are basically two kinds of communities that leaders try to build: "real communities," which are small enough that the members know and interact with one another, and "imagined communities," like nations, that are so large that its members cannot have direct interactions with more than a few. Such imagined communities,

© The Author(s) 2017
J.W. Salacuse, *Real Leaders Negotiate!*,
DOI 10.1057/978-1-137-59115-9_6

as we know from history, have exerted a powerful force on the minds of its members to the point that they are willing to fight and die for the special imagined community that they see as vital to their identity and very existence.[1]

Leaders have sought to create imaginary communities for both laudable and evil purposes. Thus, nationalist leaders like Gandhi in India sought to create the imagined community of the Indian nation in order to mobilize Indians, regardless of religion, to seek independence and throw off British rule. European leaders, like Jean Monnet since the end of World War II, have tried to convince with varying degrees of success the inhabitants of the European continent that they belong to the imagined community of "Europeans," a community which should take precedence over their allegiances to their individual nation-states, allegiances that have been a source of war and conflict for hundreds of years. On the other hand, Hitler created the imaginary community of Aryans to unite Germans and convince them of their special destiny, a strategy that led directly to World War II and the death of millions of people. Modern means of communication like the internet and social media have facilitated the task of creating and leading imaginary communities for both good and evil. On the one hand, it has allowed the creation of epistemic communities of scholars and activists to work together on issues of global importance such the environment and human rights, but at the same time it has facilitated the creation and operation of other imaginary communities, such as the "Islamic State of Iraq and Syria" (ISIS) and "White Nation," whose purposes and methods are much less benevolent.

In conceptual terms, community development for a leader is a task of integration. Integration is a process of combining various parts or elements into a more harmonious, effective, and productive unit, and by this process to somehow make the whole greater than the sum of its parts. An integrated team, whether in baseball or investment banking, usually performs its tasks, whether winning games or launching IPOs, more efficiently and effectively than one that is beset by conflict and turmoil. An integrated business corporation may seize opportunities to create value that would elude a collection of its individual star performers. An integrated law firm by mobilizing the diverse talents and specialties of its members can serve a variety of client needs and thereby generate more income for the firm than

---

[1] Benedict Anderson, *Imagined Communities: Reflections on the Origin and Spread of Nationalism*, rev. ed. (New York: Verso, 1991).

if individual lawyers work with clients only in their areas of specialization and show no concern for problems outside of that specialization. And an integrated think tank or research institute is more likely to undertake innovative studies across disciplinary boundaries than is a group of scholars laboring separately in their own offices and laboratories with little contact with one another. Lack of integration, on the other hand, can lead to friction within the organization that actually hinders the ability of that organization to serve its members and the public in the best way possible. Like the senior professor at SMU, most organizations look to their leaders to strengthen them though integration, to make them a more effective community. To achieve organizational integration and advance community development, leaders need to rely on negotiation.

Community Building from the Demand Side

Since the work of integration is largely negotiation, it is important for leaders, as in any negotiation, to understand how the situation looks to the person with whom you are trying to reach an agreement. In this case, no matter how important integration is to the organization and its leadership, that is, from the supply side—it is also useful to see how it looks from the demand side, from the point of view of followers who are to be integrated.

Psychologists have found that all people have two basic social needs: a need for autonomy and a need to belong.[2] The degree to which specific individuals will seek these two goals and the priority they attach to each depends on a variety of factors, including personality, culture, and context. Some people with what psychologists call an "independent self-construal," tend to define themselves in terms of the attributes, preferences, and traits that make them unique and autonomous from their social world, while other people having an "interdependent self-construal" tend to define themselves in terms of their social relationships and group memberships.[3] Similarly, members of an organization will generally recognize that some degree of integration is important for their organizations, and they almost always look to leaders to undertake this vital task. They will often differ however on the desired *degree* of organizational integration necessary and the price they are

---

[2] E.g., M. B. Brewer and W. L. Gardner, "Who is this 'We'"? Levels of Collective Identity and Self Presentations," *Journal of Personality & Social Psychology* 71 (1996): pp. 83–93.
[3] H.R. Markus and S. Kitayama, "Culture and The Self: Implications for Cognition, Emotion, and Motivation," *Psychological Review* 98 (1991): pp. 224–253.

willing to pay for it in terms of reduced personal autonomy. As a result, the dilemma that all followers face in an organization is: How much should I cooperate with the leadership to allow integration to happen and how much should I assert my own individual interests so that I can pursue my own professional and personal goals? That, in effect, is the follower's dilemma, and every leader needs to recognize that all of the organization's members address this question either consciously or subconsciously every day.

The follower's dilemma creates a constant tension—between the drive to assert individual interests and the drive to assert organizational interests. It is the dilemma of choosing between individual independence and organizational integration, of responding to the universal human needs of autonomy and belonging. The principal task of an organizational leader is to convince all members of the organization that their primary interests lie in successful organizational integration and that they should therefore cooperate with, support, help and, indeed, initiate efforts to integrate the organization's members into a dynamic team. Many highly talented individuals may have a tendency towards "independent self-construal." So leaders of high-talent organizations may find that they are called upon to lead a higher percentage of people for whom autonomy is a primary goal than they would find in other kinds of organizations. As a result, you need to shape your integration strategies accordingly.

Integration happens as members come to feel that they are part of a community, that they share certain things, that as a group they hold certain values, ideas, and especially interests in common. More important, integration is driven by a growing realization among an organization's members that an integrated organization meets their interests better than one that is not integrated. Integration evolves as working relations are established among the organization's members. A relationship is a feeling that one person has of being connected or linked in some way to another person. In an integrated organization, those links and connections are multiple and strong. In organizations that lack integration, those relationships either do not exist or are dysfunctional. In that regard, an integrated organization is like a complicated electronic circuit that links together the various electronic components that allow a computer to function properly. One of the tasks of a leader is to help to create that sense of community, to help its members identify and articulate what they have in common, to remind them of what they share together. A leader, like a computer engineer, works to establish, maintain, and strengthen the circuitry—the relationships—that allow the organization to function as an integrated mechanism, rather than to be a jumble of unconnected components sitting in a box on a work bench.

At the same time, leaders must recognize that the needed *degree* of integration may vary, depending on the nature of the organization, the particular goal it seeks to achieve, the nature of the external environment at a given time in history, and the perceived interests of the organization's members. Forcing integration for its own sake without regard to the perceived interests and needed independence of the organization's members to do their jobs appropriately may in the end reduce the effectiveness of the organization. The balance between individual independence and organizational integration, which is at the heart of the follower's dilemma, is one that a leader has to manage carefully and constantly.

Negotiating a Sense of "We"

In order to integrate a group, many leaders first strive to give the group a distinctive collective identity, a special sense of "we." In the realm of politics, leaders, to gain power, may either limit or expand that sense of "we." Thus Adolph Hitler limited the "we" to "Arians," while Nelson Mandela, in fighting for democracy in South Africa expanded the concept to South Africans of all races.

In business, corporate leaders seek to give a sense of "we" to all employees, a sense that they are somehow special, in an effort to more closely integrate them and hopefully lead them to greater efficiency and profitability. The leaders of international organizations, whose employees may come from as many as a hundred different countries, will seek to give them a sense of their identity derived from the mission of the organization as a means to overcome cultural, political, and ideological differences that they may have brought with them from their countries of origin, differences that if not controlled may seriously impede the operations of the organization.

Preparing to Negotiate Community

Successfully negotiating community requires leaders fundamentally to do two things: (1) analyze the group or organization they lead in order to understand the barriers to community in their particular organizations; and (2) develop a strategic plan of action for the negotiation. We will first consider the possible barriers and then suggest strategies.

Barriers to Community

Here are some of the principal barriers to community that leaders encounter in organizations:

(1) No Perceived Common Interests

Interests drive negotiations. If the people you are supposed to lead feel they have few common interests, they are not likely to work in an integrated fashion. The prevailing attitude among them will be: "You do your thing and I'll do mine." Star doctors, lawyers, asset managers, or management consultants who are compensated exclusively and richly on the basis of revenues generated from their own patients, clients, or accounts, will often feel that firm-wide activities like staff recruitment and strategic planning have little interest for them and therefore will seek to spend as little time as possible on those activities.

(2) Lack of a Felt Shared History

A sense of a common history is a powerful force for the integration of groups, whether they are professional organizations or nations. All countries encourage or require the teaching of history in schools in order to create a sense of unity and community among its citizens. One of the first challenges to integrating an organization is often the fact that its members do not feel that they have any shared history. Or they may believe that if there is a history of working together, it is really not important with respect to what each individual in the organization is doing today.

(3) Too Much Bad History

The members of an organization may indeed have a shared history, but they may view that history negatively. As a result, their organizational history may serve to divide rather than to unite, to separate rather than to foster a sense of community among the members of the organization. A nation that has endured a civil war will often find that the memory of the pains endured and the humiliation experienced in the conflict will remain in the memory of its people for generations and serve as a continuing cause of divisiveness. Similarly, the remembrance by an organization's members of past internal quarrels, struggles for power, heated arguments over policy, and contested personnel decisions can become part of the organization's folklore and serve as a continuing source of hostility and distrust among people who otherwise might have considered themselves colleagues. That distrust and hostility effectively serve to inhibit a sense of community. For example, the contested decision by the Columbia University administration to ask the New York City Police to intervene in the student sit-ins and protests of 1968 led to internal divisions that persisted long after the Vietnam War had ended.

(4) Poor Internal Communication

Just as the integration of an electronic apparatus requires connection among its components, a sense of community in an organization needs an ongoing process of communication. Poor or nonexistent communication within organizations means that individual members do not know what other members are doing, and so the necessary connection for integration among them is missing.

Perhaps even more pernicious than no communication is unequal communication, a situation where some organization members receive vital firm-wide information and others don't. Knowledge is indeed power. A situation of unequal distribution of information will mean that some members who are privy to vital information will gain influence in the organization, and that those without access will feel disempowered, a result that will only heighten the lack of a sense of community.

(5) Cultural Differences

An important barrier that inhibits organizational integration is a difference in culture among its members. What do we mean by culture? *Culture* consists of the behavior patterns, attitudes, norms, and values of a given community. Nations have cultures and so do organizations. At its most basic simple level, culture is simply "the way we do things around here."

Individuals working in organizations develop a culture from one or more of three distinct sources: from their national background, from their previous organizational experience, and from their professional training.. Thus, differences in culture within organizations are not the product of national differences alone. They are more often the product of different organizational and professional cultures.

Some organizations, like Goldman Sachs, with a deep sense of history and tradition, have over time developed a culture that its members value and that gives the organization strong cohesion. On the other hand, new organizations or organizations that have been formed by the merger or acquisition of existing firms often find that their members have different cultures:different behavior patterns, attitudes, norms, and values about work, organization, and life that effectively prevent them from functioning as a community

Professionally trained people—whether they are doctors, lawyers, management consultants, or clergy—have not only gained specialized knowledge and skills from their education, they have also gained a culture: a set of distinct behavior patterns, attitudes, and values about their work, the organizations in which they do their work, and indeed about life itself. In organizations composed of people with different professional training and background, for example, lawyers and engineers or scientists and management consultants, differences in culture may arise that cause internal conflict or inhibit effective action.

Culture can influence the way work is done, indeed the very way work is perceived by the members of an organization: how meetings are conducted, how people communicate with one another, how work is rewarded, and how teams function. In an organization like Goldman Sachs, whose culture has evolved over more than a century and is carefully taught to its new members, this common culture gives a strong impetus for organizational integration. Similarly, the "H-P way" developed by the founders of Hewlett-Packard was a powerful cultural force that gave the company a strong sense of cohesion. An organization without a common accepted culture may experience constant conflict, miscommunications, disappointed expectations, and therefore dysfunction in the form of poor performance and the failure to take full advantage of opportunities in the market.

(6) Spoilers

Different individuals within the same organization may view the prospect of integration differently. Some may see it as a way of enhancing the organization and therefore promoting their own interests. Others may view it as a threat to their interests and therefore seek to prevent it. For example, organization members who are profiting from the status quo handsomely would not want to see greater integration among firm members if that meant that the leadership would gain support to make policy changes not in their interests. These people are "spoilers." A spoiler's basic tactic is to prevent change by blocking agreement—that is, integration—by the other members of the organization. Sometimes a leader can easily identify spoilers by their actions; sometimes spoilers effectively hide their intentions and actions from the leadership and from the other members.

(7) Divide-and-Conquer Leadership

In many organizations, the barrier to community is the leadership itself, either past or present. An age-old leadership strategy is "divide-and-conquer," a method used not only by colonial rulers but by many modern-day managers. Divide-and-conquer leaders view unity among a group's members, whether they are Nigerian tribes or portfolio managers, as a threat to their own power. Therefore, in order to gain or preserve their influence, some leaders will deliberately seek to foster competition among their subordinates and actively prevent actions that would otherwise facilitate integration among the organization's members.

So instead of encouraging full and open communication within the organization, a divide-and-conquer leader will provide information selectively to certain groups and not to others; instead of encouraging cohesion among the organization's membership, a divide-and conquer leader will favor some groups over others—for example, the traders as opposed to the deal-makers in an investment bank—and thereby assure the loyalty of the favored group in future contested decisions and actions. As a new leader, you may not be a practitioner of divide-and-conquer leadership, but if your predecessor practiced this art, one of your challenges may be to find ways to undo its consequences within the organization.

Removing the Barriers to Community

The process of community development requires leaders to find ways to remove these integration barriers. You cannot sweep them away by eloquent speeches at company meetings or stern memorandums from the executive suite. To a significant extent, their removal will require you as a leader to engage in negotiation, either one-on-one or in groups, with the people you lead. People who resist integration by insisting on their autonomy at the expense of the group, are exercising their personal power to defend their interests.

Psychologists have found that the existence of a relationship between a person with more power and another person with less power tends to moderate the use of that power.[4] What you as a leader are seeking to do through one-one-one interactions is to create relationships among the people you lead and thus moderate their exercise of personal power in favor of organizational interests.

If lack of organizational integration is akin to unconnected electronic components sitting on a workbench, how should a leader of leaders go about connecting them to create integrated circuits within the organization? Here are a few techniques that may help.

Make Common Interests Apparent Through Meaningful Activity

Many professionals, such as doctors, architects, and management consultants, quite naturally focus first and foremost on the work they were trained to do, whether it is heart transplants, high-rise designs, or corporate reorganizations. They view their basic interests, both personal and professional, as doing the work for which they were trained. In most cases, their education did not equip them specifically to work in organizations, and they probably have given little serious thought to the organizational needs of their professions and their employers. They may see little connection between what they do and what others in the organization do or indeed what the organization as a whole does.

Recognizing that people respond to their perceived interests, one tactic of leaders to negotiate community is to make their colleagues in the organization appreciate that their interests will be advanced if the organization becomes more integrated. One way to achieve this goal is to involve them in activities that will enable them to perceive this potential for interest advancement. For example, their participation in committees related to the governance of the organization may foster a sense of community, even though some leaders may view this activity as interfering with leadership prerogatives. Governance committees make clear to the members of the organization that they have a definite stake in an integrated organization, and it is also an excellent way to educate and inform members about

---

[4] S. Chen, A.Y. Lee-Chai, and J. A. Bargh, "Relationship Orientation as a Moderator of the Effects of Social Power," *Journal of Personality and Social Psychology* 80 (2001): pp. 173.

organizational issues and needs. Governance committees and activities are therefore tools for achieving community.

In addition to participation in governance, planning exercises are another means to foster integration. For example, a leader may launch a strategic planning process that calls for the involvement of the organization's members in examining the threats and opportunities in the external environment and what actions the organization should take to deal with them. This process might involve off-site retreats, where the members can focus intensively on the organization's future and also come to know their colleagues better. Rather than leading the retreat discussion yourself, you might think about engaging an outside facilitator to orchestrate the process as a means to foster an atmosphere of free, open, and creative discussion.

Through participation in governance and planning, individual members in an organization will come to see that their interests are closely aligned with those of the organization. It also allows the organization to fully tap an invaluable resource—the knowledge, experience, and talents of its own members. In the end, governance and strategic planning with the involvement of colleagues may produce much better results than if you, as the organization's leader, did it all yourself. What you are doing in effect is structuring a "grand bargain" among the organization's membership, a grand bargain that consists of member involvement in the governance of the organization in return for a genuine commitment by individual members to organizational purposes.

If team members' involvement in both organizational governance and planning is to truly facilitate integration, it must be done according to an agreed-upon set of principles. Such principles as openness of discussion, transparency of deliberations, avoidance of personal attacks, and real participation in decision making will not only make the process efficient but also make clear to members the seriousness of the exercise in which you are asking them to engage.

If you are a traditional manager, you may be uncomfortable with intensive involvement of the organization's members in governance and strategic planning—the hallowed functions reserved to "top management" in most corporations. While you acknowledge the need for greater integration, you may be tempted to try to achieve it through simulated member participation, through governance committees that have no real responsibilities, and through planning exercises that have no meaning. If that is your inclination, resist it. The people you lead will almost certainly detect such charades in an instant, with the result that their participation will cease and your own credibility as a leader will suffer.

Make History

A common history is an integrating force in organizations. One of the functions of a leader is to be an organizational historian, to make its members understand and appreciate its history—the challenges faced and met, the temporary defeats that were eventually surmounted, the debt that the present owes to the past. In your internal and external communications, use frequent references to the organization's history as a reminder that it is bigger than the sum of its current members, in this way leading them to understand that they are part of an integrated whole.

Many organizations gain a powerful sense of integration from a distinguished history. Their members' ability to become a community is enhanced by a pride in that history. In many cases, members' status both within and outside the organization and their own sense of self-worth, indeed their very identity, are derived from that history. For example, Goldman Sachs's history not only endowed the firm with a remarkable degree of integration but it also gave those people who became Goldman Sachs partners special status and distinction in the financial world.

In other organizations with a distinguished history, from the New York Yankees to the Boston Symphony Orchestra, a felt perceived history among the member has also been a powerful force for integration. Wise leaders in high-talent organizations foster that sense of history in a variety of ways, including publishing firm histories, inviting distinguished senior members to address new recruits, displaying historical memorabilia in firm offices, assuring that new members understand the firm's history, and referring to important organizational historical events in their own communications with other members as well as with the public.

Not all organizations have as distinguished and as long a history as Goldman Sachs, the Boston Symphony, or the New York Yankees. A leader in those kinds of organization therefore will not have a long history to help in the task of community building. Nonetheless, any organization, unless it was created today, has some history, and it is the task of the leader to know and understand that history, to mine the past however short, and to learn how it may be used to foster and build a sense of community. A leader becomes a kind of cheerleader who identifies the successes of the past and interprets their significance for the future.

Bridge the Cultural Divide

Differences in cultures tend to isolate individuals and groups from each other. In short, cultural differences create a gap—a divide between people and organizations. For example, the differing cultures of psychologists and computer engineers in a consulting firm may mean that the two groups of professionals have difficulty communicating with one another, understanding one another, and working collaboratively together. The differences are often profound, finding their roots in their different educational backgrounds and indeed in their very identity as professionals.

An effective leader needs first to understand the nature of the cultural differences that divide the organization's members and then seek to find ways to bridge that gap. Leaders of organizations with differing cultures must think of themselves as bridge builders. As the English poet Philip Larkin has written, "Always it is by bridges that we live."[5] Accordingly, effective joint action among people and organizations of differing cultures requires a bridge over the culture gulf. One way to build that bridge is by using culture itself. If culture is indeed the glue that binds together a particular group of people, the creative use of culture among people of different backgrounds is often a way to link those on opposite sides of the gap. The essence of the technique is to create community with the other side.

A first step is to make explicit the cultural differences that exist within organizations—to put those differences on the table so that the members of the organization can know that differences in perspective and approach are not the product of individual perversion as some would like to think but rather of legitimate cultural differences that are supported by the different organizational or professional backgrounds of its members. A second step is to formulate a process whereby the members can agree on rules for handling cultural differences within the organization. Here the challenge is to determine how much diversity to allow within the desired degree of integration.

One cannot expect that highly trained professionals will abandon basic attitudes and practices that they consider fundamental to their work. In such situations, organizations might adopt the approach of *subsidiarity* of the European Union in dealing with the different local rules and practices of individual countries while at the same time fostering an integrated single

---

[5] Philip Larkin, "Bridge for the Living," in Anthony Thwaite, ed. *Philip Larkin: Collected Poems* (New York: Farrar Straus Giroux, 1988), pp. 203–204.

market. *Subsidiarity* means that local rules and laws will be respected so long as they do not interfere with the basic goals of the European Union.

An organization composed of individuals with different professional backgrounds might adopt a similar approach: The practices of each profession will be mutually respected provided that they do not interfere with the basic purposes of the organization. In short, rather than to consider all internal differences as bad and seek to suppress them, an organization might adopt an approach of mutual tolerance and allow such differences, provided they do not threaten the organization's basic interests.

In addition to bridging cultural differences, leaders need to think about ways to assure that the organization's new members become familiar with its prevailing culture, that they "learn the ropes." Community development within an organization may therefore call for an appropriate program of orientation that might include the designation of someone to act as mentor or advisor to a new member, making sure that the new member is given needed written materials on the firm's background and practices, such as copies of the firm history, procedures, and strategic plan. Such a program may also involve setting up a series of meetings for the new member with various established members so they can become familiar with the organization's culture and its diverse ways of doing things.

Become a Communications Engineer

Effective organizational communication is fundamental to integration. Without it, integration cannot take place. Without it, you lead a group of stars but not a team. As leader, you therefore need to focus constantly on tasks of communications within your organization and to develop an ongoing strategy to accomplish them. As leader, you need to see yourself as your organization's communication engineer. Not only do you need to focus on your own specific communications—your memos, speeches, and presentations—you also need to think constantly about developing and improving ongoing organizational communication systems, such as internal newsletters, regular memos or e-mails on important events, fixed schedules of meetings that will inform members of important information concerning the organization, and processes by which members can share vital information with each other.

In addition, you need to keep on your own personal agenda your role as leader and house communicator. As you circulate among your colleagues, as you meet with them about their own issues, and as you preside over committees and working groups convened to accomplish specific tasks, you need to keep thinking of how you can use those occasions to transmit important organizational information that will facilitate the process of integration.

Leaders need to be cheerleaders for the organization both inside and outside. You need to proclaim the achievements of individual members so that the entire organization and its supporters will know about them, understand their significance for the organization and for them personally, and take pride in those achievements as a positive reflection on all the organization's members. As we will see in Chapter 10, these activities are also very much a part of another daily task of leadership—representation.

Create Opportunities for Community Members to Meet and Interact

U.S. Supreme Court Justice John Marshall, laid the foundations for constitutional government in the United States not only through his legal ability but equally important through his skill at leading the other Supreme Court justices to forge unanimous opinions on key issues—much to the consternation of Marshall's political enemy, President Thomas Jefferson, who had appointed many of the justices who seemed so willing to join Chief Justice Marshall in his decisions.[6] It puzzled and frustrated Jefferson that the Supreme Court justices—some of whom were his political allies—who had lifetime appointments to the Court, who were leaders in law and politics in their own right, and over whom Marshall had no real authority seemed so willing to follow Marshall's lead on important constitutional questions. In effect, President Jefferson was asking a basic question that this book addresses: How was it that Chief Justice Marshall, with no real authority over the other justices of the Supreme Court, was able to lead leaders so effectively?

One of the reasons Chief Justice John Marshall was able to lead the other U. S. Supreme Court justices to unanimous opinions on key constitutional principles that laid the foundation for the American republic was the fact that he arranged for all the justices to live together in the same Washington boardinghouse, where they shared meals together, often over a bottle of claret provided by Marshall, and discussed their cases, the politics of the day, and life itself.[7] What Marshall did through that process was to build strong working relations

---

[6] Jean Edward Smith, *John Marshall: Definer of a Nation*. p.448 (New York: Henry Holt 1996).

[7] Jean Edward Smith, *John Marshall: Definer of a Nation*. pp. 286–287 (New York: Henry Holt, 1996).

with and among his colleagues, relationships that would enable him to lead the Supreme Court as one of the most effective chief justices in the history of the United States. As a leader, John Marshall was a community developer.

Co-opt or Isolate Spoilers

In traditional corporations, CEOs often deal with internal spoilers by firing them. In other kinds of institutions, for example high-talent organizations like universities and law firms, dealing with spoilers is more difficult. For one thing, a leader may not have the legal authority to fire them summarily. For another, even if you have that power, exercising it abruptly can seriously damage the organization. Tenured university professors, partners with large equity stakes in investment banks, politically influential board members, and famous scientists with substantial research funding of their own, cannot easily be dismissed from their jobs by firing them on a Friday afternoon and having a security guard escort them to the door. How then should leaders deal with other leaders who are spoilers? You have two options: Either convert them or isolate them.

Converting a spoiler is not a matter of religious fervor; it is essentially a process of negotiation—a negotiation between the leader and the spoiler. It begins with an understanding by the leader of the spoiler's interests. Once you understand those interests, you can then proceed to discuss with the spoiler ways by which you can help him attain those interests if he helps or at least does not thwart your efforts to integrate the firm more fully.

If you fail to co-opt spoilers, your other strategy is to isolate them in a way that will do the least damage to the organization. Isolation can take many forms, depending on the particular authority that you are granted under the rules of your organization. For example, you might avoid appointing them to various governing committees, remove them if they are already members, and order your public relations office to ignore them.

Adopt a Unite-and-Lead Style of Management

Your own style of management can encourage or inhibit the integration of your organization's members. Rather than adopt a divide-and-conquer style of management so common in many organizations, a leader of leaders would be better advised to develop a unite-and-lead approach. Rather than diminishing your power within the organization, your proven ability to unite your colleagues—to form an integrated organization, to make stars a team—will serve to empower you in other dealings with them and enhance your influence. A true unite-and-lead style means that you have to demonstrate by both word and deed that you put the interests of the organization above your own.

This may mean that you will have to give up some of the traditional status symbols of leadership. Through your own example, such as by giving up a reserved parking space near the entrance to your building, by using the organization's publicity organs to enhance your colleagues' reputations rather than your own, and by walking the halls frequently, as David Packard did at HP, instead of barricading yourself in a palatial office throughout the day, you walk the walk of a unite-and-empower style of leadership. Many talented followers draw no comfort from and do not want a charismatic leader towering above them. Rather what followers in many organizations expect—and sometimes demand—is that their leader be *primus enter pares*—"first among equals."

Conclusion: Rules for Negotiating Community

In seeking to negotiate community within your organization, remember the following rules:

(1) Make the common interests of your organization's members apparent through meaningful activity.
(2) Ensure that members of your organization know and appreciate its history.
(3) Learn to understand the nature of the cultural differences that divide your organization's members and then seek to find ways to bridge the cultural gap.
(4) Focus on the needed processes of communication within your organization and develop an ongoing strategy to accomplish them.
(5) Deal directly with members who are spoilers by converting them or isolating them.
(6) Demonstrate by both word and deed that you put the interests of the organization above your own.

7

Negotiating Conflicts

Organizations and Conflict

Every organization, no matter how well integrated, is filled with conflict. Corporate vice presidents struggle with each other over the size of their budgets. Law firm partners fight over corner offices and their share of partnership profits. Research scientists battle over laboratory space, credit on research reports, and the promotion of junior colleagues. Brothers in a family business struggle over company leadership when their father unexpectedly passes away. As long as resources like money, power, space, and credit are limited, competition for them is inevitable. As a result, one finds competition and conflict in various forms throughout all organizations, from top to bottom.

You can define a conflict as "…a perceived divergence of interest[s]" between two or more parties.[1] That divergence may be minor or substantial. It may be dealt with easily: for example, two executives with differing restaurant preferences for business meetings may decide to have Thai food at this week's gathering and Mexican at the next. Or it may be seemingly irresolvable, like the longstanding, violent conflict between Israelis and Palestinians. On the other hand, the intensity of the dispute sometimes bears little relation to the size of what is being fought over. An executive's sense of prestige, status, and influence in an organization may become very much a part of a struggle over

---

[1] Dean Pruitt and Sung Hee Kim, *Social Conflict: Escalation, Stalemate and Settlement*, 3rd ed. (New York: McGraw-Hill, 2004), pp. 7–8.

© The Author(s) 2017
J.W. Salacuse, *Real Leaders Negotiate!*,
DOI 10.1057/978-1-137-59115-9_7

something that has rather small material importance. Looking back at his days as a Harvard professor, former Secretary of State Henry Kissinger remarked that "academic politics are so bitter because the stakes are so small."

In addition to resources, conflicts within organizations can also center on non-material issues like the right theories, strategies, ideologies, policies, and procedures that the organization should adopt. Having learned a body of knowledge through painstaking effort, professionals will often fight ferociously to defend ideas that they consider basic truths and to destroy concepts they consider heresies. University departments have broken in two from faculty fights over academic theory, governments have ground to a halt because of inter-departmental conflicts over policy, and consulting firms have become paralyzed by struggles over strategy. Even in a symphony orchestra, two musicians can have an ongoing feud when one always wants certain notes to be played short while the other invariably prefers that they be played long.[2]

A certain amount of competition and conflict within organizations is productive and can lead to improved performance because it causes individuals to exert increased efforts to perform at the highest levels and to engage in creative problem solving that results in better solutions. Too much conflict, however, can cause a decline in productivity and even lead to organizational paralysis. One of the traditional tasks of a leader is to manage an organization's internal conflicts in order to prevent struggles among its members over their individual interests from threatening the well-being of the organization as a whole.

There are two general types of organizational conflicts that confront leaders: (1) conflicts between or among an organization's members, and (2) conflicts between the leader and one or more of the organization's members. Sometimes a specific dispute may have dimensions of both categories. Thus, the conflicts between Ovitz and other Disney executives which ultimately led to his dismissal had its origins in the disagreement between those executives and Eisner about the decision to hire Ovitz in the first place.

Strategies for Conflict

When faced with a conflict between or with an organization's members, a leader is faced with two basic questions. The first question is: Should I intervene at all? And the second is: if I do decide to intervene, what form

---

should my intervention take? To answer both questions and carry out the leadership task of conflict resolution, a leader needs to be guided by a strategy, that is, a general plan of action to achieve a particular goal. When faced with a particular dispute, a leader has several possible conflict strategies from which to choose to help decide on intervention.

Conflict Avoidance

Many leaders simply choose to ignore conflict, either because they do not think it is important or because they believe that it will eventually resolve itself. Thus Eisner, who appointed Ovitz over the opposition of his top lieutenants, must have believed that they would adjust to Ovitz's presence in the organization and the conflict would eventually subside as a result. Conflicts, however, rarely go away of their own volition. They can continue to fester within the organization with the result that they undermine the organization's effectiveness and even the leader's own ability to lead, eventually requiring leadership action as Eisner finally did when he fired Ovitz. Thus when faced with an organizational conflict, a leader, rather than ignore it, should carefully analyze its nature and causes, gauge the depth of feeling it has engendered, and estimate its potential impact on the functioning of the organization. Failing to expend the necessary time and effort to resolve it now may mean, as Eisner and the Disney painfully learned, that the leader and the organization may have to devote even more resources to deal with it later on.

Conflict Resolution by Fiat

While leaders sometimes try to curtail conflict among an organization's members by threats, orders, and even firings, these techniques are usually of little effect in settling the underlying causes of the dispute and may actually increase dissension within the ranks. For one thing, both inside and outside of organizations, leaders may simply not have the authority to compel certain of its members to do anything, let alone yield in a fight that they believe affects their vital interests. Thus Michael Eisner as chairman and CEO of Disney, seems to have felt that he could not order his two top lieutenants to report to Michael Ovitz, his choice for president, when they flatly refused. On the other hand, he appears not to have spent much time, effort, and thought in trying to negotiate a solution with them. It may well have been that their flat refusal to accept Ovitz was merely their opening move in their own negotiation campaign to stop his appointment.

A high priority goal of any leader is to preserve and retain the organization's top talent, its most precious resource, rather than to do something that might alienate and ultimately drive it out: a result that Eisner feared if he forced the imposition of Ovitz on his two colleagues. When faced with a potentially destructive conflict in an organization or group, a leader must answer a fundamental question: How do I reduce the negative consequences of this conflict and at the same time enable the contending persons to make a maximum contribution to the organization? Faced with such situations, leaders need to become conflict resolvers. The three principal methods that leaders may employ in this regard are negotiation, arbitration and mediation.

Negotiation

Despite a leader's formal powers and authority, they are often of limited use in resolving internal organizational conflicts. In many such situations, leaders must resort to negotiation to resolve disputes that have the potential to negatively impact organizational effectiveness. An initial problem in trying to resolve a conflict through negotiation is that, as in many competitive games, you can never know the other person's goals, intentions, and interests as well as you know your own. You have to infer them from circumstantial evidence, particularly from what the other side says and how they behave. So a key skill for any negotiator is the ability to "read" the other side, to know as much as possible about their goals, interests, and intentions. To do that, you have to elicit as much relevant information as possible from them and from other sources of intelligence and then to interpret it accurately.

With that understanding when faced with a conflict, you will normally proceed to determine an approach or a strategy to deal with the problem. Two of the most important determinants in adopting a strategy are: (1) the degree to which you will take account of your own interests; and (2) the degree to which you will take account of the other person's interests. Your concern for the other side's interests may be prompted by some altruistic motivation, some belief that those interests are morally superior to your own and therefore deserve to be recognized. But in most cases, that concern will be driven by a judgment on your part that an existing relationship with the other side is valuable and must be preserved or that it is only by accommodating the other person's interests, at least to some extent, is the only way to advance your own interests. So if your goal is to hire a superstar for your firm, your negotiation will need to find a way to satisfy most, if not all, of that person's interests. Similarly, Michael Eisner's apparent refusal to impose Ovitz as Disney president on his top lieutenants was no doubt strongly influenced by his desire to preserve good working relations with them not only for the sake of Disney's continued profitability but also to preserve his own position as Disney's leader.

Arbitration

Arbitration is an ancient method of dispute resolution by which the disputants agree to submit their dispute to a third party for a decision according to agreed-upon norms and procedures and to accept and enforce that decision. It may be applied to *existing* disputes, for example between two neighboring states as to the precise location of the boundary, and to disputes that may arise in the future, for example in collective bargaining agreements to resolve workers' eventual grievances against their employer. Arbitration has various modern forms that are embedded in international treaties, commercial contracts, and employment agree-ments, among others, as a means of settling possible future disputes arising under their provisions.

Leaders may use arbitration as a means for settling disputes among organizational members. For example, if the vice president for finance and the vice president for human resources in a company disagree over the size of the human resources budget for the following year, they might present their dispute to the president for a decision and agree to abide by his or her decision. Alternatively, if a corporate CEO is confronted with a conflict between two lieutenants, he or she might propose to settle the dispute through arbitration. The difference between arbitration and a decision by leadership fiat is that the disputants have agreed to arbitration as a conflict resolution method and thus the leader's authority to decide the matter is derived not from the leader's position but from the disputants' agreement to arbitrate.

A Case of Maternal Arbitration

An interesting and rather novel arbitration to solve a leadership dispute occurred in India early in the twenty-first century. The Indian economy, like that of many countries in South Asia, is based on family enterprises.

Indeed, it is estimated that 95 percent of all businesses in India are family-dominated firms and that together they account for almost two-thirds of the country's gross domestic product. In 2003, the largest of India's family businesses was Reliance Industries Limited (RIL), an industrial conglomerate with market capitalization of US$ 17.2 billion at the time. Reliance had been founded by Dhirubhai Ambani, a farsighted business man, and had grown rapidly over the years. In 2002, Dhirubhai died suddenly of a massive stroke, leaving behind his two sons, Mukesh Ambani and his younger brother Anil. Mukesh, who served as vice chairman of RIL, saw himself as the natural successor to his father, a position that Anil sharply disputed. When Mukesh actually took over as chairman, the feud between the two brother became extremely bitter resulting in law suits and public expressions of acrimony. Because of the company's importance to the Indian economy, various members of the government urged the brothers to resolve the dispute before it irrevocably injured the business. Although Reliance was publicly traded on the Mumbai stock exchange, the Ambani family held a controlling interest of nearly 35 percent of the equity.

By mid-December of 2004, Mukesh and Anil had expressed their desire to have their mother, Kokilaben Ambani, act as an arbitrator to resolve their dispute, a solution that seems not uncommon in South Asia where a mother will sometimes play an important role in settling disputes about succession to the leadership of family businesses.[3] Notably, as participants in an arbitration, the two Ambani brothers both committed to abide by whatever settlement terms she decided was appropriate. In dealing with such a sensitive family dispute, their mother proposed a solution in which her sons would become "separate but equal" and strove with determination to arrive at a "fair and equitable" division formula. Knowing that the sibling feud could only tarnish the Reliance reputation and her late husband's legacy, Kokilaben insisted on an agreement before the third anniversary of her husband's death. To achieve this, she sought assistance from K.V. Kamath, the head of ICICI, one of the largest banks in India, and a well-respected close family friend to serve as an honest broker and mediator in the negotiation process. After careful study of similar family business separation, he prepared a report proposing that the 34.04 percent stake, held by the Ambani family in Reliance's diverse enterprises through hundreds of investment firms should be divided in a 30:30:30:5:5 ratio between the mother Kokilaben, Mukesh,

---

[3] See Janjuha-Jivraj, Shaheena. "The Impact of the Mother During Family Business Succession: Examples from the Asian Business Community," *Journal of Ethnic and Migration Studies*, 30, no. 4 (2004): pp. 781–797.

Anil, and their two sisters, respectively. The two brothers discussed the split formula through Kokilaben, with whom they each had a one-on-one closed consultation.

On June 18, 2005, Kokilaben announced that she had "amicably resolved the issues between my two sons, Mukesh and Anil, keeping in mind the proud legacy of my husband, Dhirubhai Ambani."[4] The settlement formula allowed Mukesh to keep the flagships, RIL and Indian Petrochemicals Corporation Limited (IPCL) while Anil was given control of Reliance Infocomm, Reliance Energy and Reliance Capital.[5] In addition to the separation of control of various entities carved out from RIL, the two brothers also agreed upon a non-competition clause for the next five years.

For a time after the announcement of the agreement, the conflict between the brothers seemed to subside but soon other disputed matters between them would arise so that by 2017, one could not say that the the conflict between the brothers has been finally resolved. Nonetheless it is interesting to speculate on why the brothers, who seemed to disagree on everything else, accepted the arbitration of their mother. One possible explanation may lie in the way the brothers framed their dispute. They may have viewed it not as an ordinary *business* dispute which might entail the intervention of the courts, but as a fundamentally a *family* conflict. It was therefore natural to seek the intervention of a respected and trusted family member to help resolve it. In the Reliance Industries case, that respected, trusted family member was their mother. With their father's death, she became the leader of the family and it was natural that the family's leader serve as arbitrator in what was essentially a family dispute.

Mediation

In most cases of conflict between an organization's members, a leader will seek resolution by resorting to mediation. Mediation is an age-old conflict resolution technique that can be found in all societies, from African villages to international diplomacy, from urban neighborhoods to legislative corridors. Mediation is essentially the intervention of a third person in a dispute in order to help the disputants achieve a voluntary

---

[4] http://news.bbc.co.uk/2/hi/south_asia/4106236.stm
[5] http://www.economist.com/news/business/21610238-mukesh-ambani-indias-most-powerful-tycoon-could-make-his-country-better-place-he-would

agreement about the matters in conflict. History offers many examples of seemly intractable conflicts that the parties, left to themselves, could not resolve, but with the assistance of a third person—a mediator—were able to settle. President Theodore Roosevelt mediated an end to the Russo-Japanese War in 1905 and won a Nobel Peace Prize for his efforts. Jimmy Carter in 1979 intervened as a mediator in the dispute between Egypt and Israel and helped the two countries to achieve the Camp David Accords, which formally ended their state of war and opened diplomatic relations between them for the first time. Former Senator George Mitchell spent two years mediating the conflict between Catholics and Protestants in Northern Ireland, ultimately helping them to conclude the Good Friday Agreements of 1999 that laid a foundation for peace in a part of the world that had endured bloody sectarian fighting for many years.

In each of these cases, the mediator was a leader who assisted other leaders to negotiate a voluntary settlement of their conflict. In each case, a mediator helped the parties in dispute to do something that they seemed incapable of doing alone. Depending on the situation, the inability of two nations, two organizations, or two fully mature and competent individuals to solve their conflict by themselves can be attributed to a variety of factors, including poor communication, high emotions, deep distrust, lack of objectivity, the fear that any conciliatory gesture will be interpreted as weakness, and simply the lack of the skills necessary to negotiate a solution. For all these reasons, two vice presidents, two senior law partners, or two research scientists by them-selves may not be able to move toward a resolution of their conflict. Indeed, it often happens that the more they try to solve the problem by talking to each other the more they worsen relations between them and heighten tensions within their organizations.

The entry of a third person—a mediator—into the dispute often moves it toward resolution because the mediator brings to the situation the skills and resources that the parties themselves lack. The mediator's communication skills, objectivity, creativity, stature, and positive relationship with disputant are some of the key resources that may help settle the conflict.

An organization or group's members quite naturally look to their leaders to resolve internal quarrels that threaten organizational interests. Indeed a continuing state of internal organizational conflict is usually seen as a failure of leadership—a failure of the leader to take the necessary steps to end the conflict threatening the organization. Both within and outside of organiza-tions, leaders seek to act as mediators to resolve conflicts that may arise among the persons they are supposed to lead.

A key question for any leader is: What exactly am I supposed to do as a mediator? What actions should I take to resolve conflict among two squabbling law partners who both want the same corner office or two quarreling investment bankers who both want to chair the same business development committee? First, your very presence in their dispute is likely to change the nature of the interaction between the two disputant—hopefully for the better. The two squabbling law partners will probably conduct their discussion in your presence in a more unemotional, less hostile way than they would if the two of them were left alone. Indeed, without your presence, they may not want to talk to each other at all. On the other hand, you need to realize that mediators often fail, as President Bill Clinton did when he attempted to mediate the dispute between Israel and the Palestinians in the last year of his administration. Moreover, mediators can sometimes make the conflict between the parties worse or prolong its existence. Research has shown that energetic third party intervention can be counterproductive in those situations where the disputants are capable of moving toward settlement of their conflict by themselves.[6] So a first question you should ask when confronted with a conflict among the persons you lead is whether you should become involved at all. Are the parties able to move toward a solution to the conflict by themselves, however painfully? If not, do you have the skills and resources to help resolve the matter as mediator?

To help you answer that last question and better understand how to play the mediator role in your own organization, let's look at a specific conflict that arose between two vice presidents at a communications equipment manufacturer.

Robyn versus Luis

Assume you are the CEO of a publicly traded manufacturer of communications equipment that has had low, stagnant profits for the past five years. Hired just six months ago, you have been given 18 months by the firm's chairman to turn the company around and increase profitability. You have been working energetically with the company's vice presidents to develop a plan of action to fix the problem. In order to control costs, you and your vice president for finance, Robyn Kendal, have decided to impose a 5 percent

---

[6] Dean G. Pruitt and Sung Hee Kim, *Social Conflict: Escalation, Stalemate, and Settlement* 229, 3rd ed. (New York: McGraw-Hill, 2004).

limit on budget increases on all departments next year. Kendal is working with the company's seven other vice president to implement the budget cap.

You know that cutting costs alone will not achieve a sustained improvement in profitability. Company productivity must also increase. Luis Molina, the company's vice president for human resources, has proposed to you a new human resource development plan emphasizing employee training and evaluation as a way to improve productivity. Molina's proposed plan is based on the human resources system in the company's Canadian subsidiary, the firm's most profitable unit. You encourage Molina to develop a new human resources model based on the Canadian system for the entire company as you head off to begin a two-week tour of company facilities.

Two weeks later, on the day after you return from your trip, Robyn Kendal and Luis Molina appear at the door of your office and ask for a meeting. Puzzled, you invite them in. Reminding you of the directive to limit increases, Kendal reports that whereas all the other vice presidents have reluctantly agreed to hold budget increases for their departments to 5 percent, Molina has refused and is insisting on an 8 percent increase. Molina argues forcefully that he needs the additional 3 percent, about $500,000 more, in order to implement the human resources development that you and he had previously agreed upon, a plan that he and his staff have been working on nights and weekends to finish. Kendal insists, as she and you had previously agreed, on the need to reduce costs in order to improve company profitability; Molina argues strongly for the need to increase profitability in order to raise company profits on a sustained basis. As the discussions proceed, Robyn and Luis's emotions rise, with Robyn suggesting that Luis is not a "team player" and Luis telling Robyn not to be so "rigid."

Robyn's and Luis have come to you as their leader because they want you to do something about their conflict. These two leaders, while seeking to validate their individual positions and advance their own seemingly divergent interests, do appear to agree on one thing: one of your responsibilities as a leader is to settle conflicts among the people you lead. But before you plunge ahead to judge like Solomon, as both Robyn and Luis seem to want you to, you might first step back to consider more deeply this apparently simple situation. With greater reflection you'll see that several factors complicate finding an easy solution.

First of all, any decision you make on the issue of budget increase risks alienating one of these two key vice presidents, persons whose effort and support you will need if you are to achieve long-term profitability for the corporation. You also need to realize that you have contributed to creating this conflict by encouraging Robyn to impose a budget cap and Luis to develop a new personnel plan without communicating clearly to both the need to cut costs *and* increase productivity at the same time. Your own status and prestige as the company's new CEO, six months into the job, may also be affected by how you handle this conflict situation. Other managers will be watching to see how you deal with this problem, and they will make judgments about you and the effectiveness of your leadership accordingly. If you give Luis what he wants, will you doom any effort to impose needed budgetary discipline on the company? If you support Robyn, will you stifle creative efforts to increase productivity? In addition, Robyn and Luis have their own authority, prestige, and leadership at stake since they have pushed their staff members to develop new plans and since Robyn has, through tough negotiations, succeeded in persuading the other vice presidents to go along with a budget cap in their respective departments. To complicate matters further, you have only a year left to turn the company around. As you consider the situation you begin to understand that this seemingly simple problem about a 3 percent difference in budgets is not as simple as it first appeared. How do you start to resolve it?[7]

The First Step: Understand Interests

As a leader, your first step is to come to understand the interests of the persons you lead. Both Robyn and Luis have a diverse set of interests in this budget conflict. Robyn, as vice president for finance, is clearly interested in the financial health of the company and the achievement of increased profitability. She also seeks your respect and support and wants you to see her as an important and vital player in your plans to turn the company around. Robyn also has a strong interest in preserving her authority and respect with the other vice presidents with whom she has negotiated budget limitations and with her staff who have worked to develop this approach to cost containment. If you decide to give Luis what he wants, you may undermine Robyn's status with both groups.

Like Robyn, Luis has professional, organizational, and personal interests at stake in this conflict. As a senior manager, he certainly has an interest in the company achieving increased profitability and in maintaining your respect and support for him in that position. He also probably believes that the

---

[7] A dramatized form of this case, *Robyn and Luis*, written, directed, and produced by Jeswald W. Salacuse is available on video from the Program on Negotiation at Harvard Law School (www.pon.org)

successful implementation of the new human resources plan will bring him professional advancement, increased recognition, and ultimately improved compensation. An 8 percent increase in budget will give additional resources to his department and increase his power and influence within the company. Luis also wants to maintain the respect of the other vice presidents and of his own staff, and he certainly feels that an adverse decision in his conflict with Robyn will diminish his standing. This fight is not just about $500,000. It is about the influence and prestige of two of your key vice presidents.

You are not a disinterested bystander in this conflict. As a leader, you also have a variety of interests that you need to delineate and understand clearly. You certainly have an over-riding interest in increasing the company's profitability by reducing costs and increasing productivity. Indeed, preserving your position as CEO of the company depends upon it. You are also vitally interested in maintaining the support and loyalty of these two vice presidents who are both important to your plans to turn the company around. If you grant Luis an 8 percent increase, you risk Robyn's disaffection, the deterioration of what up to now has been a good working relationship, and perhaps eventually the loss of a valued collaborator. If you stick to the 5 percent cap, you retain Robyn's loyalty, but risk losing Luis. A compromise solution, for example giving Luis only 6.5 percent, may satisfy neither, demoralize both, and demonstrate your weakness to all.

Your Role as Leader-Mediator

Having analyzed the interests of the various parties in this dispute, you next need to think about the role that you should play in trying to resolve it. One possible role is that of judge or arbitrator. The two vice presidents have brought you a problem, have each stated their respective arguments, and have asked for your decision. After all, you are the leader of this organization. Your job is to make tough decisions that will advance the company's interests. So decide!

There are certainly many times when the people you lead will bring a matter to you for a decision, and the best thing you can do is to listen carefully, study the matter, and then make a decision. For example, if Robyn and Luis had a difference of opinion on how to interpret your directive about projects that would be exempt from the 5 percent budget cap and had appeared in your office for clarification, you could have proceed to give it. Having heard your decision, your subordinates would have walked out of your office and proceed to implement it. But is that the case here?

Your decision on whether to judge a dispute or mediate it depends largely on two factors: the nature of the dispute in question and the nature of the parties involved. The issue of whether you decide or mediate a dispute among people you lead depends to a significant extent on how deeply they are invested in the conflict and on how extensively their interests, personal and professional, are impacted by any decision that you make. One of the purposes of your conversation with them is not only to understand the facts of the dispute but to make an evaluation of the depth of their feelings and interests about the conflict. In cases where they are deeply invested, your best approach is to try to mediate a solution to the dispute. The more deeply that the parties are invested in the dispute, the more you as leader will need to mediate it and the less likely that an outright decision by you will end it. Similarly, the more an organization allows its members autonomy of action, the more likely it is that a resolution of conflicts among them will require mediation rather than a judgment from you as leader.

What is it that mediators do to settle a conflict between other persons? In general terms, a mediator *helps* the parties resolve their conflict, which in most cases means assisting them to negotiate a solution. A mediator, unlike an arbitrator or a judge, has no power to impose a solution. At the outset, you need to recognize that a single, magic mediation formula does not exist. Different mediators do different things. Theodore Roosevelt, Jimmy Carter, and George Mitchell, all successful mediators, each used different techniques to mediate the disputes they confronted. For one thing, mediators intrude into a conflict to different degrees, depending on the nature of the dispute, the parties, and their own skills, resources and judgment. In general terms, there are three general areas that a mediator may seek to address: process, communications, and substance. You as a leader-mediator should think about each of these three areas.

Process

At the most basic level, the leader as mediator may simply work to shape a more productive process of interaction between the parties in the dispute, such as Robyn and Luis. For example, recognizing that a sudden meeting in your office after your return from a two-week trip is probably not the most auspicious moment for settling a conflict, you might arrange for the three of you to discuss the issue in an atmosphere more conducive to conflict resolution. The physical site where mediation takes place can have an impact on the conflict dynamic. The site's neutrality, privacy, and security are factors that are conducive to a settlement. It is for this reason that Camp David, the retreat of U.S. presidents, has been a favored site for conflict mediation. Bearing in mind the importance of the mediation site and the timing of your intervention, you might for example invite Robyn and Luis to your private club for lunch or drinks or to return to your office at a more convenient time to share a sandwich, asking them to think creatively about ways of solving the problem in the meanwhile and acknowledging your own responsibility in causing this conflict.

One process technique that many mediators use is to *caucus* individually with the disputants so as to learn of their underlying interests and concerns. With their agreement and before meeting together with Robyn and Luis, you might want to talk to them individually about the problem. In a one-on-one session, they may be more frank about their interests and concerns, less confrontational and emotional, and thus give you insights into how best to resolve the conflict. Research suggests that when hostility between the parties is high, bringing them together too soon may serve to exacerbate the conflict, rather than begin a process toward resolution.[8]

Another process approach is to explain to them your thinking about the need both to reduce costs and improve productivity. While accepting responsibility for not having made your goals clear earlier, ask them to try to find a solution themselves and then to report back to you within a week. You might also gently suggest some basic ground rules to follow in their one-on-one strategic conversation. In effect, you are seeking to create a more productive process of discussion between the two vice presidents and then letting them take it from there.

As you help develop a process, you should also work to increase the parties' motivation to solve their problem. You can do this by talking optimistically about the possibilities for resolution, by using your relationship with each one to encourage them to work sincerely to find a solution, and by seeking ways to build trust between them, for example, by speaking positively about the important role that each person plays in the organization and the significant contributions that each has made to its success.

---

[8] Ibid., pp. 234–235.

Communications

Merely creating a better process may not be enough to settle the conflict. As leader-mediator, you may have to find ways to improve *communications* between contending parties, like your two vice presidents, Robyn and Luis. For example, you may have to help the two sides understand and acknowledge the legitimacy of each other's interests and needs: that Robyn has a legitimate interest in maintaining the confidence of the other vice presidents, that Luis has an interest in increasing productivity, that cutting costs alone will not solve the company's problems. You might seek their advice on criteria to measure results, incentives to make the plan work, and sanctions in case it fails.

One important way by which a mediator can improve communication between the parties is to help them define the precise issues in dispute and to aid them to stay focused on those issues during the discussion. A conflict is often characterized by parties' misperceptions of each other and distortions caused by hostility. By defining the issues, the mediator can move the parties toward active problem solving and away from personal recriminations. More than merely defining the issues, the mediator can facilitate settlement by reframing them in a way that appeals to the interests of both parties. Thus in the case of Robyn and Luis, the issue is not whether Luis is to receive a 5 percent increase or an 8 percent increase but what budgetary actions can the company take in the next fiscal year to increase profitability. In addition to reframing issues, another mediator technique is to sequence issues, to develop an agreed-upon agenda as to the order in which the parties will address the issues in dispute. Sometimes you can create momentum towards a solution and build confidence between the parties by taking up and resolving the easier issues before addressing the more difficult ones.

Substance

Finally, if the people you lead remain locked in their positions, as Robyn and Luis are, you might offer *substantive* suggestions as to how the two vice presidents might solve their problem. Here you might ask the parties to engage in a brain-storming session to come up with creative solutions that would resolve the conflict by allowing both Robyn and Luis to satisfy their interests.

If Robyn and Luis are unwilling to engage in this exercise and persist in holding fast to their positions, then you as mediator-leader should put forward ideas on possible options and ask for their views on them.

Depending on the level of emotion and hostility between the parties, you may wish to hold this discussion individually with each of the disputants in separate meeting, since they are more likely to be receptive to new ideas and to engage in genuine evaluation of new options in a private session with you alone than in the presence of the other party for fear that any flexibility will be seen as a weakness to be exploited.

Some suggestions that might emerge with your encouragement could include: (1) transfer to Luis's department two staff members from the company's Canadian subsidiary (i.e. payment in kind); (2) create a special budgetary category for "special projects" or "capital projects" that have to be approved by the CEO and the board and are not considered part of the annual operating budget; (3) tie the continued grant of 8 percent to criteria and penalties for failure to meet them; (4) fund the additional 3 percent from the president's budget, not the basic operating budget; and (5) grant an increase for six months with the additional six months funded only upon presentation of evidence that the plan is achieving productivity.

Mediation Power Tools

In most cases, a leader-mediator is not willing to solve a conflict at any price. "Peace at any price" cannot be the motto of an effective leader because in most cases a leader-mediator has a definite goal in mind: to help resolve the conflict between followers in a way that is in the best interests of the organization or group. As a leader, you have a point of view about the conflict and the way it ought to be resolved. If for example, you believe that Luis's new human resource plan will actually increase employee productivity, you will seek to resolve the plan in a way that will give Luis the resources he needs while protecting Robyn's status and authority as vice president of finance. On the other hand, if you feel that Luis's plan will have no impact on company profitability, then you are likely to want to move in the direction of action that does not give him all that he is asking but will still preserve his morale and your working relationship with him.

In most of the disputes you mediate, you are therefore not truly neutral. You have a point of view, a definite objective in mind. Absolute neutrality is not essential to effective mediation. Jimmy Carter succeeded in mediating the conflict between the Israelis and the Egyptians at Camp David despite the fact that Israel and the United States were historically close allies and that the United States had resupplied Israel with arms in its 1973 War with

Egypt. What is more important than neutrality is that the two disputants accept you in the role of mediator to help resolve their dispute. Mediator acceptance is more important than mediator neutrality.

In order to achieve your goal of settling the dispute in a way that is in the best interests of your organization, you will have to change the behavior of one or both of the disputants. As a leader of other leaders, you usually do not have the legal authority to order them to change their behavior in a particular way and even if you did the consequences of such an order can be extremely negative for your continuing relationship with them, for the organization as a whole, and for your future ability to lead it. Lack of legal authority or the inadvisability of using it does not mean however that you as a leader of leaders are without power. Depending on the situation, you may have greater or lesser social power that you can use to influence the behavior of other persons.

Drawing on the work of social psychologists, one can identify specific bases of social power that a mediator might use in interactions with disputants to change their behavior in desired ways.[9] Six in particular are important. They include: (1) reward, (2) coercion, (3) expertise and information, (4) legitimacy, (5) reference, and (6) coalitions and networks. These six elements are a mediator's power tools. Let's look briefly at how to use them.

(1) Reward

A mediator uses reward power by offering some positive benefit to one or both of the disputants in return for a desired change of behavior. Part of the United States' effectiveness as an international mediator has been its ability to offer increased aid to disputants who resolve their conflicts, as was the case with the Egypt–Israel peace treaty that resulted from the Camp David mediation conducted by President Jimmy Carter. Leaders by virtue of their positions have access to resources that they can use to reward disputants. Thus in dealing with Robyn and Luis, you as CEO may have special funds that you can tap to finance the new human resource plan without forcing Robyn to lift the 5 percent budget cap especially for Luis. The risk of granting a reward to disputants in your organization is that others in the organization will view your largesse as

---

[9] See, e.g., Jeffrey Z. Rubin, "International Mediation in Context," in Bercovitch and Rubin, eds. *Mediation in International Relations: Multiple Approaches to Conflict Management* (New York: St Martin's Press, 1992), pp. 254–565.

weakness, a reward for bad behavior, or as setting a bad precedent that others may exploit in the future.

(2) Coercion

Leaders have the power to punish as well as reward, and mediators have used the threat of punishment as a means to change disputants' behavior. In 1995 when the United States intervened to stop the fighting in Bosnia, Assistant Secretary of State Richard Holbrooke induced the Serbs to accept a settlement by threatening their chief supporter, Slobodan Milosevic the President of Yugoslavia, to have NATO bomb Serb positions in Bosnia. You as leader of leaders may also have various means of coercion at your disposal. Like rewards, coercive acts have both costs and benefits. You need to calculate them carefully before moving to coerce a disputant in your organization. Remember that the leaders you lead also have resources that they may decide to employ against you if you become too heavy handed.

(3) Expertise and information

In some cases, a mediator's ability to influence the parties is derived from the mediator's expertise or specialized knowledge. In those situations in which the leader by virtue of his or her position is presumed by the disputants to have superior knowledge, the leader-mediator's recommendation as to what the parties should do is supported by the power of expertise. So your statement to Robyn that you have studied Luis's plan carefully and that you as an experienced corporate officer believe it has an excellent chance of success draws its force from your expert power. You need to recognize, of course, that many of the people you lead also exercise expert power in their day-to-day lives. The ability of doctors, lawyers, management consultants, and money managers, to name just a few, to influence their patients and clients is derived from their expertise. As a result in their own areas of specialization, they may not be willing to accept your recommendations if they decide that your expertise is no greater than theirs.

(4) Legitimacy

You gain the power of legitimacy from a supposed right to ask someone to do something. As a result of your position as leader of an organization, you have certain rights to make demands on and act toward other organization members in particular ways. Indeed, your ability to intervene in a dispute between members stems from the legitimate rights you hold as their leader. The extent of your legitimacy power will depend on the organization, the situation, and the nature of the dispute in question. While it may be legitimate for you to intervene in a dispute in order to resolve it and to make recommendations, your legitimacy power may not extend to actually directing the disputants to change their behavior toward each other in particular ways.

(5) Reference

Reference power arises out of your relationship with the person you are trying to influence. It is based on the fact that the target of influence values that relationship with you and therefore will be reluctant to do anything that might damage it. For example, if one of the disputants is someone you hired and mentored over many years, your reference power with that person may be significantly greater than over a person of the same experience level but who had joined the organization a year ago. As we said at the beginning of this book, leadership is fundamentally a relationship between the leader and the persons who follow them. To the extent that you as a leader have developed strong personal relationships with those persons, you gain important tools of influence in times of conflict.

(6) Coalitions and networks

In trying to settle a dispute, your own resources may not be enough. You may therefore have to reach out to other persons to help you influence the disputants. Building coalitions and mobilizing existing social networks are important power tools for the mediator to use at the appropriate time. For example, in trying to settle conflict between senior management consultants in your firm, you as a newly chosen managing partner may have less influence over the disputants than a long-time partner who had actively mentored and aided one or both disputant over the years. By involving that person in helping you resolve the dispute, you are using coalition power to change one or both of the disputant's behavior. Any time you are working to solve a conflict among those you lead, you should always ask a fundamental question: Who else can help me with this task?

Effective leader-mediators rarely use just one of the power tools alone. They often need to be used in combination in order to achieve desired results. So in persuading Robyn and Luis or any of the other people that you lead to accept a solution to a conflict that they themselves cannot or will not settle, you as a leader-mediator may have to employ a sophisticated mixture of rewards and coercion, reference and legitimacy, as well as expertise and coalitions.

Conclusion: Rules for Negotiating Conflicts

Leaders who are called upon to resolve conflicts within their organizations should remember the following rules:

(1) Seek to understand the disputants' underlying interests, not just their stated positions.
(2) Consider carefully the process that you will use with the contending organizational members and the precise role that you ought to play in that process.
(3) Evaluate the way the disputing parties are communicating with one another and seek to improve their processes of communication.
(4) Make sure the dispute resolution process and communications are right before you jump in with substantive solutions to the conflict.
(5) Consider carefully the six mediation power tools of reward, coercion, expertise and information, legitimacy, reference, and coalition and networks that you may employ and how they might be applied most effectively in the conflict you are facing.

8

Negotiating Education

Leaders and Education

Education is one of the daily tasks of any leader. Indeed, the word "educate" is derived from the Latin "*educere*," which means to lead forth. Whether an organization's members want to recognize it or not, the job of any leader is to help them learn. Modern management scholars have urged traditional corporations to become "learning organizations," to adapt to rapidly changing business environments, to constantly rethink and reinvent the way they do business. That advice is really not revolutionary. Successful organizations have always engaged in learning, and high-talent organizations are often by nature learning organizations. Management consulting companies, law firms, research institutes, universities, investment banks, and symphony orchestras have always recognized that their basic capital is their members' collective knowledge, a wasting asset whose value can only be maintained by the continued and constant learning of its members. On the other hand, when companies disappear from the business scene, some observers are sometime quick to attribute their disappearance to "globalization" and "foreign competition." Upon closer examination of individual cases, the real reason may be the failures by the leadership of those companies to create learning environments in their organizations so as to promote innovation for the improved products and services constantly being demanded by the changing markets they were trying to serve.

Despite the importance of learning to the continued and enhanced effectiveness of organizations, many, if not most leaders, do not view education as one of their important functions. As a result, they rarely devote the time and energy that the education function deserves. I saw this attitude quite clearly during a leadership program I taught a few years ago for 200 of the top executives of a large multinational pharmaceutical company. As part of an exercise, I placed around the room seven flipcharts, each labeled with one of the seven tasks of leadership. I then asked the program participants to go the chart with the leadership task that they like to do best. The flipchart that drew the least number of executives was labeled "Education." The reason for their lack of interest in this vital leadership function is not completely clear. However, there are at least two possible explanations. First, their own education and training did not stress that education was part of their role as business leaders and therefore did not equip them specifically to act as educators. Second and, perhaps more important, the company's incentive system did not reward them for successfully educating their subordinates; consequently, they devoted time and effort to activities that the company did reward. The visible payoff for successful education efforts are often in the distant future, not immediately in the next fiscal quarter, the time horizon often of most concern to shareholders looking for a rapid increase in a company's profitability. Nonetheless, the long-term prosperity, if not the survival, of an organization is crucially dependent on the continued learning of its members. It is up to the leader to see that the required learning takes place. To do that, a leader must first accept that education is very much a part of a leader's role.

The Leader's Role as an Educator

Incorporating the task of education into a leader's role begins with understanding the nature of education. The goal of education, whether it takes place in a highschool classroom or a high-talent organization like an investment bank, is that persons learn. Useful learning can take place in many ways. For many people, the basic model of education is the traditional classroom. The old-fashioned classroom learning model is a simple, one-way process. The teacher imparts knowledge and the students absorb that knowledge as best they can. A lot of what passes for continuing education and corporate in-house training still relies heavily on that model.

In fact, few really good educational programs operate in that fashion. Students in the most effective educational environments learn in many ways: from knowledge conveyed by the teacher, from insights gained from other students, from their own study, from their own research and experimentation, from their observations of the outside world, from discussions and dialog among students and teacher, from one-on-one executive coaching, from trying to answer questions that they had never asked before, and from trying to apply their knowledge to real or simulated problem situations, to name just a few. A truly successful teacher understands that students learn in many ways and therefore seeks to manage that learning process in all its complexity to assure that the students maximize real learning from the constantly changing dynamics taking place in a particular learning environment, whether it is a classroom, laboratory, conference room, or office. Like gifted teachers, leaders, in carrying out the daily task of education, need to be *managers of the learning process* within their organization. The management of learning in organizations and with other leaders, as in classrooms, may require a variety of techniques, depending on the learning problem encountered, the persons taught, and the demands of the organization served. Sometimes, you as leader do the teaching. Sometimes you need to find others to provide the learning.

Negotiation and Learning

While recognizing the importance of education as part of a leader's function, you might ask: In view of the subject of this book, what role does negotiation play in carrying out a leader's educational functions? The answer to that question is that any educational relationship between instructor and student requires a basic bargain—an agreement—between instructor and student. That bargain is the product of an implicit or explicit negotiation between the two parties concerned. Indeed, without such a bargain, no effective learning can take place. Many organizations, in the name of education, require their employees to attend training programs against their will. While the employees may dutifully sit through what they consider an ordeal, quietly checking and answering emails or surreptitiously reading newspapers, little real learning takes place because the intended students and the instructing institution have not negotiated an agreement upon which the educational effort needs to be based. Other organizations buy "off-the shelf, general purpose training programs" developed by consulting firms and external trainers. These efforts also fail to impart real learning in the organizations that pay for them because no negotiation took place between potential instructors and potential students in putting them in place.

Why is negotiation important to the success of organizational education? For two reasons. First, the negotiation takes account of students' interest in shaping an educational effort, a vital requirement for securing student commitment and buy-in to the educational process. Second, through the negotiation process the trainers learn about the special nature of the organization concerned and are therefore better able to orient the training process to the real needs of the organization.

So if an organizational leader is to succeed in fostering learning in the organization, he or she must negotiate an educational deal. That process begins with an understanding of the organization's educational problems, including the nature of the interests of potential students who will participate in any educational effort.

Diagnosing the Learning Problem

As managers of the learning process, leaders must constantly be alert to the existence of learning problems within their organizations. The process of organizational education usually begins with a recognition by the leadership of a lack of needed learning by some or all members of the organization. Leaders first must identify those situations where optimal performance by the organization or by individual members is hindered by lack of needed knowledge or skills. Once you have detected a problem, you can't develop an effective solution until you have accurately diagnosed fully its causes and its consequences.

An organizational learning problem is not always readily apparent. Indeed, its symptoms can often be interpreted in ways that have nothing to do with learning. Like a physician examining a patient, you have to be constantly alert to symptoms, but more important you need to understand their causes. In 2002, administrators of a 1700-bed medical center and hospital in New Jersey grew increasingly concerned by tensions and conflicts between its patients and its medical staff, as well as between its nurses and doctors. The conflicts between patients and staff were particularly troublesome since they threatened to erode the hospital's patient base and therefore its revenues as patients looked elsewhere for care. The hospital was operating in an extremely multicultural environment. Approximately 80 percent of its affiliated doctors were emigrants to the United States, primarily from India, Pakistan, Russia, and Africa. Its nursing staff was drawn primarily from Latin America and the Philippines. While its patients were largely Hispanic, they also included a wide range of ethnic groups from throughout the world.

The hospital administration was receiving growing numbers of complaints from patients about insensitive, rude, and in some instances discriminatory treatment from doctors. The doctors often found it hard to communicate with patients, many of whom didn't speak English and therefore couldn't clearly communicate their symptoms, problems, and feelings. In addition, conflicts within the nursing and support staff seemed to be increasing.

The perceived tensions between medical staff and patients were merely symptoms of a problem that the hospital was facing. It was up to the hospital leadership to understand the causes and then figure out what to do about them. Different leaders might have interpreted the symptoms in a variety of ways. Tensions in relationships and their resulting negative impact on the delivery of medical services might have been caused by any number of factors —too heavy a workload placed on the staff, ineffective management systems, inadequate staff training, low nursing salary levels that dampened morale, or generally poor working conditions.

After undertaking a needs assessment, the hospital leadership found that the cause of the tensions was none of these. Instead, it concluded that its entire staff, both doctors and nurses, did not have the skills and knowledge to work and communicate in a multicultural environment. Although doctors and nurses may have had world-class skills for performing heart bypass operations and treating cancer, they lacked the ability to communicate with a multicultural patient population whose exceptionally diverse backgrounds, cultures, and languages created significant barriers for medical diagnosis and treatment. While the medical staff as individuals each had received excellent medical training in their home countries, their education had not specifically addressed how to communicate and treat people from other cultures.

Having diagnosed the nature of the problem, the hospital then had to decide what to do about it. As a first step toward a solution, the leadership concluded that it needed to mount a special program conducted by outside experts to teach the entire hospital staff about cultural diversity and the ways of communicating and working in a culturally diverse environment. Although organizing seminars and workshops on diversity for the nursing and support staff seemed a relatively simple matter, organizing sessions that the doctors would attend was an entirely different matter. Teaching the highly educated, the hospital leadership realized, could be a major challenge. Indeed, when it comes to educating elites, the more highly educated they are the bigger the challenge it is to teach them.

Several years ago, I encountered a learning problem similar to the New Jersey situation on the other side of the world—in Sri Lanka. In 1993, the Sri

Lanka Securities Commission invited me to visit that island nation off the coast of India to advise it on ways of improving its judges' knowledge about securities and financial law. Sri Lanka was then in the process of developing a stock market, and the government and the Securities Commission considered the courts vital in maintaining the market's integrity. Both the stock market and the laws supporting it were all very new and had been based on American and English models. Most Sri Lanka judges knew nothing about them and had no training in how to understand and apply this arcane area of the legal system. My host, the Chairman of the Sri Lanka Securities Commission, believed it essential to educate them, and he hoped that my visit would lay the foundation for the development of a special training course for all senior judges in the Sri Lankan judiciary. The Chairman realized that the country's judiciary had a learning problem when its judges botched the first few cases to come to court under the new stock market and securities laws. The chairman was a leader undertaking the daunting task of trying to educate high-ranking judges over whom he had absolutely no authority. He knew that the only way he could achieve that goal was to negotiate an agreement with the Supreme Court, the leaders of the Sri Lanka judiciary, to introduce a training program for judges in the new stock market and securities legislation. My lecture to the Supreme Court judges was to be the first step in that negotiation.

A First Step: Understand the Interests of Your Students

It is a fundamental rule of negotiation that to reach an agreement with other persons you have to understand their interests. A leader who seeks to negotiate an educational deal within the organization must also come to know the interests of the persons to be educated. Both the hospital administrators in New Jersey and the Securities Commission chairman in Sri Lanka understood this principle and acted accordingly.

Knowing your students is important for two reasons—one concerns *what* you teach and the other affects *how* you teach it. The first is about substance and the second is about process. In the case of the New Jersey hospital, the hospital leadership, after completing a needs assessment and consulting with outside experts, gained a clear idea of the content and goals of a training program: to impart to doctors and staff an understanding of intercultural communication techniques for use in treating people from other cultures. Knowing *how* to teach these techniques effectively to the various professional audiences within the hospital was, however, a much more difficult problem.

Having worked with doctors for many years, the New Jersey medical center's leadership knew their potential audience well enough to realize that physicians, because of their education, status, and position, would not be an easy group to reach, let alone teach. Since the highly educated draw a significant amount of their power, influence, and status from the fact of their advanced education, they usually resist strongly anything that puts their knowledge and expertise into question. To ask doctors to assume the role of students would suggest that their education was not complete. The hospital leadership was keenly aware of this educational problem and so was my host in Sri Lanka. In both situations, in order to arrive at an educational deal, the leadership had to develop an educational vehicle that would recognize the dignity and status of participants as highly trained, skilled professionals, not ordinary students.

My visit to Sri Lanka began with a dinner meeting of its Supreme Court judges, to whom I was to talk about securities law and its role in creating and supporting vibrant capital markets. The chairman of Sri Lanka's Securities Commission was extremely nervous about the meeting and about what I, an unknown and therefore unpredictable American professor, would do and say. As the time for the dinner approached, the chairman kept reminding me, as if I were one of *his* students, "Now remember, they're not students. They're judges of the Supreme Court. You can't treat them like students!" And of course, he was right. If what I said and how I said it at that dinner had made them feel like "students," as that term is understood in Sri Lanka—rather than Supreme Court judges, which is what they were—then I would have met resistance rather than acceptance to anything I told them.

The relationship between teacher and student in virtually all cultures implies a power relationship, a relationship in which the teacher by virtue of position exerts influence over the student. Educated people often resist the role of students because they see it as a diminution of their own power and status, a negation of their education, intelligence, and influence. In their view, those things are their primary assets, so don't expect the educated to give them up easily. Leaders who insist on trying to establish a teacher–student relationship with the people they lead will often meet resistance to what they consider a subordinate role and that in turn translates into resistance to anything they are trying to teach. So if the first rule for any leader who seeks to teach followers, is "Know your students," the second rule is the Sri Lankan corollary: "Don't ever treat them like students."

The New Jersey hospital followed both rules in setting up its diversity training for doctors. Knowing the sensitivity and pride of doctors in their education and high status, the hospital leadership realized that trying to put doctors and nurses in the same room at the same time to attend lectures on diversity would fail miserably since it would suggest that doctors and nurses have a similar status and level of education. The doctors would simply have refused to attend, claiming that they had no time for seminars and that their patients came first. While the hospital administration would have no problem in securing attendance by nurses at a diversity training program since they were used to attending periodic training as a condition of their employment, the hospital leadership did not have the same leverage over doctors. It therefore recognized that teaching doctors about diversity would require a special program for doctors and for doctors alone.

Knowledge of their audience also led the hospital leadership to understand that any diversity training for doctors would not only have to be separate and special but that it also had to be done in such a way that it respected both the status and the learning traditions of the medical profession. What this meant, for one thing, is that parachuting an outside expert, who did not hold an M. D., into the hospital to give lectures on diversity to a room full of doctors would be met with resistance, instead of the receptivity that is necessary to real learning. Indeed, that turned out to be the case. As the hospital began to make plans to organize diversity training throughout the medical center, many doctors made it known that they were not going to participate. They simply did not have the time to spare. The hospital nonetheless proceeded to hold training sessions for all of its other staff members.

As training proceeded with a positive response from nurses, technical staff, and administrators, the hospital leadership began to talk with leaders among the doctors about how its physicians might learn to better communicate with their ethnically diverse patients. Through these discussions, the doctors came to recognize that the hospital had a serious communication problem that was complicating and in some cases endangering patient care and treatment. Finally, they arrived at a "medical approach" to the problem: "grand rounds."

Hospitals have traditionally conducted periodic grand rounds", a time when affiliated doctors would present and examine particularly difficult medical cases and the physicians in attendance would suggest diagnosis and treatment approaches that might be considered. Grand rounds, while never called "training" or "education," were nonetheless important means for doctors to learn. Traditionally, grand rounds were done as a group of doctors moved around the hospital wards, examining patients with particularly difficult medical conditions. Nowadays, grand rounds often take place in a conference room or auditorium.

Through effective negotiation, the New Jersey hospital leaders persuaded the physicians' leadership that a doctor should prepare and present a grand rounds case involving the diagnosis of a non-English speaking, Hispanic patient by an attending physician who did not speak Spanish, an increasingly common phenomenon in the hospital's emergency room. To assist in preparing the case, the hospital administration offered the doctor the opportunity to consult with intercultural communication specialists—the same ones who had been training the nursing and administrative staff. At the grand rounds session, over lunch, the doctor presented the case, invited and received comments from the other doctors in attendance, and then asked the diversity specialist to comment, which she did. In that setting, the doctors of the New Jersey medical center began to learn some of the basic skills of communicating with their ethnically diverse patients. It was through the framework of grand rounds that the hospital leaders created and managed a learning process that taught some valuable skills and ideas to physicians, without treating them as students.

The case of the hospital in New Jersey and my own experience teaching professionals around the world suggest some other lessons about negotiating learning.

A Second Step: Use Existing Frameworks and Mechanisms

One important way of not treating educated professionals as students is to employ their own education frameworks and mechanisms. As the New Jersey case has shown, employing the grand rounds framework to educate doctors proved effective, whereas using a traditional "training course format" would have proved a failure. Similarly, as I found in Sri Lanka, holding a dinner meeting to discuss problems of judicial administration, rather than a seminar to teach judges about securities laws, proved effective, precisely because it was a framework that the judges knew and trusted, a framework that did not place them in the role of traditional students. Every group of professionals, whether they are lawyers or doctors or bishops, has its own mechanism for sharing information—for educating themselves. If you seek to educate them, you need to identify those frameworks and mechanisms and figure out how to use them for the educational purposes that you as leader want to achieve.

The name you give to the process matters. As we saw, doctors were willing to attend a meeting labeled as "grand rounds," but refused to go anywhere near something that might be called "diversity training." Indeed, in many situations, if you are educating the highly educated, you should probably avoid the use of the word "training" altogether, since training implies a teacher–student relationship and clearly treats those in attendance as students. Terms such as "executive review," "senior management conference," "executive meeting," and "strategic network" serve to elevate the importance of the gathering, to assure those attending that they are involved in something worthy of their status, and to remove it from being denigrated as just simply training, thereby encouraging other leaders to attend. Of course, if you can also serve food, as the New Jersey doctors and the Sri Lankan judges experienced, that too helps attendance.

One-On-One Education

The role you assume as leader-educator can influence your ability in actually teaching people something. Seeking to become the teacher, lecturer, or instructor of other leaders will in most cases generate significant resistance from those you are trying to teach. For one thing, that approach raises the problem of your credentials. When faced with a person who claims to have something to teach them, educated and smart people, confident of their own abilities, immediately ask what it is that you know that they don't already know. So the question doctors in the New Jersey hospital would have asked, when faced with a "diversity expert" who would lecture them on communicating with patients, is: What is it that the expert, who has never seen their patients let alone treated them, can tell them about caring for sick people that the doctors don't already know. Similarly, if you are the managing partner of a law firm or investment bank, your fellow partners, whose education and experience is better than yours, will often resist, if not resent, your lectures to them on law or finance, even though they never tell you that directly. For another thing, since a teacher–student relationship often implies an asymmetrical power relationship between student and teacher, the people you are trying to teach will often view your assumption of a teacher's role with them as a challenge, if not a direct threat to their autonomy—yet another reason to resist you and what you are trying to teach. Certainly, the doctors in the New Jersey hospital, conscious of their high status and power within the organization, opposed attending lectures by a diversity expert, not only because they questioned the expert's credentials to teach them anything about practicing medicine, but because to do so—to sit in a classroom and listen to lectures like students in school—they feared, would have diminished that status and power in the eyes of others.

Any Oxford don will tell you that the most effective way to teach students is not in a lecture hall but in one-on-one tutorials that are a tradition at that great university. Similarly, one of the most effective means of delivering your message to the members of your organization, particularly those in leadership positions, is in one-on-one conversations. For example, one study examined the results of a conventional managerial training program on managers and supervisors at a health agency, which was followed by eight weeks of one-on-one executive coaching. It found that while the training increased productivity by 22 percent the one-on-one executive coaching (which included goal setting, collaborative problem solving, practice, feedback, supervisory involvement, evaluation of end results, and a public presentation) increased productivity by 88 percent, a significantly greater gain compared to training alone. The authors suggest that the training provided a period of abstract learning of principles, while the coaching facilitated concrete involvement in a project specific to each participant's work unit. As such, executive coaching is an important way of ensuring that knowledge acquired during the training phase actually emerges as skills that are applied at work.[1]

It is in a one-on-one setting that you are most likely to achieve the greatest receptivity to your message. First, a one-on-one session acknowledges the equality, individuality, and autonomy of the other person. Second, because you are communicating with a single person, rather than with a group, you can tailor your message to the needs, attitudes, and concerns of that specific person, and that person alone. Third, through the feedback you receive, you will gain new insights into the other person's interests and concerns and therefore adjust your presentation accordingly. And finally, a one-on-one structure instead of a group setting allows you to deal with oppositional coalitions more easily. People in groups tend to form coalitions, subgroups that adopt a common viewpoint or position. The doctors in the New Jersey medical center mentioned earlier initially formed a coalition to oppose diversity training for physicians. In negotiating an educational deal, you always need to be alert to the possibility that some or all of the persons you seek to educate will form a coalition, either consciously or unconsciously, to oppose a policy, goal, or direction that you are seeking to

---

[1] Olivero, Gerald, Denise K. Bane, and Richard E. Kopelman. "Executive Coaching as a Transfer of Training Tool: Effects on Productivity in a Public Agency," *Public Personnel Management*, 26, no. 4 (1997): pp. 461–469.

advance. More than one new and inexperienced leader has had the unsettling experience of coming up with a new idea for the organization, calling a meeting to present it, and then as the meeting progressed watching helplessly as a coalition of the people the leader is supposed to lead begins to form slowly but inexorably in opposition to that brilliant idea. A more experienced leader would have first persuaded key colleagues of the wisdom of the idea in one-on-one sessions before the general meeting took place so as to have a basis for building a coalition in favor of the idea and to prevent the formation of a blocking coalition. Similarly, if you are going to educate those you are supposed to lead, particularly members of high-talent organizations, you might think about doing it one member at a time.

Advice and Consent, not Command and Control

In one-on-one meetings with other leaders, you can assume a variety of roles as an educator. You can lecture. You can give a sermon. You can plead. You can deliver the riot act. Depending on the situation and the person involved, any of these methods of communication may serve to educate. But there are two other roles that you should consider: the role of advisor and the role of client.

Advising is essentially a one-on-one relationship through which one person (the advisor) seeks to help another person (the client) determine a course of action to solve a particular problem. Implicit in the notion of advising is that the problem in question and the precise course of action to be taken remain the decision of the person receiving the advice. Advising respects the autonomy of the person advised. Advisors have many different names: consultants, counselors, guides, coaches, mentors, and assistants, among others.

One of the basic functions of many of organizations, such as law firms, investment banks, management consultants, and medical practices, is to provide advice to other persons. At the same time, advice is an important tool for managing and leading those same organizations. Subordinates influence their boss's decisions through advice, and most boardroom decisions are the product of advice from many sources, both inside and outside the corporation. Even in traditional corporate structures bosses, too, know that it is often better to advise employees on a particular course of action, rather than to give them direct orders. While "advice" from the boss is in some cases merely a disguised command, in many situations, particularly when authority has been broadly delegated within the organization, a manager plays an advisory role. Generally speaking, the more decentralized the operation and the more educated the employees, the more important advice becomes in leading an organization. To the extent that "command and control" forms of leadership do not work in an organization, the wise leader seeks to rely on "advice and consent" leadership.[2]

As a method of educating other leaders, advice and consent leadership can operate in two fundamentally different ways: sometimes times you, as a leader, play the role of advisor and in other circumstances you assume the role of client, the person seeking advice. Whether you assume one role or another depends fundamentally on the willingness of the other person to let you become his or her advisor. That in turns depends on your relationship with the persons you are seeking to lead. Sometimes your position in the organization entitles you to provide advice to its members. Thus, as chairman of an investment bank facing increasing competition from large financial organizations, your advice as to how to confront this new competitive challenge—for example, by transforming your partnership into a corporation and then making an initial public offering of shares—is both expected and considered legitimate by your partners. Of course, like any advice, your views do not bind your partners. They are free to reject them as a way of solving the firm's problems.

In certain other situations, it may be more effective to advance learning with other persons by asking *them* to advise *you*. Generally, people like to give advice. They usually believe that they have a rich store of ideas and information and are willing to share them with others, either because they find that another person seeking their advice is flattering to their egos or because through their advice they can influence others. As a leader, you can put that instinct to work to advance learning among members of your organization when you use it as a means to open a dialog on a matter that the person from whom you ask advice needs to be educated.

Senator Joseph Biden did just that in the waning days of the Cold War when as a member of the Senate Foreign Relations Committee he was trying to persuade Andre Gromyko, the Soviet Foreign Minister, to accept certain modifications in an arms control treaty that the Untited States and the Soviet Union were in the final stages of negotiating. Detecting Gromyko's resistance to any changes, Biden, instead of advocating modifications, took another tack: he asked for Gromyko's advice. He said: "Mr. Minister, I

---

[2] See Jeswald W. Salacuse, *The Wise Advisor: What Every Professional Should Know About Consulting and Counseling* (2000).

understand your views, but I have Senate colleagues back home that need to be convinced that this treaty will not harm American security. Perhaps you can give me some advice on how I explain certain of the provisions to them." As Biden pointed out some of the more problematic provisions, Gromyko responded by telling him the arguments that he should use with other senators. In each case, Biden responded that, yes, he understood Gromyko completely, but that some of the more difficult senators would respond in this way or that. As the dialog proceeded, Gromyko, said at one point: "Yes, I see what you mean. Perhaps we can modify the language of the treaty in this way to take care of that point." By asking Gromyko to become his advisor, Biden in the end educated Gromyko about the difficulties of ratifying the treaty in the U.S. Senate and thereby secured changes that he needed.[3]

Similarly, in the New Jersey hospital facing severe problems of communicating with a multi-ethnic population, the process of education began when the leading hospital administrator met with the head of medicine and asked for his advice on how to improve communication between patients and the hospital staff, including the doctors. It was during that conversation that the idea of using grand rounds was suggested. The Sri Lankan Chairman launched the process of educating the country's judges about the stock market and securities laws when he met with the Chief Justice of the Supreme Court asked for his advice on improving securities law enforcement.

Framing the Problem

Education is the process of learning about something. The effective leader-educator must determine what that something is and then communicate it to the persons to be educated. Any teacher will tell you that how you define your subject matter—how you *frame* it—is the difference between engaging your students and turning them off. Similarly, negotiators know that framing is an important tool for reaching agreement. Framing is the use of analogy, metaphor, or characterization to define a problem or describe a situation. A frame can orient people's thinking in either productive or unproductive ways, and the frames that work best are those that take account of the interests of those whom you seek to influence. The Goldman Sachs's leadership framed the fundamental question about the firm's future as "What

---

[3] William Ury, *Getting Past No: Negotiating With Difficult People* (1991): pp. 61–62.

should be its strategy in meeting increasing competition from huge financial firms with a global reach?", not "Should we turn ourselves into a corporation and sell our shares to the public?" For the New Jersey hospital, the question was not framed as "How can we teach doctors to communicate better with a multi-ethnic population?", but "How can we as a hospital improve our treatment of patients from an increasingly multi-ethnic population?" For George H.W. Bush, the question posed to other leaders at the time of the 1991 Gulf War was not "How do we drive Saddam Hussein from power?", but "What actions should we take to protect the security of the world and the principle of territorial sovereignty that is the foundation of the international system?"

As a leader seeking to foster learning in your organization, you should give careful thought to how you frame the problem that you want to educate others about. First, in order to secure receptivity, at least initially, try to frame the problem under discussion in a way that accords with or at least does not threaten the interests of those you are trying to educate. That includes avoiding framing the problem in a way that is critical of others or blames the problem on them. Consequently for a law firm, posing the question as "How can we get departments in our firm to cooperate with one another more effectively in order to better serve our clients?" may be better than "Why do the partners and associates in the business transactions area have such a hard time working with the lawyers in litigation?" Framing the problem in a way that is threatening to those you are trying to educate will only cause them to raise defenses to what you are saying and thus impede real education.

Second, frame the question in such a way that it invites genuine participation and engagement. Real education begins by engaging the other person's mind. The right question can do that. The wrong question can stop education dead in its tracks. So Senator Biden did not frame his question in a way that was critical of the Soviet Union or of Gromyko personally. He did not say, for example, "Why can't you Soviets be more flexible on questions of weapons verification?" That question would have provoked a defensive reaction from Gromyko, not a genuine search for a solution. Asking for Gromyko's advice on how to explain the treaty to other U.S. senators truly engaged Gromyko's mind in a way that educated him about American concerns and interests.

Third, the effectiveness of a frame often depends on the name you give it. Calling the discussions among doctors about the problems of diagnosing the illnesses of persons from different cultures "grand rounds," instead of diversity training, was a key factor in gaining acceptance by doctors of the hospital leadership' efforts at promoting learning in an important problem area.

Never Give a Solo Performance

Good teachers know that education requires the active participation of students. Similarly, as a leader who would educate others, you need to find ways to actively involve them in the process of education that you are seeking to facilitate. Several reasons justify such an approach. First, other leaders, by virtue of their experience and education, individually have valuable knowledge that needs to tapped and shared to advance the education of the entire group. One of your tasks as leader-educator is to mobilize and exploit that knowledge for the common good and to help to diffuse it within the organization.

Second, as every good teacher knows, students understand and retain best those ideas that they themselves have discovered. Education is a process of discovery in which students actively participate.

Third, the purpose of education in any organization is not knowledge for knowledge's sake but knowledge to solve problems and improve the organization's performance. The persons you are seeking to educate are more likely to apply their new-found knowledge to the work of the organization if they themselves have been involved actively in its development and discovery than if it is just handed to them. They will more readily "buy into" and take ownership of new ideas and knowledge if they have actively participated in its development than if they have been isolated from the process and are merely passive recipients of that information.

What this means is that one of your basic tools as an educator within your organization is not the declarative sentence but the question. Socrates, one of the greatest of all teachers, developed this approach to a fine art, an approach we know of today as the "Socratic method." The Socratic method's goal is to actively involve students in the learning process. The question serves as the foundation of that approach because it taps students' knowledge, leads them to discover the knowledge for themselves, and convinces them of its applicability to life. For many leaders, the idea of asking questions of those they lead rather than telling them what they need to know is anathema, the very opposite of what good leadership is about. For them, leaders are supposed to have the answers to problems. They are the font of wisdom. While this approach is questionable in traditional corporations, it is bound to encounter resistance in educating those who feel they are already educated. So the next time you are preparing an elaborate and colorful PowerPoint presentation in order to teach something to the people you lead, ask yourself whether your method is actually the best way to educate them, to implant new ideas and knowledge that will be internalized, retained, and actually acted upon. The ultimate test of good teaching is not whether the professor has delivered a brilliant lecture but whether the students have actually learned something.

Conclusion: Seven Principles for Negotiating Learning

As you go about negotiating learning in the organizations you lead, bear the following principles in mind:

(1) As a leader, think of yourself as a manager of the education process in your organization.
(2) Seek to understand the educational needs of your organization and the educational interests of its members and find ways to accommodate those interests in your educational efforts.
(3) Work to negotiate a basic bargain with the organization's members upon which to base your educational efforts.
(4) Think carefully about how to frame your educational efforts. Try to use the established and accepted educational frameworks and methods of the group you are hoping to educate. Examine particularly whether the frame you adopt takes account of the interests of those you are trying to educate. Consider carefully the label you give your efforts.
(5) To the maximum extent possible, do your educating one-on-one, rather than in groups.
(6) In the face of resistance, assume the role of advisor or client.
(7) Use questions to educate.

9

Negotiating Movement

It is one thing for a leader to determine a direction for the organization, it is quite another to cause people to actually move in that direction. Moving people toward a goal, a traditional function of all leaders from national presidents to factory superintendants, is the aim of the fifth daily task of leadership—motivation. *Motivation*, derived from the Latin word "to move," is basically a force within persons that incites them to act. Individuals are not robots. They have their own separate will to take action. The task of any leader is to find and apply the means that will trigger—that will incite—others to take the desired action for the benefit of the organization or group. Human actions may be driven by external forces such as governmental orders or by internal factors, factors within each of us that cause us to act in particular way. That internal trigger is called "motivation." In fact, motivation is the internal driving force behind all our actions.

Interest-Based Motivation

The interests and feelings of those you lead are at the heart of the motivation challenge. People act when they believe it is in their interests to do so. That belief in the desirability of action may be based on a person's rational calculation of costs and benefits, on emotional factors, or on ideology or a religious conviction. The techniques of motivation vary from leader to leader and from situation to situation. Political leaders have traditionally sought to motivate their followers through oratory. Winston Churchill, by his speeches

© The Author(s) 2017
J.W. Salacuse, *Real Leaders Negotiate!*,
DOI 10.1057/978-1-137-59115-9_9

to the British people during World War II, strengthened their motivation to endure the German bombardments of England and to struggle on to victory. Martin Luther King's ringing words motivated both black and white Americans to fight for civil rights. President Franklin D. Roosevelt's radio fireside chats helped the United States to face the trials of the Great Depression. And, in the aftermath of the terrorist attacks on the World Trade Center on September 11, 2001, New York Mayor Rudolph Giuliani through his words and actions provided emotional support to New Yorkers in a time of great tragedy and motivated them to take up normal life again with courage and calm. In times of crisis, people seem instinctively to look to their leaders to motivate them, encourage them, and strengthen them to do the right thing for themselves and for the group.

The task of motivation is by no means the exclusive province of national leaders in times of crisis. Effective leaders in all organizations and groups, large and small, think about it every day. They think about it with respect to motivating particular individuals or entire groups of people within their organizations. The basic question that is constantly on a leader's mind is: How do I motivate the people I lead to act in ways that are in the best interests of the organization? In order to answer that question, you have to think hard about their interests, about what is important to them. Your negotiation about motivation should be interest based.

Management literature and business consultants have sought to answer the motivation puzzle for many years as they have defined a wide variety of "incentives," from bonus plans to flexitime, that will hopefully motivate employees to work determinedly in the interests of their companies. Like alchemists seeking the secret of turning lead into gold, they have sought to discover the universal motivator. For the past several decades, one favored incentive for corporate managers has been the stock option, a device that seeks to motivate managers by aligning their financial interests with those of the corporation and its shareholders. According to the motivational theory underlying this incentive, if a corporate manager's financial interests through the stock options owned are tied to the interests of the corporation, that manager will be motivated to work hard to increase shareholder value and thereby his or her own financial fortunes. Corporate America seems to have viewed the stock option plan as the universal motivator, the one-size-fits-all incentive that achieves the ultimate corporate goal of maximizing shareholder value. While stock options have certainly served to motivate hundreds of thousands of employees and executives over the years, they have also led to abuses and manipulation to the detriment of the company, as the Enron and Worldcom cases demonstrate.

Monetary rewards such as stock options are not the only form of incentive that can move people. Other intrinsic and psychic rewards can also be powerful. For example, in 1988, Amnesty International invited Reebok to be a sponsor of its "Human Rights Now! World Tour!" featuring musicians Bruce Springsteen, Sting, Peter Gabriel, Tracy Chapman, and many others. The tour visited 23 cities in four continents and had the impact of inspiring its own employees. As one commentator noted,

...the event probably didn't sell any shoes. But because the concerts were held at a critical time in Central Europe and in authoritarian regimes of the Third World, they had a huge political impact that inspired the imagination of Reebok employees, suppliers, and franchisees who were engaged in the project. By thrusting the company into the leadership ranks for the global human rights movement, the concerts gave the company's stakeholders a reason to be proud of what they do.[1]

Despite economists' emphasis on the importance of monetary incentives, there is probably no such thing as a universal motivator. Leaders need to shape their approaches to motivation to take account of a variety of factors, most important of which is the nature of the people you are trying to motivate. What that means in practice is that leaders need to negotiate motivation with the people they lead.

Negotiating Motivation

The purpose of motivation is to influence human behavior in a desired way. The constant preoccupation of leaders is to influence and often to change significantly the behavior of the people they seek to lead. To achieve that goal, leaders use incentives. Behind their use, is always an explicit or implicit negotiation. The terms of that negotiation are usually quite simple. The leader offers to do X, if the followers will do Y. Through this negotiating process, the leader hopes to lead the members of the organization or group to act in ways desired by the leader. So if a CEO is seeking to increase profitability in order to satisfy the board of directors and the shareholders, he or she might offer those who succeed in improving their performance and thereby contribute to an increased profitability, stock options as a bonus at the end of the fiscal year. If the general manager of a major league baseball

---

[1] Craig Smith, "The New Corporate Philanthropy, June 1994," *Harvard Review on Corporate Social Responsibility* (2003): p. 172.

club is seeking to attract bigger crowds to games through higher team standing in the league, he might offer contracts with bonuses to pitchers who win more than 20 games and sluggers who hit more than 50 home runs during the season. And if the leader of a software team needs team members to work nights in order to finish a project, he or she might offer them Fridays off with pay so that they can spend longer weekends with their families.

As you negotiate incentives to motivate the people in your organization, you should constantly bear in mind the following three questions:

(1) Will the incentive you are planning to offer actually bring about the behavior you are seeking or will some other incentive be more effective? For example, will a stock option program actually motivate your computer science engineers to design new, innovative programs or will giving them more autonomy in their work bring about that result?

(2) Even if the incentive will induce the desired behavior will it also lead to other, undesirable conduct? For example, although the stock option incentive may result in increased profits from quarter to quarter, will it have a negative impact on long-term corporate profitability by causing employees to devote less time and energy to projects having a long-term but distant payoff?

(3) And finally, is the benefit to be derived from the incentive worth the cost that the organization will have to pay for the incentive?

This X-for-Y motivation negotiation plays out at all levels and in a wide variety of contexts, from international politics to internal family conflicts, like the one I saw my two-year old granddaughter Olivia, whom our family calls "Livi," negotiate with her mother.

Motivating Livi

On a beautiful, warm summer afternoon, my daughter and I were sitting, chatting on the backyard deck of my house, when Livi, with a book under her arm, toddled up to us, plopped down next to her mother's chair and, extending the book, said "Read, Mommy. Read." She had a rubber pacifier in her mouth, which her mother had been encouraging her to abandon. Seeing this situation as an opportunity to motivate Livi to give up the pacifier, my daughter said, "I'll read to you if you give me the pacifier." Livi met that request with a very energetic shaking of her head. Here then, in conflict resolution terms, was a perfect illustration of deadlock, of standoff, of stalemate. The scenario that I watched was like the western nuclear powers telling Iran they would not lift the trade sanctions against that country until Iran had eliminated all its capabilities to enrich uranium that might be used to make an atom bomb. Faced with a no-reading sanction imposed by her mother Livi did not cry and she did not throw a temper tantrum. Instead, she looked at her mother a moment, gauging the determination of her adversary, and then suddenly reached up to her mouth, and took out the pacifier, but instead of handing it over, she laid it very carefully on the ground next to her own leg where she could grab it in an instant if she needed. She then looked up at her mother and said, "Read, Mommy. Read."

In the negotiation over motivation, Livi had made a counter offer, an offer in negotiation theoretical terms that was "interest based." She was in effect saying to her mother "Your primary interest is not that I give you the pacifier, but that I not use it, at least while you read to me. I have satisfied that interest. Now can we make a deal to have you read to me?" Iran, like Livi, countered demands from the western nuclear powers to abandon and destroy all facilities to enrich uranium, with a counter offer that it would instead not use those facilities to enrich uranium for 15 years, a concept that would become the basis for Iran's 2015 nuclear deal with the West. Like Iran, Livi succeeded in making a deal to lift the sanctions and so she ultimately persuaded her mother to read to her on that summer afternoon.

In seeking to motivate many members of your organization, particularly those who are highly trained, the first thing you need to recognize is that they usually do not view their professional activities—whether they are doctors in a hospital, architects in a firm, computer programmers, or violinists in a symphony orchestra—as just a job. It is a profession, a calling, a commitment to an area of endeavor that has necessitated long years of training and practice. In most cases, they view that commitment as life long. Moreover, to a significant extent, they derive their identity, social status, and indeed very purpose in life from their positions as doctor, lawyer, or violinist.

This conception of their role in life has two important consequences for leading them. First, they often have strong alliances and senses of affiliation with others who pursue the same calling. Indeed, that sense of affiliation with fellow professionals may be stronger than their loyalty to the institution that pays them. Thus, lawyers, economists, musicians, and actors may care much more about the opinions of other lawyers, economists, musicians, and actors than they do about the particular firm, university, orchestra, or studio that currently employs them.

Second, the traditions of their particular calling may give them a special outlook on the world not shared by others and may even lead them to believe that by virtue of their profession they are a special, privileged caste. Indeed, their professional training may have deliberately sought to give them that sense of being special. Thus, law schools emphasize that they are teaching students to "think like lawyers," as if lawyers somehow think not only differently but better than other people, and medical schools are infamous for giving their graduates the belief that they have a status superior to other healthcare professionals.

The strong sense of the role, profession, or calling that professionals in your organization feel has important implications for motivating them. First, monetary incentives alone may not be significant motivators. Other factors that affect the role they have chosen in life can also be powerful forces. These incentives include associating with persons of the same calling, learning new skills and knowledge related to their field of specialization, recognition of their achievements by their peers or by the public, and career and professional growth. Conversely, actions that they perceive as negatively affecting their professional status may serve to alienate them and cause them to resist and challenge those who try to lead them.

The individuals in your organization may have diverse motivations for action, and it is your job as organizational leader to figure out what those motivations are. Those differences of motivation reside in the fact that different people have different interests. It is those interests that "make them tick." For example, as the president of a non-profit organization, such as a school, museum, or charity, you will find that the members of your governing board have different motivations for serving as board members. Some are committed to the cause that the organization is dedicated to, such as educating handicapped children, promoting modern art, or aiding the poor. Other board members are primarily motivated by the opportunity to associate with other civic or business leaders. Still others are driven by the public recognition that they gain in their respective communities by serving on a non-profit board such as yours.

For you as president to work with and to lead these board members, you need to understand their individual interests if you are going to motivate them to work for the organization and, equally important, to contribute money to it. Thus, an important lesson about motivation is not to assume that those you lead have the same interests and will therefore respond in the same way to the same incentives.

And while you are at it, you should also try to determine your own motivation as a leader. What is it that motivates you to accomplish the daily tasks of leadership? The answer to that question may influence the way you go about the job.

One Size Does Not Fit All

As we have seen, motivating others requires you to shape incentives through negotiation to the particular interests and concerns of the individuals you are trying to motivate and ultimately to move. There is no universal motivator for all leaders. This factor, however, presents an additional challenge for any leader and it is important to recognize it at the outset: the accusation of unequal treatment from those you are supposed to lead. Seeking to find and provide the special incentives that will motivate a particular individual may conflict with the prevailing ethic in most organizations and groups that the leadership should treat all members equally. To what extent do differentiated incentives run the risk that you will be accused of undue favoritism, of playing favorites, and therefore of undermining your legitimacy as a leader of an entire group? That question is real, and you should bear it in mind as you seek to motivate and encourage the people that you lead.

When I was dean of the Fletcher School, a history professor who I considered a rising star in her field told me that she had the opportunity to become the editor of her field's most prominent journal, but that to do so she would need significant funding over the next five years to pay for the editorial office that would be moved to the school. When I asked my associate dean for finance to find the funds for the editorial office in the school's already constrained budget, he protested that I was giving a special favor to one faculty member over all the others, that I would be accused of favoritism. Moreover, if I provided her with funding, other professors would come running to me for money to support all sorts of special projects. I was starting a process that I would regret.

The principle of equality of treatment is a fundamental imperative in any organization, but it may also be used as a bureaucratic defense against needed action and innovation. Leaders have to make judgments on the importance of actions that depart from this norm and the reasons that justify them. In this case, I felt special treatment was justified since I believed that funding the editorial office would help the history professor to become a recognized leader in her field, a recognition that would not only benefit her but the school's reputation as well. Moreover, if other faculty members had projects of equal importance, I was prepared to find money for them also, even it meant a budget deficit.

In the end, we found the money to support the journal for five years. The history professor not only did a superlative job as editor of a prestigious journal, but she also went on from there to become the president of a prestigious international academic association, while demonstrating in many concrete ways a strong commitment to the mission and programs of the school. As an incentive, the funds for her editorial office were a far more powerful motivator for excellent academic performance that if I had given her the same amount as a salary rise. Moreover, the fears about accusations of unfair favoritism never materialized because the importance of the project was understood and accepted by her colleagues.

An understanding of the interests of the people you lead comes essentially from getting to know those people extremely well, a process that usually requires one-on-one interactions with them. You need to get to know them as persons, not just as associates. That means, to the extent you are able, that you should try to get to know something about their personal lives—their families, their aspirations, their achievements, their experiences, and their disappointments. Here, of course, a leader needs to tread carefully. On the one hand, you want to know as much about those you lead as possible, but you must avoid intruding into the areas of their lives that they want to keep private. If you push too hard and too quickly to probe those areas, the people you lead may become resentful and consider you a busybody, raising defenses against your attempts to get to know them. Getting to know the people you lead is a slow process that requires the investment of a significant amount of leadership time.

On the other hand, you may find, as I have on many occasions, that by virtue of your position as leader, the people you lead feel they need to inform you about calamities in their lives, like divorces, serious illnesses, and troubled children. Like it or not, leaders have to deal with the emotions of those they lead. Your followers' emotions not only affect their ability to do their jobs but they can also influence positively or negatively the morale of entire organizations. It often falls to leaders to help employees cope with negative emotions and find ways to overcome them. Some members of an institution, however, are often less inclined to seek such emotional support than others since they fear to do so would reduce their influence and status within the organization.

Through those relationships, you gain the knowledge and the influence that facilitates all of the seven tasks of leadership. At the Camp David negotiations between Egypt and Israel in 1979, President Jimmy Carter worked hard to develop strong personal relationships with Egyptian President Anwar Sadat and Israeli Prime Minister Menachem Begin. At one point, the negotiations reached an impasse, and Begin decided to leave Camp David and return to Israel with his delegation.

On the morning of his departure, President Carter went to Begin's cabin and, as a parting gift, gave him photographs personally autographed to each of Begin's grandchildren. When Begin saw the children's names written in Carter's hand, he became emotional, perhaps as he thought about their future in a country that was still at war. Moved, Begin, under Carter's urging, decided to stay and continue negotiations toward what became a peace treaty with Egypt. Carter's gift had made Begin think of the long-term interests of his grandchildren and, by extension, future generations of Israelis. As a result, Carter motivated him to persevere in the search for peace.[2] Carter's ability to motivate the Israeli prime minister came from his relationship with and knowledge of Begin, not just as an Israeli politician, but also as a person.

As you get to know the people you lead, through conversations in the hall, shared lunches, and drinks after work, you build a relationship with them, a personal connection between them and you. That personal relationship itself becomes a vehicle for motivation. We are usually more willing to do things for people we care about and who seem to care about us than we would for people with whom we have no relationship. Indeed, our loyalties in organizations are generally to the colleagues with whom we have positive relationships, rather than to the abstract and disembodied thing known as "the firm," the "company," or "the institution."

Carter worked very hard to build personal relationships with both Begin and Sadat, and those relationships helped him motivate both leaders to work equally hard to achieve a peace agreement that has proved to be enduring. Similarly, Lyndon Johnson became master of the Senate because of the network of complicated relationships that he painstakingly built with each of its members over several years. Those relationships gave him the ability to influence and motivate desired action through individual incentives directed at each of the Senate's 100 members, persons who were themselves leaders in their own right, so as to achieve the legislative goals that Johnson wanted. On the other hand, Johnson would not have been able to dominate the U.S. House of Representatives because of its size—its 435 members. Johnson, who had served in the House, recognized the implication of the difference immediately. When he gazed at the Senate Chamber after his election to that body, he was heard to murmur "Just the

---

[2] Jimmy Carter, *Keeping Faith* (New York: Bantam Books, 1982), p. 399.

right size!"[3] He knew instinctively that the number of people you have to motivate has a direct impact on your ability to lead them. The more people you have to motivate the more complicated the task of leadership.

Motivation, Not Manipulation

Much of what passes for advice on motivation in management literature is often about employee manipulation—stratagems to induce workers to produce more, labor longer, and work harder. So, for example, leaders are urged to find reason to praise employees whenever they meet them or to present them with tokens of appreciation. In practice, as leaders apply these techniques more and more frequently throughout their organizations, the praise and presentations often become matters of pure form and ritual, deprived of significant meaning. Sometimes, incentives are insincere and border on the fraudulent. Eventually employees come to recognize manipulation for what it is and either ignore it or react negatively when they realize that their leaders are manipulating them.

In his dealings with Sudanese officials, Egyptian President Anwar Sadat invariably said to them: "You know, my mother was Sudanese." He apparently assumed that his Sudanese connection would motivate them to be well disposed toward him and by extension to Egypt. While it was perfectly true that Sadat's mother was born in Sudan, over time he came to refine his gambit by stressing his connection to a particular part of Sudan. So in dealing with a southern Sudanese, he would say that his mother had come from southern Sudan. To an official from western Sudan, he would say that his mother had come from western Sudan, and an eastern Sudanese would hear that Sadat's mother came from eastern Sudan. Eventually, the origins of Sadat's mother became a standing joke among Sudanese officials. They saw it as an insincere stratagem to manipulate them, and they treated it as such.

Trying to manipulate followers has real dangers since members of the leader's organization are usually more capable than most of recognizing manipulation for what it is. Your ability to manipulate your followers is further limited by the fact that they may be smarter than you are and have probably read the same management books that you have. One of the dangers of manipulation is that it may serve to *de*motivate the people you are trying to motivate. Insincere forms of motivation and attempts to

---

[3] Robert Caro, *The Years of Lyndon Johnson: Master of the Senate* (New York: Alfred Knopf, 2002).

manipulate others will often result in them behaving in ways that are the opposite of what you desire. In fact, your perceived efforts at manipulating people you are trying to lead may result in a reduction of their trust in you, thus diminishing your ability to lead. For example, your insincere statements of support or praise meant to motivate others may cause them to question the truth and sincerity of your statements on other matters as well.

Convincing Conviction

Your ability to motivate the people you lead begins with your own strong belief in the goal you are trying to achieve. As leader of the Senate, Lyndon Johnson, was fond of saying: "What convinces is conviction." As a result, before seeking to convince others of the rightness of a particular position, he first worked hard to convince himself.[4] It is important therefore for any leader seeking to motivate other leaders to achieve a level of "convincing conviction," whether it is to build a coalition to go to war or to start a risky new area of practice in a consulting company. The very fact that you demonstrate an energetic and enthusiastic drive toward a particular goal will have the effect of motivating others toward that goal or at least cause them to think seriously about it. On the other hand, your failure to demonstrate convincing conviction will be interpreted by others as your having serious reservations about a proposed course of action so perhaps they should, too.

Convincing conviction is reflected not only in your words but also in your actions. By modeling in your own acts the behavior you want others to follow, you motivate them to act in that way. Thus Mayor Rudolph Giuliani's calm courage following the terrorist attacks in New York City on September 11, 2001 motivated New Yorkers to emulate him as they struggled to re-establish normal lives in that city. Giuliani's convincing conviction caused New Yorkers to face the future with courage and confidence.

While convincing conviction is an important force for motivation, *how* you convey your conviction to others is equally important. Indeed, you may do it in such a way as to demotivate the people you are trying to motivate. Most of the people in your organization usually have their own strongly held convictions about the future and the world around them. To try to

---

[4] Ibid., p. 889.

overpower them with your own ideas, without regard to their own thoughts and feelings, is likely to alienate, not motivate them.

While seeking to motivate others through your own strongly held views, you also need to avoid conveying the message that you, as leader, are the primary source of ideas, the principal and perhaps only problem solver, and that if they will just shut up and do as you say the organization or group will prosper. Conveying these messages, intentionally or unintentionally, will in most cases demotivate, not energize, the people you are trying to lead.

Many people grow impatient with the apparent chaos and lack of order in universities, artistic organizations, research institutes, and other organizations composed of smart, talented, and creative people. "Why can't you just tell them what to do?" critics ask. "All they need are tough leaders who aren't afraid to tell them what to do." As a leader, you may of course tell your followers anything you wish. The problem is that smart, talented, and educated people don't have to listen to you if they don't want to. They certainly don't have to obey you.

Several years ago, I invited Judge John R. Brown, a great federal appellate court judge who played a key role in helping to desegregate the American South, to speak at the Southern Methodist University School of Law. After his speech, at an informal luncheon, Judge Brown, a flamboyant and congenial individual, began to talk about the need to reform legal education. At one point, he said, "Why, if I were dean, I'd tell the faculty to...."

"Judge," I gently cut in, "I don't think you understand the nature of the job."

The job of leading organizations, unlike that of a judge, is not just about ordering people to do things. It is about encouraging and guiding them toward a desired end, rather than directing and controlling. It is fundamentally a political process of persuading other people, building coalitions, and engaging in lengthy, sometimes tedious, dialog. You need convincing conviction, yes, but you need to express that conviction in ways that respect the autonomy, ideas, and interests of those you are trying to lead.

Looking Ahead and Feeding Back

The task of motivating leaders is essentially one of looking ahead and feeding back. Leaders motivate their followers by envisioning a future that will benefit them and communicating that future to them in a convincing way. Leaders are, as Napoleon wrote, "dealers in hope." Hope, the belief that good things will happen in the future, is a powerful motivator. Although the future is a mystery for all of us and leaders are really no more prescient than anyone else, people in organizations tend to look to their leaders to provide guidance about the future, in effect to make a prediction. Your ability to convince them about the future that lies ahead and the hoped for personal and organizational benefits it will bring is an important force for motivating the people you lead to work toward that envisioned future.

But simply pointing the way to that desired future is not enough. You also motivate those you lead by showing them how well and how far they are moving toward the desired goal. In management terms, you are providing them with *feedback* on their performance. The purpose of feedback is to help the people you lead evaluate their past performance and understand how they may perform better in the future.

Orchestra leaders, senior law partners, university deans, consulting team leaders, chiefs of surgery, and any number of other leaders have as one of their basic functions providing feedback on the performance of those they lead. Each profession has its own traditions and each organization has its own procedures for accomplishing it, but all look to their leaders to provide or at least orchestrate the feedback process. While a follower receiving a leader's feedback may view it as a method of reward or punishment, from the organization's perspective its purpose is to improve performance and enable the organization to attain its goals. It is vitally important that the leader also sees it from this perspective.

Conclusion: Rules for Negotiating Movement

In order to motivate the people you lead, keep in mind the following simple rules:

(1) Learn as much as you can about the people you seek to motivate, as well as the interests driving their actions. Usually, the best source of that information is the person in question.
(2) On the basis of that knowledge, seek to understand and develop the particular incentives that accord with those interests and may therefore move that person to act in a desired way. Thereafter, seek to shape a basic bargain to be negotiated with organization members so as to secure the behavior you desire in return for the incentive granted.
(3) In order to provide motivating feedback, arrive at a common understanding with the person you seek to lead of the standards to be applied in evaluating performance.

(4) Agree on future goals in the short, medium, and long term for that person, and show how those goals relate to those of the organization.

(5) Agree on a plan of action that is specific, doable, and clear.

(6) To the extent practicable, build into that plan of action incentives that will motivate high performance.

(7) Motivate your followers by envisioning a future that will benefit them and communicating that future to them in a convincing way.

10

Negotiating Representation

Leaders must not only focus their efforts on the people they lead, they must also concentrate enormous attention on the world outside their organizations. In fact a constant complaint of many corporate CEOs is that the demands of outside constituents, such as shareholders, industry groups, politicians, government agencies, financial analysts, and civic organizations prevent them from devoting sufficient time to the internal working of the firm and that therefore they feel less connected to their company's actual business than they should.[1] In my own experience as dean of two different graduate schools over 15 years, the demands of orchestrating and conducting external fundraising, alumni relations, negotiations with university officials, and activities with national and international professional organizations took up so much of my time that I often had to sneak back to the office on Saturday and Sunday mornings to attend to the internal paper work and decisions that I had put off during the week. Equally troubling was that I seemed to be getting further and further away from my professional specialization, international law, which had been the reason for entering academic life in the first place.

A principal task of all leaders is to represent their organizations and groups to the outside world. In those negotiations, leaders are not negotiating for themselves as principals but rather for their organizations as agents. Organizations and groups need representation because they can only impact

---

[1] See Michael Porter, Jay W. Lorsch, and Nitin Nohria, "Seven Surprises of New CEOs," *Harvard Business Review on CEO Succession* 59–86 (Boston, MA: Harvard Business Press, 2009).

© The Author(s) 2017
J.W. Salacuse, *Real Leaders Negotiate!*,
DOI 10.1057/978-1-137-59115-9_10

the outside world through individuals who act of their behalf—through agents, through individuals who *represent* them. For all leaders, the way to impact the outside environment is through negotiation. While numerous individuals within an organization may represent it at various times in various circumstances, an organization's most important acts of representation require the intervention of its leader. Most of the time, successfully representing an organization requires the leader to negotiate with a wide array of external actors. Thus, to secure peace, presidents and prime ministers have had to negotiate treaties with presidents and prime ministers of foreign countries; to obtain new resources, corporate CEOs negotiate acquisitions with the CEOs of other firms; to fund new science labs or expand language programs, university presidents negotiate grants from foundations; and to attract new investments to their states, governors travel abroad to negotiate with foreign companies.

Leaders in every organization have a special role in representing it. A leader's task of representation is not only something that the outside world expects, but it is also something that members of their organization demand. A leader is usually a principal link between the organization and its external environment. As such, leaders negotiate, speak, and act for the people they lead. Leaders *represent* their organizations. In this capacity they are agents carrying out a variety of tasks on behalf of those they lead— seeking bigger budgets, making important deals, securing the promotion of valued associates, and presenting a positive public image. This task not only demands effective negotiation and communication skills, but it also requires leaders to manage the constant tension between the often competing demands of the organization's internal and external constituencies. In this regard, leaders are often "people in the middle," who must somehow mediate between the demands of those they lead and the demands of the outside world.

Some leaders, by virtue of their public persona, become the embodiment of their organizations or groups to the outside world. So Nelson Mandela, who led South Africa to a multiracial democracy, was seen during his lifetime by many people as the symbol of that country. Steve Jobs became the face of Apple, and Richard Branson, the curly-headed, bearded, blond Englishman, came to represent Virgin Atlantic Airways in the eyes of the public. But in any organization, large or small, famous or little known, representation is always a task of leadership. As a leader, you must therefore not only focus your efforts on the people you lead, but also concentrate significant attention and energy on the world outside your organization—a fact that often leaves you little time to deal with internal challenges effectively.

While the internal tasks of leadership and the external tasks of representation may appear to be conceptually distinct and some leaders treat them as such, in reality they are very much intertwined. As we shall see, your effectiveness as a representative of others can influence your ability to lead them, and your effectiveness as a leader can influence your ability to represent the people you lead. Steve Job's ability to represent Apple to the public was certainly strengthened by the corporation's financial results achieved under his leadership, and his leadership within Apple was enhanced by the reputation he attained with the external public.

The Functions of Leadership Representation

For any leader, the task of representation is complex and multidimensional. One can however reduce it to three basic functions that leadership representation serves in the life of an organization or group:

(1) Resource acquisition
(2) Relationship management
(3) Image projection.

Let's examine each one briefly. As we shall see, to carry out each function, real leaders have to negotiate.

Resource Acquisition

For the members of most organizations, the most important function that leadership representation serves is the acquisition of needed resources. Whether it is investment capital, markets, or human talent, most organizations expect their leaders to play a key role in securing the resources that are vital to its operations. So corporate boards want CEOs to make profitable acquisitions of other companies, faculty expects university presidents to raise funds from alumni, and lawyers want their firm's managing partners to be "rain makers," to play an active role in securing new clients and new business. Although many organizations' members, from salespersons to financial officers, are also actively involved in resource acquisition, the organization's leader plays a particularly important role not only in overseeing this vital function but in actually becoming engaged in it through acts of representation, particularly when the resource to be acquired is large. Indeed, the failure of the leader to be present and active in a particularly significant external negotiation or act of representation sends a signal that the organization does not consider the matter to be important and that the particular external constituency is not important either—a message that may obstruct the acquisition of the needed resource, whether it's a new client for the firm or a new investment from a hedge fund.

Relationship Management

All organizations have a dense web of relationships with the outside world, and those relationships are vital in attaining its fundamental objectives. Here, too, many are involved in building and maintaining those relationships on an ongoing basis. Nonetheless, in all organizations, the leader plays a special role in building and maintaining certain vital relationships with external groups. Thus, state university presidents work hard to preserve good working relationships with their state's legislators in the hope of securing sufficient funds to run their institutions, managing partners of consulting firms actively cultivate relationships with executives of major corporate clients, and conductors of symphony orchestras nurture relationships with executives at recording companies. Usually, this kind of relationship management requires leader to negotiate one-on-one with those they want to influence. When those relations become troubled by conflict, for example as a result of actions by other members of the group or organization, it is often the organization's leader, and only its leader, who must negotiate a solution to the problem. For example, if a country's foreign minister has through words and actions insulted the president of another country, it may be the job of that foreign minister's boss, the prime minister, to negotiate a settlement that will placate the president's hurt feelings.

Image Projection

Through their acts of representation, leaders serve to create and project an image of their organization to particular constituencies and to the public in general. By speeches, public appearances, attendance at conferences, and interviews in the media, a leader communicates many messages, conscious and unintended, about the nature of the organization that he or she represents, which together constitute its image. Indeed, some leaders, like Steve Jobs and Richard Branson, gained such high profiles that their personal image becomes in the eyes of the public the very image of the organizations they represented. In fact, the leader of an organization is so closely connected to its image that boards of directors in selecting leaders will often consider not only the candidate's talents and abilities but the image of the organization that their very appointment will project to the public. For example, in one search for a university president, many members of the board of trustees of a prestigious university rejected an otherwise excellent candidate because he was then dean of a veterinary school and the trustees were concerned that the appointment of a veterinary school dean, rather than a leader in more traditional "academic" subjects, would diminish the university's reputation for academic excellence. The search for a "charismatic leader," so valued by organizational governing boards, is often driven not so much by the potential effect of a candidate's charisma on the internal operations of the organization as by its hoped-for positive impact on important external constituents like shareholders, customers, alumni, and the media.

The precise boundaries between these three functions often are not always clear. The same representational act may involve more than one function. For example, the managing partner of an investment bank who makes a speech to a group of securities analysts is engaged in performing all three functions: relationship building and image projection with the long-term hope of resource acquisition through the new business that the speech will generate. In order to understand the complexities of leadership representation, let's look at a specific case.

A Japanese Act of Contrition

In 2004, the Japanese financial authorities discovered that Citigroup's private bank in Japan had consistently engaged in improper and illegal transactions over a period of time. It therefore took the draconian step of closing all of Citigroup's private banking operations in the country, a step that would reduce the revenues of the world's largest bank by $100 million a year. Coming on the heels of other scandals in Citigroup's far flung operations, the closure of its private banking business in Japan was a particularly harsh blow that needed a serious response by the bank's leadership.

In response, Charles Prince, who had been appointed CEO the previous year and had taken on the task of trying to change the bank's culture, fired three of the bank's top executives in New York, as well as several employees in Japan. He then flew to Tokyo to meet with Japanese authorities to negotiate the reopening of Citgroup's closed banking operations. At a large press conference, he took responsibility for Citigroup's actions, promised appropriate reforms, apologized for the bank's behavior, and then in a traditional Japanese act of contrition, bowed deeply from the waist, eyes fixed on the ground. News photographers captured this unique moment of Prince's bow of apology, and it appeared on television and in the press around the world. As the *New York Times* would comment: "It was a bow seen round the world, an unusually public *mea culpa* by the top executive of a financial giant that has typically circled its wagons when criticized or preferred closed door resolutions of problems."[2]

Prince's visit to Japan was an example of a leader engaged in representing his organization through negotiation. His bow from the waist had meaning to the world only because of the institution he represented, his position within that organization, and the situation in which he found himself. Charles Prince bending from the waist to look for something that had fallen on the floor of his office would have been a totally unremarkable event. Prince's bow, in the context in which executed it, attracted the attention of the world's media.

In considering this incident, one might well ask: Why did Charles Prince bow? What role did it play in his negotiating strategy in seeking to reopen Citigroup's operations? Prince knew that if the Japanese authorities were to allow the reopening of Citigroup's private bank he would have to convince them of Citigroup's firm intent to clean up its act. He also knew that conveying that message in any meaningful way was complicated by cultural differences between the two countries. Cultural differences between the Japanese and the Americans constituted a barrier that Prince had to overcome in his negotiations. In order to connect with his Japanese audience, he therefore chose to adopt a Japanese form of apology in the hope of convincing them of the genuineness of his and Citigroup's intent to change. Prince did not decide to bow on the spur of the moment. It was the subject of intense discussion among Citigroup's top executives before the trip to Tokyo because they knew it could have serious consequences. On the one hand, it was hoped that the bow would convince the Japanese regulators and public of the seriousness of Citigroup's regret for the actions of its employees in Japan. On the other hand, there was also the possibility that the Japanese might interpret Prince's bow as an insincere, blatant attempt to manipulate them and therefore impede the success of his negotiation. It was only after

---

[2] Todd Zaun, "An Apology May Be Just the Start for Citibank Japan," *New York Times,* December 26, 2004, Section 3, p. 2.

serious thought that Prince decided to use the traditional Japanese public bow to express his institution's apology for its actions.

Prince's action communicated a message. The messages communicated, however, differed, depending on the audience. While the Japanese were impressed by Prince's bow as an act of sincere regret, certain business executives in the West questioned the appropriateness of the leader of the world's biggest bank "groveling" in front a foreign audience. It was just not dignified.

Prince's negotiations in Japan were in pursuit of all three leadership representation functions: resource acquisition, relationship management, and image projection. First, Prince's ultimate goal was for Citigroup to acquire the resource of once again participating in the Japanese private banking market, but he knew that Citigroup could not do that without repairing its relationship with the Japanese regulatory authorities and rebuilding the bank's image with the Japanese public, tasks that he also had to accomplish during his visit if the bank was to regain the resource that it had lost.

Choosing Your Shots

Leaders have an incessant host of competing demands on their time. One of the questions that leaders must answer constantly is which of the multitude of external demands should they personally devote attention to. Which particular acts of representation should the leader personally conduct and which acts should be left to others in the organization to attend to? Which opportunities for representation should be avoided completely? That was precisely the question I was asking myself constantly as dean as I struggled to find time in my daily schedule for what I considered "work"—the internal demands of the two schools I led.

Three basic criteria can help you decide these important questions. The first is the importance of the goal to be achieved through a leader's personal act of representation to the interests and well-being of the organization. The second is the extent to which another person can, as effectively as the leader can, carry on the representation. And the third is the perception of the concerned external constituents of your failure to personally participate in the expected act of representation.

In the Citigroup case, re-entry to the Japanese private banking market was extremely important to both the financial goals and the reputation of Citigroup, and no one but Charles Prince, the bank's CEO, had the status, prestige, and power to assure the Japanese that the bank did indeed regret past improper behavior and was committed to changing its culture. Certainly, if any other Citigroup executive had showed up in Tokyo to make amends, the Japanese would probably have been insulted and would most certainly have questioned Citigroup's intentions and sincerity.

Similarly, to the extent that you as leader and representative of your organization are negotiating agreements with leaders of other organizations, you may have to devote an inordinate amount of time to the task, since they are precisely the kind of people who assume that your personal attention and care are their due. In addition to your words, your personal attention and care send a clear message to representatives of other organizations about the importance you attach to the event and to them personally. Certainly it was George H. W. Bush's personal, one-on-one negotiations prior to the 1991 Gulf War that helped to influence world leaders to join their countries to the coalition led by the nation that Bush represented.

The Leader's Mandate

In order to negotiate effectively on behalf of your organization you need a *mandate*. You need an authorization—general or specific, formal or informal—from the people you lead that you are empowered to act on their behalf. You also need some means of assuring the people with whom you are dealing that you are indeed acting for the organization you lead, and not just for yourself. If you are engaged in merger negotiations, you need some assurance that your organization will approve the agreements you make. If, like Charles Prince, you are seeking to re-enter the Japanese private banking market, you have to be able to assure the Japanese authorities that the reforms you promise will in fact be executed by the organization you represent.

Your mandate is crucial to your ability to lead outside the organization for two important reasons. First, the other side's belief that you have a mandate means that they will deal with you seriously as a representative of those you lead. Both the Japanese authorities and the public took Prince seriously because they assumed that, as chairman and CEO, he had Citigroup's mandate: that he was indeed speaking for Citigroup and not just for himself. Second, the existence of a mandate gives assurance you will be able to induce your organization to act in conformity with what you have represented to others that it would do.

In dealing with you as a representative, the question in the back of the minds of others is: Will you be able to deliver? Prince could speak with confidence to the Japanese, knowing that he had the power and authority within Citigroup to implement what he and the Japanese authorities had agreed to with respect to Citigroup's operations in Japan. The Japanese were fairly confident that he would be able to deliver what he promised. On the other hand, history is filled with examples of leaders with apparently strong mandates who made promises and agreements with others only to find that their followers rejected them later on. Woodrow Wilson attended the Paris Peace Conference in 1919 as a strong president of a victorious country in World War I and played a dominant role in shaping the Treaty of Versailles and the Covenant of the League of Nations; however, the changed political climate in post-war United States caused the Senate to refuse to ratify them.[3] The reason for Wilson's failure was that he had either lost his mandate or had exceeded the one that had been granted to him.

In view of the importance of a mandate to your ability to negotiate on behalf of the people you lead, an important question is: How do I get a mandate? The existence of a mandate does not automatically come with the position you hold. Some leaders assume that by virtue of their position and title they are fully empowered to act on behalf of the organization or group that they lead. Your position may give you a mandate to deal with minor matters, such as making a speech on behalf of the organization, but in matters that affect the vital interests of the people you lead you will ordinarily have to obtain a specific mandate from them and then work hard to preserve it.

So the managing partner of an investment bank will have a mandate to make speeches about its activities by virtue of his position, but will need to obtain a specific mandate from his partners to engage in merger discussions with another bank. Indeed, leaders often assume to their sorrow that their position has given them a broader mandate for representation than they in fact have. This is particularly true in leading people who believe they have the ability to defend their own interests and are reluctant to turn that task over to their leaders unless they are sure that their leaders will carry it out in a way that will satisfy those interests. Their trust in the leader to protect their interests is an important factor in influencing them to grant or withhold the necessary mandate.

---

[3] See generally, Margaret Macmillan, *Paris 1919: Six Months that Changed the World* (New York: Random House, 2002).

A mandate to represent is different from legal authority to carry out a specific task. A leader with a mandate may not have specific legal authority to carry out the action being discussed with an external organization. Nonetheless, both the other side and the leader know that this mandate is sufficiently strong to secure the necessary legal authorizations when the time comes. A powerful CEO who is conducting merger negotiations with another firm may not have specific authorization to carry out a merger, and indeed the law and corporate charter will certainly require approval by both the corporate board of directors and the shareholders; however, by virtue of his relationships with those he leads both the CEO and the negotiators on the other side know that he can obtain the necessary legal authorization if a deal is made.

To a large extent, your mandate depends not on your position and title but on the nature of your relationships with the people you lead. In this respect, leaders may play a variety of roles. Some leaders are "good soldiers," who merely carry out the orders of the people they represent and rarely go beyond them without first checking with their principals. Other leaders are more like architects, who after gaining a basic idea of the interests and aspirations of their followers, set out to design a future through their negotiations with other organizations and firms, confident that they will be able to convince their principals to accept that future when it is revealed to them. And still others are tribal chiefs, who make arrangements and deal with other organizations, knowing that they have the power to convince or threaten their followers to approve. One can find examples of all three styles of representation among successful leaders. As in other key leadership tasks, gaining a mandate from the people you lead begins with understanding their interests. As managing partner of a law firm, you may strongly believe that acquiring a firm specializing in intellectual property is essential to build your client base, but unless you understand how that acquisition will impact the interests of your partners, you cannot begin to build a mandate. Once you understand their interests, you need to engage them, often on a one-on-one basis, to think about the future competitive position of the firm and the strategies for facing that competition.

No mandate is permanent. A leader may gain a mandate to represent other people but lose it in an instant. Those who grant a leader a mandate can take it away just as quickly as they gave it. In the euphoria of victory, President Woodrow Wilson may have had a broad and strong mandate from the American public when he entered the Paris Peace Conference. Within a year, however, the euphoria diminished as the United States considered the post-war world and its role in it, factors that led it to reconsider and ultimately reduce Wilson's mandate to commit the United States to the League of Nations.

So a challenge for any leader is not only to obtain a mandate but to maintain it. You can lose your mandate through your own actions or through the actions and events attributable to others. To maintain your mandate, you must keep your followers informed of what you are doing in your negotiations as their representative and continually assure them that in negotiating with others your fundamental goal is to advance the interests of the people you represent.

One of the factors that led to the refusal by the United States Senate to ratify Wilson's work in Paris was that Wilson, a Democrat, had steadfastly refused to include any Republicans on the U.S. delegation that accompanied him to Paris. This slight infuriated the Republicans, who had strongly supported the United States involvement in the war. While Wilson did not trust them and thought that their participation in the Peace Conference might allow them to obstruct his broad ambitions for a new post-war world order, their absence would eventually contribute to their successful efforts to block ratification of Wilson's work in Paris.[4]

Republican participation in the U.S. delegation would have done at least three things to strengthen Wilson's mandate. First, it would have kept Republicans and their allies informed of the process and therefore served to counter negative allegations and rumors by opponents. Second, the Republicans would have become part of the process and the resulting product, and therefore they would have had less legitimacy to repudiate the Paris agreements. Third, their presence in Paris would have enabled Wilson to stay aware of opposition concerns and plans, thus allowing him to develop his own strategies for countering them. On this point it is well to remember the words of Lyndon Johnson, a far earthier and savvier political strategist than Wilson: "It is better to have your opponents inside the tent pissing out than outside the tent pissing in."

Involving the people you lead in representation helps to assure and strengthen your mandate. To a large extent, your followers' perception of the external environment depends on your ability to communicate its reality to them. Their own participation helps to convince them that your reports on the external environment are correct. The presence of Republicans in the U.S. delegation in Paris would have helped to convince them more than Wilson's mere reports that the Treaty of Versailles was the result of hard

---

[4] Ibid., p.5.

bargaining with the allies in World War I and not just the product of Wilson's lack of will and strength at the negotiating table.

When Wilson returned from France to find strong opposition in the Senate, he decided to build the necessary mandate by going directly to the American people to convince them of the need to support the agreements that he had made in Paris. He therefore embarked on an exhausting speaking tour across the country, delivering two and even three speeches a day to enthusiastic crowds. In the end, the tour did permanent damage to his health but did not achieve the end he sought. Although Wilson's speeches engendered popular enthusiasm for the Treaty of Versailles and the Covenant of the League of Nations, the opposition in the Senate prevailed and the treaties were never ratified.

The simple fact was that Wilson needed a mandate from the Senate, not just the American people, because it was the Senate, not the American people, who had to ratify the treaties to make Wilson's vision of a post-war order a reality. The lesson here is that a leader must know from whom he needs a mandate in order to accomplish a given act of representation.

Remember that no mandate is permanent. Even though you have obtained a mandate from the people you lead, numerous events may intervene to change those perceptions and weaken or strengthen your mandate to represent them. In the euphoria of the allied victory in World War I, the American public seemed ready to give Wilson a broad mandate to set the foundations for a new post-war era. As that euphoria waned with time and as America faced the domestic issues following the war, Wilson's mandate to achieve his goals weakened and opposition to him grew.

From the above, the two lessons for negotiating representation are clear:

(1) Don't take your mandate to represent people for granted.
(2) Work constantly to preserve and strengthen your mandate.

In representing others on matters that affect their interests, as a leader you have to work constantly to assure yourself that you continue to have their support.

A User's Guide to Negotiating Representation

Your effectiveness as a leader depends on your understanding what your followers want. Followers expect their leaders to fulfill two fundamental obligations towards them: their duty of *loyalty* and their duty of *care*. What followers expect, if you represent them, is that (1) you will place their interests above your own, and (2) that you will look after those interests carefully.

In the modern era, when "market forces" seem to determine so many issues, the notion of loyalty has a quaint, almost old-fashioned ring. In business and government today, self-interest, not loyalty, seems to be the driving force. Who, after all, serves another out of loyalty? Doctors work hard to heal the sick, but few would say that they are "loyal" to their patients. For international consultants, who often see themselves as "hired guns" in an age of laptop computers and cellular phones, loyalty to the client may appear to have gone the way of manual typewriters and carbon paper—a quality that once was useful but has now been replaced by something else. Anyway, when it comes to leadership, isn't it the followers who are supposed to be loyal to the leaders, not the other way around?

The Loyal Leader

In representing other people, leaders always have two sets of interests in mind: their followers and their own. In any act of representation, there is always a potential conflict of interest. In negotiating a merger, a CEO will be concerned about increasing shareholder value and possibly preserving jobs, but she will also be concerned about her own financial position after the merger. As a result, that CEO may spend more effort negotiating her compensation package than on increasing the payout to shareholders. All followers are aware of this potential conflict of interest, and they worry that their interests will suffer as a result.

Having experienced down-sizing, plant closures, and large-scale layoffs, employees have generally come to believe that in representing their organizations company leaders always let their own interests prevail over those of their followers. It is perhaps this perception that has most damaged leadership in American corporations. In short, corporate employees and shareholders often consider corporate CEOs to be less than totally loyal to their interests.

While corporate shareholders and employees have limited means to defend their interests against self-interested leaders, certain members of other types or organizations, particularly those with wealth, talent, and power often are more able to assure themselves of their leader's loyalty. For one thing, they do everything they can to make their leaders realize that the mandate come from them, not a position or title, and that they can withdraw or modify it at any time. So, before a leader embarks on important acts of representation, he or she needs to clear it with elite followers. Whereas the leadership of Daimler-Benz and Chrysler might negotiate a merger quickly and secretly, as they did in 1999, without gaining the approval of other executives, shareholders, or even board members, no managing partner of an investment bank, law firm, or consulting company would dare to undertake a similar action without seeking the preliminary approval of key members of their organizations.

Second, followers seek to assure the loyalty of leaders who represent them by requiring periodic reports of representation, establishing mechanisms for overseeing representation, and for actually participating in key representational acts, like mergers, initial public offerings (IPOs), large bank financings, and new public relations campaigns.

The effective leader of elite followers understands these concerns and seeks to assure them of his or her loyalty in representing them. Instead of resisting efforts to oversee and participate in the execution of his or her representational mandate, the effective leader of those kinds of organizations seeks to assure them of loyalty to their interests by consulting with others constantly and by proactively advancing mechanisms that will facilitate their oversight of and participation in the leader's key tasks of representation. Instead of taking the attitude that you are the boss and representation is none of their business, you will be better off if you recognize at the outset that representation is very much the business of the elite followers you lead, especially when their interests are at stake. And because their interests are at stake, you will do a better job of representation if you include them in the process from the outset.

Interest-Based Representation

Whether you are engaged in resource acquisition, relationship management, or image projection, the ultimate purpose and result of negotiating representation as an organizational leader is to advance someone's interests. The fundamental question that you as a leader must ask is *whose* interests am I seeking to advance? Many leaders do not consider that question and those that do, often facilely respond: "Why my organization's interests, of course!"

The problem of representing interests is complicated by three factors: (1) organizational disunity; (2) dysfunctional organizational interests; and (3) leadership self-interest. First, often the members of an organization or group may not agree on the precise interests to be pursued through representation. So, you need to ask: To what extent are the people I lead unified with respect to the interests they want me to pursue? To the extent that there is disunity, you will have to engage in extensive internal mediation among diverse interests groups before you can effectively pursue those interests through external representation.

Second, the members of the organization may be united in their perception of their desired interests, but the leader may judge that those interests are unrealistic or will not really benefit the organization in the long term. In that case, the leader, in order to be an effective representative of the persons he or she leads, will have to seek to transform those interests through discussion and negotiation, often on a one-on-one basis. So a second question you must ask is: To what extent do I accept and seek to pursue the stated objectives of my followers and to what extent do I seek to change or transform them?

And finally, all leaders have a dual agenda: their organization's interests and their own personal interests. Often they confuse the two, either unconsciously or deliberately. To the extent that their acts of representation are driven by their personal interests, rather than by group interests, leaders risk damaging the organization and ultimately their own legitimacy. So a third and final question you need to keep in mind constantly is: To what extent am I pursuing the organization's interests and to what extent am I pursuing my own personal interests?

The effective leader needs to ask these three questions constantly in order to carry out the important leadership task of negotiating representation.[5]

The Other Side of the Table

To effectively negotiate representation for your organization or group, you also need to be aware of the representational role played by the people with whom you are negotiating on the other side of the table. Whether or not the person with whom you are negotiating is a principal or a negotiating agent has important implications for your strategies and tactics in the negotiation. In particular, if you are facing an agent of the other side, instead of a principal, you should try to determine in as much detail as possible at least three vital factors: (1) the agent's mandate; (2) the agent's relationship to his or her principal; and (3) the agent's own interests. Let's consider each briefly.

---

[5] See Joel Cutcher-Gershenfeld and Michael Watkins, "Toward a Theory of Representation in Negotiation," in R.H. Mnookin and L.E. Susskind, eds., *Negotiating on Behalf of Others—Advice to, Lawyers, Business Executives, Sports Agents, Diplomats, Politicians, and Everybody Else* (Thousand Oaks, CA: Sage Publications 1999), pp. 23–51.

The Agent's Mandate

Just as your mandate determines what you can and cannot do on behalf of the organization or group you are representing, the agent on the other side of the table is similarly constrained or empowered by his or her mandate. It is therefore important to find out what that mandate is. Sometimes the other side's agent may willingly disclose the full extent of the mandate; in other situations, the agent, for tactical reasons will not be forthcoming. Through questioning and observing behavior, you may be able to discover the limits of your counterparty's authority. For example, within a short time after the negotiation begins, you may gain a fairly accurate idea of how often the other side's agent has to refer back to the principal for decisions and how much latitude the agent has to explore new ideas and possible solutions to negotiating problems.

The Agent's Relationship with the Principal

It is also important to determine the nature of the relationship between the other side's agent and the principal. For example, is the relationship a close and personal connection imbued with significant trust and confidence between the two? Or is it formal and impersonal? Does the person negotiating on behalf of an organization's principal hold a high position within the organization, like Charles Prince, or is he or she a low-level employee without significant influence? The answer to these questions will tell you about ability of the agent to be flexible in the negotiation, to persuade the principal to accept new ideas, and to be able to actually implement what the two of you have negotiated at the bargaining table. Moreover, the willingness of an agent with a close relationship to the principal to accept new ideas, justifications, and arguments may be indications that the same ideas, justifications, and arguments will be acceptable to that agent's principal.

The Agent's Individual Interests

In addition to determining the interests of the principal on the other side of the table, you should also consider the agent's individual interests and how those interests may affect the negotiation. For example, if you are across the table from a corrupt official who is seeking a bribe from your company in order to grant you a government contract, you will have serious ethical and legal issues that in the end might force you to abandon the negotiation. But not all personal interests of agents are illegitimate or illegal. The desire of an official for the respect due his or her office, not to be embarrassed in front of superiors or colleagues, or to be acknowledged for his or her contributions to the negotiation process are legitimate individual interests that you should try to satisfy during the course of the negotiation.

Conclusion: Rules for Negotiating Leadership Representation

Although leadership representation is a complex, multifaceted process, the following simple rules will help you navigate its intricacies.

(1) Remember that every act or statement that you make, whether in public or in private, has the potential to affect your organization's relationships with the outside world. Nothing you do is purely personal. A leader is always on stage.
(2) Seek to understand the interests of the people you represent.
(3) If those interests are diverse and disunited, seek to unify them or at least build a winning coalition among the persons you lead around a particular set of interests.
(4) If those interests are dysfunctional or unrealistic, seek to change or transform them by negotiating with the people you lead.
(5) Beware of confusing your self-interest with organizational interests.
(6) Work to build and maintain a mandate from your followers for your representation. Remember that no mandate is permanent.

11

Negotiating Trust

Trust is vital to leadership. It is vital not just because that is what followers want. It is vital because it is difficult and in most cases impossible to lead people who don't trust you. Without trust of those they lead, leaders will not be able to direct, integrate, mediate, educate, motivate, or represent the people in their organizations. In short, trust is the linchpin, the essential element for carrying out effectively the daily tasks of leadership that I have previously discussed. In some situations, leaders can lead—at least for a time—without the significant trust of their followers, relying instead on their legal authority, raw power, deception, or control mechanisms designed to secure compliance with their orders But over the long term, leaders like Michael Ovitz at Disney, who never gained the trust of those they were supposed to lead, or who, like Carly Fiorina, former chair and CEO of Hewlett Packard, in 2005 lost the trust that she once had of her corporate board of directors, invariably also lose their positions as leaders.

The Meaning of Leadership Trust

Shortly after I became dean of the Southern Methodist University (SMU) Law School, a senior member of the faculty congratulated me on the appointment, saying "I'm glad you are dean because I trust you." At first I was flattered by his confidence in me, but then I began to think: "Wait a minute! That's it? He's glad I'm dean *just* because he trusts me? Nothing about my vision? My energy? My knowledge of legal education?" He had said

© The Author(s) 2017
J.W. Salacuse, *Real Leaders Negotiate!*,
DOI 10.1057/978-1-137-59115-9_11

nothing about those things, and I don't think he felt they mattered much as far as selecting a dean was concerned. For him, the most important and probably the only thing that qualified me to become dean was that he trusted me. After working in leadership positions for over 35 years, I have learned that my former colleague was not unique in the way he evaluated leaders. What followers seek above all are leaders that they can trust.

But when the law professor said that he trusted me, what exactly did he mean? He obviously felt that as dean my actions would somehow be trustworthy. But what exactly did he trust that I would do or not do as dean of the school. As I began to think about his statement, I came to realize that what he really meant was that he felt that as dean he could trust me to act in a way that would advance his interests or at least not harm them. He was willing to invest his trust me, confident that I would treat him fairly with regard to such vital interests as his salary increases, teaching assignments, office space, and research funding.

In this regard, the SMU law professor was no different from other people in evaluating their leaders: They are concerned first and foremost about their interests and how their potential leader's acts will affect them. Despite the hype about group loyalty and leadership charisma as motivating forces for followers, an individual's prime motivation for joining a group or organization is to advance his or her own interests, and the constant evaluation of those interests directly affects how he or she will behave in that organization or group. Thus, during the 2016 election campaign, many supporters of Donald Trump said that they could never vote for Hillary Clinton because they "did not trust her." What they seemed to mean by that was that they felt she could not be trusted to protect and advance their economic and social interests and that if she became president she would disregard them just the way they believed the country's political elite, of which she was a member, had done in previous years.

Leaders often confuse trust with friendship and affection. We usually trust our friends, so it's natural to think that if you can create a friendly relationship with people you lead they will trust you. Trust and friendship are two different relationships. All of us have a friend for whom we have great affection but whom we would not trust to manage a large sum of money or take care of a pet when we are away. The law school professor who said he trusted me was not really a friend of mine. We had never had a drink together, played tennis together, or gone out to dinner with our wives. Ours was basically a working relationship.

It is important to understand the difference between friendship and trust because many leaders mistakenly set out to become "friendly" with those they lead in the hope that their actions will automatically result in creating trust, and then they meet disappointment when they fail. No amount of smiling, joke-telling, and friendly daily greetings to the people you lead will develop trust if at the same time you are firing people arbitrarily and granting salary rises based on your personal whims instead of generally understood and accepted performance standards.

Human uncertainty about and vulnerability to other people are at the heart of the trust problem. In social life, the future actions of others we encounter are always both uncertain and potentially harmful to our interests. We can never totally control the actions of other people. The risk of injury is ever present in your interactions with others. In theory, when you arrive for work in the morning, the colleague in the next office may either greet you or kill you.

If you are an accountant in the finance department of a corporation, you can be fairly certain of receiving a friendly greeting from your co-worker in the next office in the morning when you arrive for work. On the other hand, if you were a Tutsi official in an office full of Hutus at the height of the 1994 genocide in Rwanda, a friendly greeting would be less certain. In the former situation, because of your long-time relationship with your co-worker and the social context in which you are both living and working, you feel assured that your colleague will smile and wave to you as you walk by her office every morning. The risk of harm to your interests, if you consider it at all, is negligible. Although you can never know with absolute certainty what your co-worker is thinking and planning, you trust her not to attack you as you go by her office in the morning. In the second situation, knowing the enflamed hostility of the Hutu toward the Tutsi and aware of the mass killings of Tutsi taking place throughout the country, you determine that any interaction between you and a Hutu presents the risk of physical danger to you. In short, as a Tutsi you do not trust the Hutu because you believe they threaten your interests and you act accordingly by not going to the office at all and instead hiding in your home.

Trust is essentially confidence that your given interactions with other people will not harm your interests. At its base is an evaluation about risk and about expectations for the future. By trusting someone, you make yourself vulnerable to harm from their actions. The more you trust a person the more you allow yourself to be exposed to the risk of harm. While you may trust your business partner to work hard for the partnership and to give all business opportunities that she finds to the partnership instead of exploiting them personally, you might not trust her, as you might your brother, to manage your estate for your children after you die. In this sense, trusting in someone is similar to making an investment. As with buying 100 shares of stock on the New York Stock Exchange, when you decide to trust someone, you are aware of the risks, but you judge that the probability of gain outweighs the risk of loss. Moreover, just as we are willing to invest more money in some stocks than in others, we feel we can trust some people more than others.

For all followers, every action proposed by a leader has both the potential for benefit and the risk of harm imbedded in it. If followers consider their leaders trustworthy, they will more readily come to believe in their recommendations, values, and visions than if they distrust them. Goldman Sachs's IPO, Woodrow Wilson's League of Nations, and Lyndon Johnson's civil rights legislation would bring benefits and losses and risks and rewards in varying degrees to many of their followers. Their followers' willingness to support or oppose those proposed measures was a function of how they evaluated the measures' impact on their interests. That evaluation in turn was influenced by the trust they were willing to place in their leadership. In the end, Goldman Sachs sold its shares to the public and the Senate adopted civil rights legislation because a sufficient number of members in those organizations trusted their leadership. On the other hand, the Senate refused to approve the League of Nations in part because they had lost trust in Woodrow Wilson.

More than just facilitating the task of direction, trust between leader and followers and among followers can increase organizational effectiveness and productivity. For one thing, it enhances creativity by encouraging members to openly share ideas and information without fearing that the leadership or other members will use those ideas and that information to harm the interests of the individuals providing them. It also facilitates cooperative action for the benefit of the group. Persons who trust each other, whether they are musicians in a chamber group or analysts in a money management firm, are more likely to achieve a higher level of performance, whether it is making beautiful music or insightful investment recommendations, when they cooperate than if they do not.[1] Trust allows people to focus more intensely on the task at hand, rather than on their troubled and suspicious relationships with one another. And finally, trust in an organization reduces the transaction costs of carrying out its activities. Generally speaking, the less trust that exists in an organization, the more it must devote resources to

---

[1] Gilbert W. Fairholm, *Leadership and the Culture of Trust* (1994).

compliance and monitoring procedures to ensure that activities desired by the leadership are carried out.

Negotiating for Trust

In view of the importance of trust in leading organizations and groups, any new or potential leader may well ask: How do I gain the trust of the people I am supposed to lead? The short answer to that question is: You negotiate for it. That statement has at least three implications. First, the trust necessary to lead does not automatically come with your leadership position. At the outset, you need to realize that you gain trust only if another person is willing to give it to you freely. No matter the degree of your power and legal authority over the people you are to lead, you can't compel them to give you their trust. They may follow your orders out of fear, but that doesn't mean they trust you. So leaders who declare to their followers "Trust me!" almost never get what they are looking for. Secondly, trust requires knowledge and information. No one can trust another person until he or she knows something about that person. The law professor said that he trusted me, not because I held the title of dean, but because he and I had worked together as colleagues for two years during which we came to know and evaluate one another. Second, gaining trust through explicit or implicit negotiation takes time. Third, as in any negotiated deal, the people who grant you their trust expect something in return. Fourth, in negotiating to gain the trust of your followers you will need to rely on many of the same strategies, techniques, and tactics that you use elsewhere in negotiating your leadership duties. And fifth, and finally, once you have struck a leadership bargain you will have to manage it effectively if you expect to retain the power to lead.

The power to lead others—that is, the ability to influence the behavior of others—is based on the relationship that exists between leader and followers. As with communities discussed in Chapter 4, relationships may be either real or imagined. A relationship implies a *connection* between the parties, a complex set of continuing interactions characterized by a degree of cooperation and, in many cases, trust. Leaders like Winston Churchill and Martin Luther King formed real relationships with thousands of people with whom they came in contact throughout the course of their political lives, but through their speeches they formed imagined relationships with millions of others who, although they had never met them, felt that they knew and had a relationship with "Winston" and "Martin."

Gaining the trust of followers is just the first step in traveling the leadership road. Equally important is the need to retain that trust as the leader goes about the business of leading an organization or group. Trust between leaders and followers is never permanent. Either because of the leader's actions or external circumstances, leaders can lose the trust of their followers rapidly. In those situations, trust just seems to evaporate like water off pavement after a brief shower. Many "powerful" CEOs have found that when they lost the trust of their boards of directors, they lost their power of leadership. Sometimes they were forced out the door; sometimes they held on for a time as titular leader. With trust evaporated, they don't often hang on to their title for very long, either, as President Richard Nixon learned, after winning re-election with a resounding victory in 1972 yet having to resign as a result of the Watergate scandal less than two years later. In the business world, CEOs are fired when they lose the "confidence"—just another word for trust—of their boards of directors. Thus, Apple got rid of Steve Jobs during his first attempt at leadership of that corporation and HP dumped Carly Fiorina in 2005 when it judged that the acquisition of Compaq, which she had engineered, looked less profitable than it had hoped. Just as any long-term relationship based on a commercial contract between companies or a diplomatic treaty between countries needs to be managed through the wise use of negotiation, a relationship of trust between leaders and followers requires similar careful negotiating management.

Principles of Negotiating Relationships of Trust

If the creation and maintenance of relationships of trust is important for leadership, a natural question comes to mind: What should a leader do to create and maintain them? The following principles may prove helpful.

Do Ask, Do Tell

First and foremost, relationship building requires mutual knowledge of the parties. Thus in any negotiation, the negotiators need to get to know each other. A first step in seeking to gain the trust of the people you lead is to let them get to know you in a way that allows them to evaluate your intentions and the impact that you may have on their interests. So at SMU, I could assume a certain level of trust from the faculty and staff because they had known me as a colleague for two years, but when I became dean of the Fletcher School of Law and Diplomacy at Tufts University I did not assume that the same level of trust existed because no one at Fletcher had worked with me before. The tasks of trust building at the two institutions were therefore very different. At Fletcher, I spend the first several months of my deanship in long, one-on-one meetings with faculty, staff, and student representatives and avoided suggesting any significant initiatives until I felt I knew the place thoroughly. At SMU, because I knew the community and they knew me, I started a strategic planning process in the second month of my deanship. New leaders often feel that when they arrive on the scene, they need to announce major new directions in order to assert their leadership. If you have that impulse, restrain it. It will only generate distrust among people who don't yet know you.

The precise knowledge about you that your followers are seeking is information that will allow them to make predictions about your future actions with respect to their interests. What this means is that they are not just seeking to learn about your golf game or your college exploits, but about your capabilities, intentions, and values as it affects them. One of the important ways you can convey these factors is not just through your own declarations but equally importantly by getting to know the people you lead.

Several years ago, a law school in Pennsylvania asked me to help mediate the troubled relationship between its faculty and its dean, who had been appointed two years previously. The faculty did not trust the dean and the dean, who had had a successful tenure at another institution, was mystified as to the reasons why. As I met individually with faculty members to discuss the problem, I kept hearing the same theme: "The dean doesn't know us." As conversations proceeded, I also came to realize something else: the faculty didn't know the dean. An experienced law school administrator, the dean had arrived at the law school in Pennsylvania and had immediately plunged into the task of managing its affairs, letting the faculty, who after all had played a key role in selecting him, get on with the job of teaching students and doing legal research. The faculty's lack of knowledge about the new dean and his intentions, as well as his own apparent ignorance of their interests, led to their increasing distrust of the dean. "What exactly is going on in the dean's office?" became the daily question among the school's professors. It was both a question and a statement of distrust.

By not coming to know the faculty, the dean created a strong reason for distrusting him. In effect, the faculty was saying, "If the dean doesn't know us and our concerns, how can he lead this school in a way that will meet our interests? Indeed, he must not care about our interests, so how can we trust him?" A relationship of trust between two people requires mutual knowledge. In order to begin the process of gaining mutual knowledge and thereby building a relationship of trust between the dean and the faculty, we organized a two-day retreat in the Pennsylvania countryside where faculty members could talk freely about their hopes, fears, intentions, and concerns for their law school. Ultimately, the dean and the faculty would gain the mutual knowledge, understanding, and eventually the trust needed for an effective working relationship, and the dean continued to serve in that position for many years.

The hard-and-fast rule that some negotiators have of telling the other side as little as possible is not conducive to relationship building or to building trust. A policy of "don't ask, don't tell" is not an effective rule for gaining trust and negotiating leadership. Indeed wise leaders should do just the reverse: ask and tell.

Transparency

Beyond just exchanging information, the dean needed to develop a different approach to working with the faculty. In particular, he needed to become more open and transparent in his approach to leading the law school. If mutual information is the first foundation stone of trust, transparency is the second. Openness in a leader is not just an easy smile, a charming manner, and a ready handshake. Openness in a leader refers to the process by which he or she makes decisions, for it is decisions, not smiles and handshakes, that have implications for followers' interests. Openness in a leader's style has many dimensions. First, it means sharing information with the people you lead. Many leaders excel at playing "hide the ball," of manipulating, distorting, and selectively rationing the information that they give to their followers. While that approach may enable you to achieve certain results, it will not gain you the trust of those you lead. They can readily discern when they have been provided with partial or distorted information and they will readily interpret it as your lack of confidence in them—a situation that will not engender trust in you. After all, if you don't trust them, why should they trust you?

Openness also means a willingness to involve your followers in the decisions that you make on their behalf. One cause of distrust between the Pennsylvania law school dean and the faculty was the fact that he had made decisions affecting their interests without consulting them. If trust arises from a feeling of confidence about predicting the future behavior of another person, that confidence increases when that person involves others in decision-making processes rather than excluding them. The dean therefore needed to change his approach to leading his faculty by creating mechanisms such as committees, faculty retreats, and one-on-one consultations to involve the faculty in helping to arrive at leadership decisions affecting their interests. He gained their trust by sharing control of the school with them, a technique that all leaders should consider, particularly in seeking to lead elite followers.

Openness not only helps to create trust; it also facilitates maintaining it. By being open in making a decision through consultation with and transparency towards the people you lead, you encourage them to continue their trust and hopefully to raise it to higher levels. In dealing with the Soviet Union on arms control, President Ronald Reagan quoted a Russian proverb to the Soviet leader Mikael Ghorbachev: "Trust but verify." Some critics interpreted that statement as "We don't trust you." What that proverb also means is that our trust will continue into the future to the extent that we can ascertain that you are living up to your commitments in the present. So to maintain and develop trust, it is important for leaders to show their followers constantly that they have actually done what they have promised to do.

Develop Trust by Increments

Trust in a leader does not just spring full blown into existence the way Athena sprang from the head of Zeus. Instead, followers' trust in their leaders grows one small step at a time. It evolves by increments. Over time, with increasing knowledge and experience of each other, with more and more evidence that the leader is open to his or her followers, involves them in decision making, and actually delivers on promises, followers increase their level of trust in their leaders.

In dealing with adversaries, international relations has the concept of "confidence building measures," a series of small steps that each side to a previous hostility takes in order to show the other their side peaceful intentions and thereby, over time, develop a relationship of increasing trust. New leaders seeking to build trust should adopt the same approach in dealing with their new constituents. By planning a series of small actions which is in their followers' interests and which they can deliver on, they lay the basis of increasing trust. Like an entrepreneur who gains small amounts of capital from an investor and then obtains larger and larger investments as the business demonstrates success, a leader also obtains growing trust by increments from followers.

In organizations, leaders can often begin the process of creating trust by trusting first—by taking actions that show their trust in the people they are trying to lead. Usually, by trusting first, you make yourself vulnerable to the unpredictable and potentially harmful responses of others. When the Pennsylvania law school dean agreed to participate in a two-day retreat with his faculty, his participation was an act of trust in the faculty. He was trusting that the faculty would genuinely use the retreat as an opportunity to improve relationships within the school and not simply to denounce him for his real and imagined errors over the previous two years. Recognizing his vulnerability, the faculty at the retreat responded by engaging in a dialog that was both constructive, in the sense that it avoided personal attacks on the dean, and open, in the sense that the faculty expressed their genuine concerns and aspirations. The constructive tenor of the conversation was a response to the dean's own willingness to participate, and the openness of their comments, which in turn could have rendered them potentially vulnerable to retribution from the dean on their return to the school, was the faculty's responsive act of trust in the dean. The need for the leader to trust first is another way that gaining trust is like raising capital. Usually, you can't raise capital from other investors unless you yourself have first invested some of your own money in the business.

Some leaders avidly seek the trust of their followers while at the same time actively discouraging trust among them out of fear that followers who trust each other too much will threaten their leadership. I once worked for a university president, a creative and dynamic leader, who discouraged the university's deans from meeting together when he was not present. He considered too much cooperation as a threat to his leadership, so he practiced the age-old strategy of divide and conqueror. Leaders following this strategy pit one associate against another; they selectively provide information to one group in the organization and not another; they play favorites. While divide-and-conqueror leadership has indeed sometimes brought positive results to many of its practitioners, like my former president, one may ask whether the creation of a more positive climate of trust might not have enhanced organizational effectiveness in the long run.

It is extremely difficult for you as leader to gain the trust of other leaders if you do not at the same time seek to increase trust among them. Divide-and-conquer leadership heightens members' sense of their own vulnerability and increases their need to be defensive in all their interactions—factors that inhibit trust generally. Divide-and-conquer is unpredictable by nature. Unpredictability increases members' sense of vulnerability with respect to your actions and therefore inhibits their trust in you. So if you want to gain the trust of your followers you need to find ways to encourage them to trust each other.

Developing trust among the people you lead is also an incremental process. They will not trust each other because you order them to do so any more than they will trust you because you say so. Your followers will learn to trust one another through experiences of working together that they judge to have advanced or at least not injured their interests, experiences that give them the knowledge of one another, that will give them confidence in the future actions of one other. One significant approach is to develop joint activities, such as organizational planning and implementation exercises, to give them the experience of working together and hopefully achieve the positive results that will lead to increased trust.

Another approach is joint training. The interaction that accompanies learning together can heighten trust in a group. Towards the end of the apartheid era in South Africa, international agencies organized joint training sessions in negotiation in which black and white South African leaders participated together. The experience of engaging in interactive training was a first step in building trust among the contending groups, for it enabled them to know one another personally, to develop a common vocabulary to communicate with one another, and to learn basic skills of relating to one another. The trust that began in these sessions helped to foster the final negotiations that brought a peaceful end to apartheid and the transition to a black majority government. Leaders seeking to foster cooperation among the people that they lead can use similar techniques such as planning retreats, training sessions, simulated exercises, and implementation activities that deliberately seek to bring together people who have not previously had significant experience of working together.

Obstacles to Trust

Creating trust is not just a matter of a leader's good intentions. In the course of the leadership journey, a leader, like a white water canoeist, must navigate to avoid numerous obstacles, both apparent and hidden, that threaten to prevent the development of trust or destroy the trust that exists. Here are a few of the obstacles that every leader should be alert to.

(1) Lack of time

Building trust takes time. The pressure to achieve organizational results rapidly through sudden changes and innovations when a new leader arrives on the scene often increases distrust. When possible, leaders should seek to lay the foundation of trust before introducing sweeping change.

(2) The perceived untrustworthy act

Psychological research clearly shows that actions by a leader, regardless of good intentions, that followers perceive as untrustworthy serve to undermine the development of trust.[2] In making decisions, leaders need to ask: How will my followers perceive my action? Often they may interpret a leader's inconsistent acts as evidence of untrustworthiness. While one perceived untrustworthy act will not permanently prevent the development of trust with the people you lead, you will have to work hard and persistently to overcome its effects.

(3) An overly competitive environment

An overly competitive environment within organizations, a phenomenon often fostered by leaders as a means to increase productivity and motivate followers, can also serve to undermine trust. In an overly competitive environment, members of the group view each other as threats to their interests and therefore have a disincentive to trust one another. The challenge for any leader is to foster trust and cooperation and at the same time find ways to encourage each member to make a maximum contribution to the organization. A client of mine, a new leader seeking to increase the productivity of his organization, complained, "There is just too much cooperation around here. The employees keep talking about how they are a 'family.' I don't want them to be a family. I want them to be a team." "What's the difference?" I asked. "The prodigal son!" he shot back. What he meant was that in the cooperative and trusting atmosphere of a family, its members accept each other's failings, often without complaint, whereas team members expect and indeed demand high performance from one another. In his view,

---

[2] Robert Axelrod, *The Complexity of Cooperation: Agent-Based Models of Collaboration and Competition* (Princeton: Princeton University Press).

for the purposes of increasing productivity, a team struck a better balance between cooperation and competition than did a family.

(4) Leadership mobility

Trust is personal. Followers develop trust in the leader's person, not the position or title. Because trust creation takes time, frequent changes of leadership in organizations, so common in contemporary American institutions, tend to inhibit the development of trust. Each time a new leader arrives on the scene, the process of trust creation must begin anew. Moreover, knowing that a new leader will probably not stay long in the job, members may see little point in investing the time and effort in developing working relationships characterized by a high degree of trust.

(5) The exaggerated leadership ego

All of us have egos and all of us, leaders and followers, pursue our own interests. While recognizing these facts, followers also demand leaders that will at the same work to advance followers' interests. It is only when they are certain of a leader's intentions in this regard that they are willing to grant their trust. Individuals who assume positions of leadership can manifest their egos in extreme and exaggerated ways, from the language they speak to the people they surround themselves with, from the way they decorate their offices to the way they treat subordinates. These exaggerated manifestations of leadership ego can become an obstacle to trust because they carry a strong message: "My interests come first—before your interests and before the institution's." The people they lead will not readily grant their trust to a leader whose interests are not aligned with theirs. While the so-called charismatic leader has been considered important to many organizations, the line between charisma and egomania has not always been clear. There is reason to believe that charismatic leaders tend to extreme narcissism causing them to promote projects like mergers to expand their empires without increasing their organization's profitability, projects that serve their personal interests rather than those of the organization.[3] Elite followers in particular, like research scientists and investment bankers, tend to be particularly

---

[3] Yassin Sankar, "Character Not Charisma," *Journal of Leadership and Organization Studies* 9, no. 4 (2003): p. 47.

skeptical of the charismatic leader and the exaggerated leadership ego if only because they both offend the basic notion of *primes inter pares*, first among equals, that for them is the fundamental organizational principle that protects their interests.

Conclusion: Rules for Negotiating Trust

In seeking to gain the trust of others leaders so you can lead them, you should bear in mind a few simple rules that emerge from our discussion.

(1) Recognize that people will trust you not because of your charisma, your charm, or your vision, but because they have concluded that your leadership will advance their interests. You therefore need to work to understand the people you lead and to know their interests.
(2) Trust building takes time, so be prepared to invest the necessary time in the process.
(3) Find ways to demonstrate that your interests are the same as your followers.
(4) To gain the trust of others, you must trust first.
(5) Trust building proceeds by increments. So have a plan for a sequence of trust-building measures.
(6) The provision of information and your openness to those you lead are important building blocks of trust.
(7) Be consistent and predictable in your actions as leader. Beware of the trust obstacles of lack of time, leadership mobility, an overly competitive environment, and exaggerated manifestations of the leadership ego.

12

Leadership Help — Advisors and Negotiating Leaders

It's not always lonely at the top. Despite romantic images of leaders engaged in solitary struggles to guide their organizations and nations to security and prosperity, the fact of the matter is that leaders usually have lots of help. Indeed, their success or failure is vitally dependent on the quality of help they receive. Leadership help has two basic dimensions. First, a helper may carry out actions on behalf of a leader to assist him or her in the process of leading an organization or group. Thus, a leader may delegate certain leadership functions to an assistant, for example approving business decisions made by subordinates, monitoring the operations of specific parts of the organization, or writing speeches for the leader to deliver. A second important type of leadership help is advice to guide a leader's actions and decisions, particularly those actions and decisions that relate to negotiating leadership.

Leadership and Advice

Leadership runs on advice. From the White House to the town hall, from the corporate executive suite to the factory floor, advisors, counselors, and consultants fuel the processes and outcomes of leadership actions. Throughout history, counselors to kings and emperors have influenced decisions about peace and war. Woolsey, Richelieu, and Rasputin shaped the course of events in England, France, and Russia through their advice. In more recent times, unelected advisors like Henry Kissinger, James Baker, and Robert Strauss have influenced national policy and leadership negotiations

© The Author(s) 2017
J.W. Salacuse, *Real Leaders Negotiate!*,
DOI 10.1057/978-1-137-59115-9_12

by counseling U.S. presidents. Sometimes the presence of advisors is obvious in leadership actions, but in many cases it is not. As a result, our understanding of the dynamics of a particular leader's actions and decisions is often limited and incomplete.

Two examples illustrate the important roles that advisors play in influencing leadership. The first concerns the 1978 Camp David negotiations between Egypt and Israel. The second relates to the origins of the U.S. policy on the use of torture to interrogate terrorist suspects. The Camp David negotiations between Israel and Egypt in 1978 leading to a peace agreement between two countries that had been at war for 30 years has, of course, had a major impact on geopolitics in the Middle East. The decision to hold those talks at Camp David in the hills of rural Maryland, rather than in Washington or Geneva, was an important factor that led to a successful result. The idea of holding negotiations at Camp David did not come from the leaders involved—Egypt's President Anwar Sadat, Israel's Prime Minister Menachem Begin, members of their governments, or even from their host, President Jimmy Carter. No, the idea was advanced by one of Carter's most trusted advisors—his wife, Rosalynn. During a quiet family weekend at Camp David in July 1978, as the President was lamenting with her the difficulty of doing anything positive to resolve the conflict between the Arabs and Israel, Mrs. Carter suggested that he bring Sadat and Begin to Camp David to talk through their problem.[1]

Embedded in Mrs. Carter's suggestion were two key elements of advice: (1) that the president convene a negotiation between Begin and Sadat and (2) that the negotiation take place at Camp David. Her advice set in motion a process of negotiation that would yield a peace treaty between the two adversaries and would profoundly affect the Middle East for years to come. As one examines the history of that negotiation, the fact that it took place at Camp David clearly facilitated agreement in a way that more traditional diplomatic settings, like Geneva or Washington, would not. The nature of the site for a negotiation can greatly affect its results.[2]

A less positive example of an advisor's influence was reported by the *New York Times* in a front page story in December of 2014.[3] A few months after the terrorist attack on New York City on September 11, 2001 the United

---

[1] Lawrence Wright, *Thirteen Days in September* 45 (New York: Knopf, 2014).

[2] Jeswald W. Salacuse, *Negotiating Life: Secrets for Everyday Diplomacy and Deal Making* (New York: Palgrave Macmillan, 2013), pp. 153–169.

[3] James Risen and Matt Apuzzo, "C.I.A., on Path to Torture, Chose Haste over Analysis," *New York Times*, December 15, 2014, p. 1.

States captured Abu Zubaydah, who was suspected of helping to plan the attack. At a meeting in 2002, CIA officials discussed who was to interrogate Zubaydah and how it would be done. A legal advisor at the meeting suggested the name of a psychologist, a contract employee of the Agency's Office of Technical Services, a person he did not know, working on a program to train US Air Force personnel to resist interrogation and torture if captured. In desperation to obtain vital information from Zubaydah and other prisoners, the CIA turned to this psychologist, without actually vetting or evaluating him, for guidance on interrogation methods of suspected terrorists and he would then develop a program of enhanced interrogation techniques employing torture. The legal advisor's advice, almost casually delivered in that meeting, ultimately led to the adoption by President Bush of policies permitting the widespread use of notorious interrogation techniques that Senator Dianne Feinstein, the Chairman of the Senate Intelligence Committee, would label "a stain on our values and our history."[4]

The moral of these two stories is that advice, no matter how earnestly or casually given, can have significant consequences, consequences that neither the advisor nor the leader who receives it may foresee at the time it is given and that scholars and the public may be unaware of until years later, if at all.

The Nature of Advising and Advisors

Advice to leaders comes in many forms: technical studies by a team of financial experts on the effect of raising taxes in a particular area; a briefing by an aide to a governor on whether to approve or veto a bill just passed by the state legislature; or an informal conversation with a spouse on approaches to resolving a conflict between two countries. Despite differences in form, all advice is essentially *a communication from one person (the advisor) to another (the client) for the purpose of helping that second person determine a course of action for solving a particular problem.*[5] For the purposes of this chapter, the "client" is, of course, the leader who receives advice.

One of the defining characteristics of advice is that it is not obligatory. The leader is free to take it or leave it. Advice is thus markedly different from certain other communications, such as laws, contracts, and directives, whose

---

[4] Ibid., p. 1.
[5] Jeswald W. Salacuse, *The Wise Advisor: What Every Professional Should Know About Consulting and Counseling* (Westport, CT: Praeger, 2000).

contents are intended to impose obligations on the people to whom they are addressed. On the other hand, because of the information asymmetry that often exists between leader and advisor, a dependency relationship may develop over time between the two, making it often difficult in practice for the leader to reject advice without another source of needed information on which to rely. Such dependency is often the situation existing between newly elected presidents and the senior members of the permanent government bureaucracy on whom they must rely for advice on governing. In this connection, it is worth noting that the word "client" comes from the Latin word *cliens*—"a person who has someone to lean on." Many leaders come to see their advisors as people they can lean on to help carry out the tasks of leadership.

The Use of Advisors in Leadership and Governance

Just as advice comes in many forms, advisors to leaders have many guises. Some advisors, like economic or legal advisors in government departments, are officially designated as such while others, like Rosalynn Carter may have no formal role whatsoever. Some, like the anonymous CIA lawyer, are lone individuals, while others, like international consulting firms, may be substantial institutions. Still others, like Henry Kissinger who accompanied President Nixon to China to negotiate a ground-breaking relationship with that country, are public figures, while others like the boyhood friend of a city mayor, remain private figures, no matter how important their contribution to a given leadership decision. In addition, many advisors are committees. Indeed, the advisory committee seems a permanent feature of modern organizations. The U.S. government, for example, has over a thousand officially constituted advisory committees—so many that the American Congress has had to pass a special law, The Federal Advisory Committee Act, to regulate them. The reason leaders use committees instead of individuals as advisors is not only to obtain a broad base of information but also to create a forum in which different viewpoints within the organization may be shaped into a single recommendation for action. Whether an advisor is official or unofficial, public or private, individual or collective, can profoundly affect that advisor's role in the advising process. Thus a private, unofficial advisor, like the mayor's boyhood friend, would probably feel much less constrained by a role prescription in dealing with his or client leader than would an official, public advisor, like Kissinger.

Regardless of the form of the advisor's role, leaders use advisors for two principal reasons: (1) *expertise* and (2) *validation*.

Expertise

One may explain the need for expertise from two perspectives: (1) the perspective of the individual leader and (2) the perspective of the governance system in which the leader functions. With regard to individualist explanations, the most common reason is that the advisor has expert knowledge that may improve the leader's performance in the tasks of leadership and governance. The leader is thus in some way deficient and the advisor has the skill or knowledge to make up for the deficiency.[6] For example, political leaders use advisors because of such felt deficiencies as lack of specialized knowledge, limited time to handle a heavy workload, or an overly partisan viewpoint. That deficiency in knowledge may be about the *substance* of policy matters, the *process* for making desired policy decisions, or both.

From an organizational or systemic perspective, another purpose of advisors is to enable complex organizations, like the United States government or the European Union, to reduce the transaction costs of leadership and governance that would otherwise be required to gain that expertise without recourse to experienced advisors.

Validation

In addition to acquiring expertise, leaders may use advisors to *validate* a fact, policy, or intention, either to themselves, their followers, their opponents, or the public. In in this connection, leaders need to remember that their choice of advisor can send a signal, positive or negative, intentional or unintentional, to the people they are trying to lead. Followers carefully study the people or organizations that a newly selected leader turns to for advice as clues to the kind of policies and actions the leader may take in the future.

On the other hand, a leader may deliberately select a particular advisor to send a signal to another party in the hope of influencing a favorable response. For example, in financial crises, leaders of governments seeking to negotiate economic assistance from international lenders may choose as advisors

---

[6] Y. Dror, "Conclusions," in W. Plowden, ed. *Advising the Rulers* (Oxford: Basil Blackwell Ltd., 1987), p. 170.

distinguished foreign economists known for opinions acceptable to such international lenders, not only to gain financial and economic expertise but also to encourage foreign governments and international organizations to provide aid. Similarly, candidates running for political office in the United States will select particular people as advisors to reassure wealthy donors about the policies they will follow if elected so as to encourage those donors to finance their campaigns. And leaders contemplating significant new policies or negotiation initiatives may engage certain noted advisors in the hope of persuading their followers, influential interest groups, or the public of the seriousness of their intent or the soundness of contemplated policies. Such advisors have "reputational capital" that leaders seek to mobilize to achieve desired ends. For example, during the Vietnam war, President Lynden Johnson appointed John Roche, a distinguished political science professor and former dean of Arts and Sciences of Brandeis University, as his special assistant in part to make a hopeful positive signal to the US academic community which was expressing strong opposition to his foreign policies and his presidency.

The selection of a particular person to advise a leader can also send positive or negative signals to a leader's own potential supporters and constituents. For example, choosing as an advisor a well-known expert who in the past has expressed sympathy for or assisted an adversary may cause a leader to lose the support of constituents who fear that the advisor will cause the leader to negotiate agreements that will injure the country's or the constituents' interests. Thus, an analysis of the role of an advisor on leadership and governance requires an understanding of precisely *why* a leader has engaged a particular advisor and the specific potential or actual impact that such an advisor may have on governance or the policy-making process. For example, the fact that U.S. President Woodrow Wilson, a Democrat, refused to include any Republicans in his delegation to the Versailles Peace talks in 1919 sent a message to the Republicans in the Senate that their interests did not matter, an action that later influenced the Senate to refuse ratification of the treaties concluded at Versailles. One might compare President Wilson's approach to dealing with political adversaries to that of President Abraham Lincoln during the U.S. Civil War, who instead of isolating his political rivals, included them as members of his cabinet. It follows that in selecting a particular advisor, government officials should consider whether the signal sent to supporters, opponents, and the public by such an appointment will facilitate or complicate the tasks of leadership.

Finally, leaders use advisors to validate their own inclinations, positions, and policies. For example, governmental authorities often commission advisors, individually or as a committee, to provide expert advice on a proposed program or policy in order to give that proposal added legitimacy in the eyes of the public. And during the process of making a decision, a leader may seek advice to validate a contemplated action. For example, at the 1986 Reykjavik Summit, U.S. President Ronald Reagan and Soviet Premier Mikhail Gorbachev undertook promising negotiations for large reductions in nuclear weapons. Reagan, however, insisted on the U.S. right to continue research on a space-based system, known as the Strategic Defense Initiative (SDI), to track and destroy incoming missiles during an attack. Gorbachev countered that such research should be limited to the laboratory, not performed in space. Reagan refused. In the midst of this stand-off between the two leaders, Reagan passed a note to U.S. Secretary of State George Shultz, his chief advisor at the talks, asking: "Am I wrong?" Shultz whispered, "No, you are right." That whispered validation led Reagan to maintain his position on SDI research. He therefore chose to end the Summit without an agreement, saying to Schultz, his advisor, "Let's go George, we're leaving."[7] The next year, encouraged by Schultz's advice to maintain his position, Reagan eventually led the Soviets to sign the Intermediate-Range Nuclear Forces Treaty, abolishing an entire class of nuclear weapons without requiring the elimination of SDI.

Advising as a Relationship

Superficially, the act of advising may seem essentially the delivery of information from one person to another—for example, where to hold negotiations between Egypt and Israel or how to interrogate suspected Al-Qaida prisoners. On closer examination, one sees that effective advising requires more than the delivery of information: it also necessitates a relationship between advisor and leader. As defined earlier, advising is a communication from one person to another to help that second person solve a problem or choose a course of action. For that communication to be effective in actually influencing the actions of the person to whom it is addressed, a relationship of some sort must always exist between the two individuals concerned. A relationship is a sense of connection between two or more people. A productive working relation between the advisor and the client leader entails to

---

[7] F. Stanton, *Great Negotiations: Agreements that Changed the Modern World* (Yardley, PA: Westholme, 2011), pp. 201–227.

some extent a degree of trust and confidence between the two. If a leader is to accept and act on advice provided by an advisor, that leader must have confidence in the advisor's technical competence, integrity and loyalty. Effective advisors understand this dimension of advising and therefore make efforts to build productive relationships with their clients. They build relations through their communications with their clients. Thus, their individual communications may have one or both of two basic goals: to deliver information and to build and strengthen client relationships.

Ideally, the relationship between advisor and leader is one characterized by the leader's sense of trust and confidence in the advice and behavior of the advisor. As Sir Francis Bacon wrote in his seminal essay *Of Counsel*, "the greatest trust between man and man is the trust of giving counsel."[8] The development of a relationship of trust and confidence between advisor and leader is based first on a belief by the leader in the technical competence of the advisor. Technical competence alone, however, is not enough to create the needed trust between advisor and leader. Impartiality of the advisor and unbiased nature of the advice is also important, especially in multilateral settings, like the European Union Council of Ministers or the United Nations, where the advisor working for the international institution sometimes plays the role of a mediator or "honest broker" among countries' leaders with respect to contentious issues. Even more important is a leader's belief that his or her advisor is loyal and working in the best interests of the negotiator and the organization or country the official represents. That position is important in influencing leaders to accept advice offered by their advisors. For example, in the negotiation of the EU's Lisbon Treaty, the director-general of the Legal Service, a division of the Council Secretariat, took the initiative of preparing an entire draft treaty, drawn from the experience of prior EU constitutional negotiations, and presented it to the Council's June 2007 session, a meeting of European political leaders. That draft would become the basis of negotiations leading to the Treaty of Lisbon, an agreement that would eventually serve as the EU's current constitution.[9] The director-general's initiative reduced the transaction costs of negotiating a new constitutional basis for the EU compared to a process in which individual states would have introduced their own separate drafts into the negotiation. The willingness of the members of the Council, who were political

---

[8] Francis Bacon, "Of Counsel," in *Essays, Advancement of Learning, New Atlantic*, (Franklin Center, PA: Franklin Library, 1982), p. 54.

[9] R. J. Goebel, "Introduction: A Tribute to Jean-Claude Piris: Director-General of the Legal Service of the Council of the European Union," *Fordham International Law Journal* 34 (2011), p. 1189.

leaders of the EU member countries, to accept the director-general's advice in the form of a draft treaty as a basis for negotiations was crucially dependent on the member states' confidence in his impartiality and technical competence. In role theory terms, this incident is also an example of a client, the Council membership, allowing an advisor, the director-general of the Legal Service, to redefine his role prescription in order to facilitate the work of the group.

For an advisor to preserve the necessary air of impartiality, it is important that he or she not be viewed publicly as the driving force in the policy-making process, that he or she not be seen as overshadowing or usurping the work of the leader. Thus in many instances, to be effective, an advisor must remain an unobtrusive helper, a person out of the limelight whose role in leadership decisions is not publicly known. Given the political sensitivities in many countries about unelected bureaucrats making policy, advisors to governmental leaders are concerned that they are not seen as preempting or overtly influencing the policy-making process in democracies.

Many other kinds of advisors face a similar problem of not overshadowing or pre-empting leaders who are their clients. Advisors who become too public may ultimately impair their effectiveness in two ways. First, such action may damage their relationship with their client leaders, who may resent being overshadowed and publicly diminished in status. Second, the legitimacy of the resulting leadership policy or decision may later be called into question by the leader's constituents or opponents as being not the authorized work of the leader but the unauthorized meddling of the advisor.

The Structure of the Advising Relationship

The nature of the relationship between advisor and leader can influence policy making and governance. It is therefore important for advisors to understand that relationship as well as the relationship existing between other leaders with whom they interact and their particular advisors. In certain instances, that knowledge may enable a leader productively to use the other leaders' advisors as sources of information or as means to influence those officials themselves. For example, at the Camp David talks, President Carter, faced with Menachem Begin's intransigence, began conversations with two of Begin's advisors, Ezer Weizman, Israeli minister of defense, and Moshe Dayan, Israel's foreign minister, in hopes of better understanding the Israeli prime minister and perhaps finding a way of softening his negotiating position.[10] Those conversations ultimately helped Carter to better evaluate Begin's position. Later, Dayan would also play a role in persuading Begin to accept the treaty that would emerge from the Camp David talks by suggesting to the Americans a formula to overcome a final obstacle raised by Begin to signing the treaty.

The structure of the relationship between leaders and advisors has two basic dimensions: formal and substantive. Let's consider each one separately:

The Formal Elements of the Relationship

Advisors to leaders may either be *official* or *unofficial*. Official advisors are those who have been designated as such by the organization or group on whose behalf they work. Thus, the CIA lawyer who participated in the discussions on interrogating terrorist suspects was an official advisor. Giving advice was his job. On the other hand, various unofficial and unauthorized people may seek to advise leaders, either for altruistic or self-serving reasons. Rosalynn Carter was an unofficial, but nonetheless very influential, advisor to her husband Jimmy, and she clearly assumed that role out of a desire to help her husband solve a difficult diplomatic problem facing his presidency. On the other hand, some individuals may try to assume the role of advisor to a leader in order to influence policy for self-serving reasons, a tactic often used by lobbyists for special interests. The use of unofficial advisors in policy making therefore has potential benefits as well as potential costs. The principal benefit is that it may expose leaders to new and creative ideas that result in successful leadership actions, as was the case with Rosalynn Carter's advice to use Camp David as a site for peace negotiations. In addition, in cases where the choice of a particular person as an *official* advisor may send an undesired message to a leader's constituents, using such a person as an *unofficial* advisor may blunt or minimize such negative effects. On the other hand, in certain circumstances, the use of unofficial advisors may be seen as an improper interference in governance, thereby subjecting a leader's efforts to attack and undermining the legitimacy of the policy-making process, as well as its results.

---

[10] Wright, *supra*, pp. 185–186, 287.

The Substantive Elements of the Relationship

While the precise nature of the substantive relationship between advisor and leader may take many variations, it essentially tends to follow one of three basic structural models: (1) the advisor as director; (2) the advisor as servant; and (3) the advisor as partner.

Model 1: The Advisor as Director

In this model, the advisor tends to take control of the policy-making process, directing a leader's actions to arrive at a result. In the advisor's mind (and sometimes in the leader's), the leader just needs to follow the advisor's directives to achieve effective leadership. Here, the leader is an empty vessel to be filled with the advisor's wisdom. Indeed, advisors to leaders sometimes see themselves as leading the organization through their clients.

Model 2: The Advisor as Servant

Rather than act as a director in the advising process, the advisor may play the role of a servant, responding only to the specific demands of the leader. Here, the leader remains fully in control of the process and may limit the participation of the advisor to specific questions and tasks. Sometimes, leaders have several advisors, particularly where the leader holds a high rank, such as a minister or president. In that situation, the resulting competition among advisors for the leader's attention further underscores their roles as servants.

Model 3: The Advisor as Partner

In certain situations, advisors and leaders may become partners in policy making and governance. The essence of any partnership is coownership and joint participation. When advisor and client function as partners, they jointly manage the advising process and together take ownership of the problem to be solved. At the same time, the leader has ultimate responsibility and decision-making authority for contemplated governmental or organizational action. Here, as a result of mutual trust and confidence between the two, advisor and leader draw on a common pool of knowledge and skills in order to resolve the policy problem at hand. Rosalynn Carter, who sometimes attended cabinet meetings, certainly had a partnership relationship with her husband. Other examples of a partnership between leaders and advisors include President John F Kennedy and his brother Robert during the Cuban Missile Crisis of 1962, President Ronald Reagan and Secretary of State George Shultz at the Reykjavik Summit in 1986, and President George H. W. Bush and Secretary of State James Baker during the Gulf War.

On the other hand, at Camp David, Sadat clearly saw his advisors, not as partners in his negotiations, but as servants, and the members of his delegation recognized that fact. When one of the members of the Egyptian team complained that Sadat was keeping them in the dark and negotiating behind their backs, Boutros-Ghali, Egypt's minister of state for foreign affairs, later to become United Nations Secretary-General, reminded the team of their servant status, stressing that their only function at Camp David was to support Sadat. "We must offer *al-Rayyyis* our advice," he said, using the Egyptian word for "the chief," "but the final decision is his."[11] This incident was an example of a situation in which the role prescribed for the advisor by the leader, President Sadat, conflicted with the role expectations of the members of his team. The role preference of the president clearly prevailed,

The precise nature of an leader–advisor relationship depends on a variety of factors, including the experience and personalities of the advisor and client, the nature of the issues they work on, the organizational setting in which the advising takes place, the communication style of the advisor, the type of social relationship existing between advisor and leader, the prescriptions of the advisor's role, and the advisor's own conception of that role. Thus, the facts that Secretary of State James Baker and President George H. W. Bush were old friends, that John and Robert Kennedy were brothers, and that Jimmy and Rosalynn Carter were spouses were all important social foundations upon which to build a partnership relationship in the advising process and clearly shaped the respective roles of each person.

The relationship between advisor and leader may change over time, resulting in an alteration of the advisor's role. For instance, an advisor to a leader may begin in the servant role and then, later, as the official develops confidence in the advisor, attain the status of partner. Conversely, clients of a high powered, politically-connected advisor who arrives on the scene and assumes the role of director may eventually relegate that advisor to a servant if his or her advice or advising method proves unhelpful. Both in government and the private sector, an advisor's role usually changes when the leadership of the institution changes.

---

[11] Wright, *supra*, 52.

Conclusion: Advice for Leaders and Advisors about Advising

The purpose of this chapter has been to better understand the role of advisors in the leadership process and to suggest ways that such knowledge may be useful to both leaders and their advisors in carrying out their functions. The chapter therefore concludes with brief advice for both leaders and their advisors about how best to conduct the advising process so as to enable leaders to negotiate their leadership responsibilities.

Advice to Leaders

Leaders should consciously incorporate knowledge of the role and function of advisors into their preparations, strategies, and tactics for policy making and governance. According, they should therefore approach their tasks with the following seven questions in mind:

(1) What are my specific needs for advice in exercising my leadership of the organization or group for which I am responsible? What kind of advisors, formal or informal, should I use in a particular leadership task?
(2) What resources will the people I select as advisors bring to my leadership and how will those resources help me to achieve the desired results?
(3) What are the interests—personal, organization, and professional—of my advisors? How may those interests affect the way my advisors help or hinder my efforts?
(4) What should be the nature of my relationship with particular advisors in leading my organization? Will that person serve as director, servant, or partner?
(5) What kinds of signals, positive or negative, does my choice of advisor communicate to my associates, constituents, opponents, and the public in general?
(6) Who are the advisors of other leaders and organizations important to my own leadership tasks? What is the nature of their relationships with the people they advise?
(7) How and to what extent do I need to get to know the advisors of other leaders and participants in governance and policy making? To what extent should I use those advisors as channels of communication, sources of information, or means of influence?

Advice to Advisors

Advising achieves best results when advisors consciously understand and analyze the advising process in which they are engaged and apply certain principles in carrying it out. Based on the experience of advisors in many different contexts, the following seven simple rules are addressed to advisors of leaders.

Rule 1: Know Your Client

To be an effective advisor, you need to know the client, that is, the leader whom you advise, from the very start. Knowing the client is important for two reasons—one concerns *what* advice is given (i.e. substance) and the other affects *how* it is given (process). Thus good advice must always meet the leader's needs, circumstances and values—vital information that the advisor must know before actually giving advice. Secondly, the effective advisor shapes the advising process to fit the leader's abilities, background, and situation. In order to gain needed information from the leader, the advisor must build an appropriate relationship with the leader.

Rule 2: Help or at Least Do No Harm

An advisor's fundamental purpose is to help the leader, something that inexperienced advisors sometimes forget. It is therefore important to understand in what way the leader needs help. When Hippocrates advised Greek physicians "to help or at least do no harm," he knew that the practice of medicine had the capacity for both helping and injuring the patient. Advising has the same potential. Unskilled advisors sometimes fail to appreciate the extent to which their advice can cause damage to their clients. Thus, the CIA legal advisor who casually offered the name of a possible "interrogation expert" set in motion a program that did great damage to the international reputation of the United States. In the end, it is, after all, the client, not the advisor, who pays the price of bad advice. President John F. Kennedy, who received both good and bad advice during his political career, underscored the point when he remarked that an advisor, after giving advice, goes on to other advice, but the leader whom he advises goes on to an election.[12]

---

[12] Peter Szanton, *Not Well Advised.* (New York: Russell Sage Press, 1981), p. 140.

Rule 3: Agree on Your Role

The advisor has a particular role to play in the advising process. As we have seen, an advisor may be a director, a servant, or a partner. The role that an advisor plays is a function of the relationship that the advisor has established with the leader to be advised. Role definition is not a matter of telling clients what they can expect or of imposing their roles. Instead, advisors must negotiate their roles with the clients they serve, while recognizing that those roles can change over time and according to circumstances.

Rule 4: Never Give a Solo Performance

Advising is rarely a one-person show or a solo performance. Experienced advisors know that effective advising requires the active participation of the client. One of an advisor's great challenges is to secure from the client leader the maximum contribution to the advising process, a task complicated by leader's many preoccupations and limited time. Two principal reasons argue for active leader participation. The first is that the client leader has valuable knowledge that the advisor does not have and that the advisor cannot be effective without that knowledge. Thus while policy advisors may be experts in particular fields, they often lack vital knowledge about political and personal imperatives that constrain the leaders they advise, knowledge that is vital in formulating effective advice. A second reason for the advisor to involve the client in the advising problem is that the problem to be solved is ultimately the leader's, not the advisor's.

Rule 5: Make the Process Clear and Constructive

To be effective, advice must be clear and constructive. Clarity in this sense means that the client understands the advice delivered, a task requiring the advisor to adjust advice to the client's background, experience, and expertise, a process that can only take place if the advisor knows the client. A skilled advisor also endeavors to be constructive in giving advice, particularly in understanding the leader's problems and in recommending helpful solutions. Being constructive does not mean being overly optimistic or telling clients only what they want to hear. But it does mean avoiding unnecessary negative criticism and seeking to offer helpful options to solve problems. Early in his career as an advisor to presidents, Henry Kissinger learned that a president is often surrounded by people telling him what he cannot do but that "it is better to become one of those telling him what he can do or at least offering preferable alternatives."[13]

Rule 6: Keep Your Advice Pure

In stressing the advantage of good advice, Sir Francis Bacon wrote: "certain it is that the light a man receiveth by counsel from another is drier and purer than that which cometh from his own understanding and judgment, which is ever infused and drenched in his affections and customs."[14] In theory, by virtue of their detachment and experience, advisors are able to give objective, independent counsel that is unaffected by the client's own biases, fears, and blind spots. In practice, however, an advisor's light can sometime also be impure. Advisors may give impure advice to leaders when they fail to fulfill either of two fundamental obligations to their clients: their duty of care or their duty of loyalty. The advisor's duty of care means that he or she will carefully look after the interests of the leaders they advise. The duty of loyalty means that the advisor will not place his or her own interests above those of the leader. Accordingly, not only should advisors refrain from advancing their material interests at the expense of the client but they should guard against satisfying certain psychological interests—such as their ego demands for public recognition of their role in the leadership process.

Rule 7: Have a Vision of the End and Know When to Stop

The purpose of advice is to support the leadership of a group or organization. Advice is not an end in itself. Consequently, an advisor must know when to cease advising so that the actual tasks of leadership may happen. A final rule is therefore that advisors must know when to stop. That is valuable knowledge not only for advisors, but for writers as well.

---

[13] Walter Isaacson, *Kissinger: A Biography* (New York: Simon & Schuster, 1991), p. 113.

[14] Francis Bacon, "Of Friendship" in *Bacon's Essays with Annotations*, edited by Richard Whately and Franklin F. Heard, (Boston: Lee and Shepard, 1968), p. 285.

Part III

Leadership Preservation and Loss: Negotiating to Stay on the Leadership Road

13

Challenges to Leadership

The Leadership Lease

In 1975, at a meeting of Conservative Party members of the British House of Commons chafing under the ineffective leadership of Edward Heath, a former prime minister who had led the party for 10 years, a backbench MP tellingly reminded his colleagues that the leadership of the Conservative Party was "a leasehold, not a freehold."[1] What he meant of course was that while a person may *occupy* the position of leader for a time that person does not *own* it permanently. Shortly afterwards, the indomitable Margaret Thatcher, who also attended that meeting, would replace Heath as party leader and then proceed to win three general election victories to become the longest-serving British prime minister in the twentieth century. In 1990, however, she too would learn the same lesson as Heath about the leadership leasehold when, faced with strong opposition from Conservative members of Parliament concerned about her growing unpopularity with the public, she was also forced to resign as prime minister and party leader. Countless other leaders of corporations, countries, educational and scientific institutions, from Richard Nixon to Steve Jobs, from General Douglas MacArthur to Hewlett Packard CEO Carly Fiorina, whose positions had once appeared as secure as freeholds, have also found themselves suddenly and usually unceremoniously dumped, ejected from the leadership premises when their leases on leadership unexpectedly ran out.

---

[1] Alan Clark, *The Tories* (London: Weidenfeld & Nicolson, 1998), p. 379.

© The Author(s) 2017
J.W. Salacuse, *Real Leaders Negotiate!*,
DOI 10.1057/978-1-137-59115-9_13

Leadership is an asset that leaders of organizations and groups gain by various means discussed in this book: however, it is not permanent. It is a depreciating asset that no leader can hang on to forever. Although most leaders cling desperately to their positions, they often lose sight of their temporary nature of their positions and have to be reminded of that fact by both followers and opponents. Long-serving leaders like Thatcher and Heath, not to mention Churchill and Roosevelt, struggled mightily to prevent their leadership leases from ending and adopted various negotiation strategies, sometimes with success, to delay the inevitable, but never to defeat it. They devised these strategies, as in any negotiation, to overcome specific challenges facing their continued hold on leadership power at a given moment.

Numerous forces threaten and challenge a person's leadership of a group, institution, or nation. In fact, some of these forces may begin to emerge even before a person gains the power to lead. Leaders therefore need to understand the forces that may end their leadership positions and learn how to deal with them. In many instances, they seek to find solutions to those challenges in negotiation. This chapter will examine the nature of those challenges, and the final chapter will consider how leaders use negotiation to protect their leadership positions.

In general, one may divide the threats and challenges to leadership power into two basic categories:(1) internal challenges, whose origins are to be found in the physical and psychological situation of the leader's person and (2) external challenges, whose sources lie outside of the leader's person in the context in which the leader must operate. Let's look first at the internal challenges.

Internal Challenges to Leadership

The ability of a leader both to do the job effectively and to maintain the support of people necessary to gain and hold onto the leadership job is crucially dependent on the leader's mental and physical state. In this regard, the leadership behavior of human beings parallels that of animal herds in the wild that will exclude one of their number from leadership or even from the herd itself when that animal becomes too weak or too old to fight off challenges from younger, stronger competitors.

Leaders are, after all, mortal and subject to the same physical and mental ills as anyone else. Thus the physical and mental condition of candidates for leadership positions is always an important factor in granting leadership to anyone. When that necessary physical or mental status is questioned or uncertain, a candidate for leadership is often denied the job of leader. For example, during the 1972 presidential election campaign, Democratic nominee Walter Mondale chose Senator Thomas Eagleton as his vice presidential running mate. When it became publicly known that Eagleton suffered from depression and had in the past been hospitalized for that illness on several occasions, facts that he failed to reveal either to Mondale or the public, he felt compelled to withdraw his candidacy. As part of their electoral campaigns, candidates for U.S. president and other elected offices release their medical records or statements from doctors affirming that they are physically fit for the job. Many organizations request or require a person chosen for leadership to undergo a medical examination.

Once in power, leaders often like to demonstrate their good health and strength through public demonstrations of their physical activity since they seem to assume that such demonstrations reassure the public of their fitness to lead. Thus, during his presidency, Bill Clinton often jogged with the press in tow, and in August 1966, as China's Mao Zedong, at the age of 73 was about to launch his cultural revolution, he staged a much publicized "long distance swim" in the Yangtze River to show that he was still physically strong and fully in charge of the country. Leaders assume that such demonstrations of physical strength, by reaffirming their physical vigor for all to see, will have a positive effect on their ability to lead, including their negotiating power with both supporters and opponents.

On the other hand, when leaders suffer illness, they will often do everything they can to hide their condition from both supporters and competitors since they fear that such knowledge will weaken their hold on leadership and therefore their ability to negotiate the necessary tasks of leadership. History gives us numerous examples of this particular leadership negotiation strategy. For example, throughout his years as president, Franklin Delano Roosevelt successfully hid from the public the fact that as a result of polio he could not walk, fearing that if his incapacity became widely known Americans would no longer support him as their leader. While the public was aware of John F. Kennedy's problems with his back, he successfully projected an image of youthful physical vigor while hiding the fact that he had other serious ailments, including Addison's disease, a life threatening loss of adrenal function.[2] In 1919 while Woodrow Wilson was in the midst of conducting

---

[2] Lawrence K. Altman and Todd S. Purdam, "In J.F.K. File, Hidden Pain and Pills," *The New York Times*, November 17, 2002.

a national campaign to secure public approval of the agreements he had negotiated at the Versailles Conference following World War I, he suffered a massive stroke that left him incapacitated. His wife Edith, with the help of his doctor and other members of his White House inner circle, hid his condition from the public and may even have made decisions in his name in order to preserve his hold on the U.S. presidency. He never fully recovered.

Concealing health problems is not a leadership strategy of American presidents alone. In June 1953, Prime Minister Winston Churchill at age 78 suffered a disabling stroke which he hid from both the public and the members of his government, whom he viewed as potential threats to his leadership since they had the power to replace him as leader of the governing Conservative Party and therefore remove him from his position as prime minister. Through strenuous efforts, he recovered in time to address the Party at its fall conference, a convincing demonstration that rumors about his ill health and inability to govern were unfounded. As a result, he would continue to hold the position of prime minister for another two years, until 1955, when he retired. After his retirement, he lived for another 10 years.

Wilson, Roosevelt, Churchill, and Kennedy realized that while widespread knowledge of their physical infirmity might garner them a significant amount of sympathy from the public, such sympathy would only reduce their power to lead and to negotiate with both allies and opponents. For all four men, physical strength, or its appearance, not public sympathy, was a key component of the power to lead.

In general, such efforts to demonstrate physical and mental strength or to hide physical and mental infirmities can be viewed as a sort of negotiation between the leader concerned, aided by his close confidants and advisors on the one hand, and the leader's supporters, opponents, and the general public on the other. In that negotiation, Churchill, Roosevelt, Kennedy and Wilson seemed to have followed the principle of *caveat emptor*, let the buyer beware, like deal makers in business who do not feel required to reveal to their counterparts at the negotiating table all of the weaknesses of the product or service they are selling. Just as negotiators may use a variety of tactics and strategies to convince potential buyers that they are getting a good deal if they sign the contract, physically and mentally impaired leaders use comparable strategies and tactics to convince their constituents that the leader has all the resources, both physical and mental, needed to lead. I have previously defined negotiating power as the ability to influence the decisions of other people in a desired direction; consequently, the existence of negotiating power depends crucially on how the other side in a negotiation *perceives* the resources commanded by a person, organization, or country. Roosevelt, Kennedy, and Churchill, all skilled political negotiators, knew that public knowledge of the full extent of their disabilities would reduce the public perception of their strength of leadership and therefore their ability to govern.

In addition to actual physical and mental infirmities, the internal threats to leadership include various self-induced psychological conditions that may serve to limit or curtail a leader's tenure and effectiveness. Thus, the material advantages and powers that accompany a leader's position may result in a their reduced sensitivity to the concerns of other people, heightened ego and an inflated sense of self-importance, and delusions of grandeur, conditions that may adversely affect a leader's judgment, encourage risky decisions, and cause violations of rules and laws; precisely the attitudes of the Salomon Brother leaders, discussed earlier, that led to the abrupt firing of its chairman and CEO John Gutfreund, by the Salomon board of directors. As in the Salomon Brothers case, these internal factors may also make leaders reject negotiation as a problem-solving device in situations where it is called for, viewing the need to negotiate as a sign of weakness and therefore as a challenge to their leadership. In addition, other internal factors may cause leaders to voluntarily leave their positions because of burn out, family and personal responsibilities, or simply the desire to do something else. In my own case, after a total of 15 years' experience as the head of two different graduate schools, becoming president of a university seemed the next logical step in my career; however, after considering a couple of presidencies and thinking hard about what university presidents actually do, I decided that I would find greater professional and personal fulfillment in returning to full-time teaching and writing, so I resigned as dean of the Fletcher School and have never regretted that decision.

External Threats and Challenges

Many of the most serious challenges and threats to leadership arise from the context in which a leader must function. Some can directly cause leadership loss while others may indirectly lead to it. Thus, a corporate leader's failure to deal effectively with technological changes in the market, to curtail employee criminal behavior, or to increase company profitability can be seen as indirect causes for the removal of a CEO. The direct cause is the action of the board of directors in firing the CEO. Here are some of the more significant direct challenges to a leader's power to lead:

Leadership Expiration Dates

Like most leases, many leadership positions come with a fixed expiration date. Thus political leaders, like presidents, are elected for a fixed term of years, the length of tenure of corporate presidents is often specified in their employment contracts, and the leadership term of heads of law and consulting firms may be limited by their organizations' mandatory retirement policies. Leaders sometimes successfully avoid these constraints by winning re-election, renegotiating their employment contracts, and bargaining with governing boards for a waiver of mandatory retirement policies in their own particular situations. Similarly while the constitutions of some countries, like the United States, have sought to limit the power of their presidents to remain in office indefinitely by enacting mandatory term limits, some leaders, claiming their continued leadership necessary for the welfare of the nation, have sought to hold on to the power to lead by maneuvering to have their wives or other close relatives elected as president or by negotiating with a pliable legislature to amend the constitution to weaken or eliminate term limits.

Loss of Allies and Constituents

No leader comes to power by virtue of his or her talents and abilities alone. Leaders gain power through the support of specific allies and constituents. Thus, the members of the board of trustees of a university or museum who have chosen a specific person as president are usually allies and supporters of that person, at least at the outset of his or her tenure. Michael Eisner was an enthusiastic supporter of Michael Ovitz and that support translated into the selection of Ovitz as president of Disney. Winston Churchill, Edward Heath and Margaret Thatcher became prime ministers of the United Kingdom, not because of their undoubted intelligence and determination but because they had the support of the majority of the Conservative Party members of Parliament, which at the time of their selection had become that body's dominant political group. Similarly, Gamal Abdel Nasser became Egypt's leader after the overthrow of the monarchy because he had the support of the Egyptian army.

Once in power, all leaders continue to need the support of important allies and constituents in order to remain in power. The basic problem for any leader is that over time he or she may lose the support of key allies and constituents. That loss may happen for a number of reasons. Allies may die or resign from the positions that enabled them to support the leader, or because of changes in circumstance they may decide that it is no longer in their interest to support the leader as they once did. Thus Michael Eisner, once a close friend of Michael Ovitz, determined when faced with internal anti-Ovitz forces within the Disney organization that it was no longer in his interest to support Ovitz as president of Disney. Similarly, Carly Fiorina lost the leadership of Hewlett Packard (HP) because the composition of its board in 1999 when she was hired was not the same in 2005 when she was fired.

Thus leaders, to maintain their power, need constantly to be concerned about four things: (1) to maintain the support of old allies; (2) to get rid of or thwart actual or potential opponents and former allies who no longer support the leader; (3) to replace departing allies with equally strong supporters; and (4) to build new alliances with other centers of power. Each of these tasks requires skilled negotiation on the part of the leader. Failure to attend to these tasks may lead to loss of leadership. The case of Carly Fiorina at HP is illustrative.

Fiorina was chosen as CEO of HP in 1999 by a board consisting of 14 members, three of whom were relatives of HP founders and another three who were current or retired HP employees. Thus, potentially, over 42 percent of the board that chose her consisted of people with large HP share ownership and strong personal commitments to HP policies and practices of the past, factors that might cause them to resist major new policy initiatives that Fiorina might attempt. By 2001, through various efforts by Fiorina, the board size had shrunk to 10, a reduction of almost 30 percent from the board that had appointed her. Those who left the board included David Woodley Packard, a son of one of the HP founders and a large HP shareholder. As a result, the board seemed more amenable to initiatives that departed from past traditions.

In 2002, Fiorina launched negotiations to acquire Compaq, a computer maker, in an effort to increase HP's market share and improve its stock price. Certain members of the founders' families concerned about the negative impact of such a merger on the value of their shares sought to stop the acquisition by launching a proxy fight, a strategy that had the effect of depressing HP stock even more. Fiorina was able to win that costly fight, with the result that opponents of the merger left the board. In effect, Fiorina engineered the departure of several old board members but she had to accept as their replacements five former shareholders of Compaq, who had become HP shareholders as a result of the merger.

If Fiorina assumed that her position of HP leader was secure as a result of the change in board membership, that assumption would be proven wrong within three years. In the aftermath of the merger, the market price of HP stock declined and dividends did not increase. However, the annual compensation of directors doubled from about $100,000 to $200,000 per person, a desperate effort, it would seem, by Fiorina to secure director loyalty to her as HP chairperson and CEO. As a negotiating tactic, that gambit ultimately failed because the primary interest of the HP directors was not director compensation but share price since they held or represented large amounts of HP stock. At the time of Fiorina's appointment in 1999, the price of HP stock was $53.43 per share but by September 2002 it had fallen to $12 per share. Ultimately, because of the failure of the stock to rebound significantly after the merger, the new board, whose interests were basically to increase shareholder value, both their own that that of the shareholders they represented, abruptly fired her as HP chairperson and CEO in February 2005. While the indirect causes of her dismissal were the brutal proxy fight and the weak HP stock price, the direct cause was the loss of allies on the board of directors, whose members no longer saw it in their interest to retain her as the company's leader. In essence, the board ceased to be dominated by Fiorina's allies so she lost leadership support and ultimately her job as the company's chairperson and CEO. Fiorina was never able to build another alliance to replace the one she had lost.[3]

Competing Internal Centers of Power

The development of competing centers of power within the organization or group that a person leads can also become a threat to that person's leadership. Dictators, of course, are always alert to competing groups within their governments and move brutally to suppress them. Mao used the Cultural Revolution in China to purge potential sources of opposition to his rule, and Stalin did the same thing during his entire reign in the Soviet Union. In more recent times, the world has witnessed the President of Turkey, Recep

---

[3] For background on this case, see Bruce Bueno de Mesquista and Alastair Smith, *The Dictator's Handbook—Why Bad Behavior is Almost Always Good Politics* (New York: Public Affairs, 2011), pp. 51–57.

Tayyip Erdoğan, in response to an attempted coup in 2016, jail hundreds of people thought to have participated in the coup and fire thousands of government employees suspected of opposition or insufficient loyalty to his rule. These leaders each saw competing centers of power within their countries as threats to their leadership so they moved ruthlessly to deal with them. In their view, to do nothing would have allowed competing centers of power to limit or entirely curtail their own power to lead.

Centers of power that compete with existing leadership can develop in any organization or group in any setting. When Steve Jobs, having been expelled from Apple in 1985, returned to the organization, then in dire straits, 10 years later at the request of the company's board of directors to serve as "advisor to the chairman," he became a strong competing center of power against the CEO Gil Amelio, and would ultimately work successfully to replace him as CEO in 1995. According to his biographer, Jobs "had told Larry Ellison that his return strategy was to sell NeXT to Apple, get appointed to the board, and be there ready when CEO Gil Amelio stumbled."[4]

Competing centers of power may emerge for a variety of reasons, not necessarily as a deliberate plan to unseat the leader. Laws and regulations may require the development of departments to apply them and "compliance officers" to enforce them, resulting in new centers of power that a leader must manage in leading the organization. In order to achieve leadership goals, the leader may have to negotiate power-sharing arrangements with these new power centers. Similarly, advances in technology or demands in the market may necessitate the creation of information technology departments with chief technology officers to lead them, thus establishing yet another center of power within the organization that a leader must take account of in making decisions.

The Demands of External Forces

The development of various external forces from outside the organization can also threaten or result in leadership loss, particularly when they cause supporters to abandon the leader they once supported. The thrust of these events is that they make former allies realize that supporting the organization's leader is no longer in their interest, so they withdraw their support and

---

[4] Walter Isaacson, *Steve Jobs* (New York: Simon & Schuster, 2011), p. 306.

the leader falls. Defecting allies come to believe that continuing to support the leader is no longer in their interest for one of two reasons: either such support has become too costly or because support for another leader promises greater rewards.

The first reason is illustrated by the Salomon Brothers case discussed earlier. The directors of Salomon Brothers were quite satisfied with John Gutfreund's leadership and had given him strong support until the Treasury scandal erupted with the resulting threats of prosecution and negative publicity. They then realized that continuing to support Gutfreund was no longer in their interest since it not only threatened the firm's existence but also their positions as board members, their investments in the firm, and indeed their very reputations.

Similarly, when the board of trustees of Baylor University in 2010 landed as its president Kenneth Starr, a former federal judge, US solicitor general and the lawyer who had led a controversial investigation of Bill and Hillary Clinton, they were proud of their achievement, so much so that three years later they also named him chancellor, the first time in the university's history that the same person held the two positions. However, in May of 2016, the same board abruptly fired him. Responding to numerous allegations by female students that the university had failed to take seriously their complaints of sexual harassment by university athletes, Baylor, prodded by negative publicity, hired an outside law firm to investigate. After a lengthy investigation, the firm determined that Starr, a strong supporter of Baylor's high-profile football program, had mishandled complaints by female students of sexual assault against athletes at the school. Under strong pressure in the face of negative publicity, Starr was dismissed by the board of trustees from his position as president and subsequently resigned as chancellor.[5] While individual board members may have continued to esteem Starr for his personal qualities, maintaining him in a leadership position at the university had simply become too costly in terms of potential damage to their reputations and that of the institution they were charged with governing.

The lessons of these two widely separated cases is clear. When a company's market performance is failing, a financial firm faces potential criminal investigations, or a university's reputation is threatened by sexual or athletic scandals, the governing boards of these institutions may not yet have decided a long-term strategy to solve these problems but they will often determine

---

[5] Marc Stacy, "Baylor Demotes President Kenneth Starr Over Handling of Sex Assault Cases," *The New York Times*, May 26, 2016.

that a useful, short-term, temporary fix is to fire the institution's leader to relieve pressure from stockholders, alumni, the press and the public by signaling that the board has begun to take action to rectify a bad situation. In short, when the costs of remaining in a coalition supporting a leader become greater than its members can bear, they will begin to defect and the coalition will ultimately crumble. This was precisely the dynamic that both Gutfreund and Starr experienced when they lost their leadership.

Members of a supporting coalition will also defect when joining a coalition supporting another leader offers them potentially greater benefits than they are currently receiving. For example, in the United Kingdom elections of 1945, with World War II almost won, the Labour Party led by Clement Atlee defeated the Conservative Party led by Winston Churchill, the country's wartime hero, in a landslide. One explanation for the overwhelming defeat is that the British population, having suffered austerity and deprivation for the sake of winning the War, believed that Labour with their promises of social welfare programs offered them a better deal than the Conservatives which seemed to offer only more austerity. The result was that they abandoned the Conservative coalition that had steadfastly supported Churchill during the War and shifted their allegiance to the Labour Party, a coalition that supported Atlee and an end to austerity.

Negotiating Away the Challenges to Leadership

Leaders who want to stay leaders need to be alert to the challenges to their leadership, challenges that may arise at any time. They then must determine a course of action to deal with them. Many strategies to protect leadership require the use of negotiation. In the final chapter, we will examine some of them.

14

Negotiating to Hold On and Let Go

To withstand challenges to your leadership, keep in mind three fundamental principles. First, you are the leader of a particular group, institution, or nation because certain influential individuals or groups support your hold on that position. Second, those key players give their support to you not because of your charisma or their affection for you, but because they judge that doing so is in their interests. Third, their perception of their interests in your leadership may change at any time. When that happens, they may withdraw their support and thereby put your leadership in jeopardy.

A Key Question: Why Me?

Long-time leaders seem to assume that they are entitled to the position they hold. As a counterweight to that potentially dangerous assumption, real leaders should always continue to ask themselves a fundamental question: Why should the people I'm supposed to lead follow me? If you believe that your charisma, your exalted office, or your vision is reason enough, you're in trouble. While these qualities may affect how others relate to you, the truth is that other people will follow you when they judge that it's in their best interest to do so. Whether they are acting as individuals or team members, people almost always give first priority to their own interests. Just as wise negotiators work to understand and focus on the other side's interests, rather than their stated positions, effective leaders seek to understand the interests of the people they lead and to find ways of satisfying those interests. By doing

© The Author(s) 2017
J.W. Salacuse, *Real Leaders Negotiate!*,
DOI 10.1057/978-1-137-59115-9_14

so, they can better achieve both their organizational and personal goals, particularly the goal of remaining in power.

Challenges and threats to your leadership of an organization or group may begin to emerge even before you formally take power. Competitors for the leadership job you won may become your leadership opponents seeking to find ways to cripple your ability to lead. For example, even before President Obama's inauguration for his first term in 2009, many Republicans announced that they wanted "to destroy" his presidency. While you probably will not encounter that degree of vehemence from rivals as you assume leadership of a company, a charitable institution, or a civic organization, you should remain aware in the course of leading those institutions that you are almost certain to encounter challenges and threats to your hold on the power to lead. In order to protect your leadership, you will ordinarily have to engage in a three-step conceptual process: (1) **recognize** the threat; (2) **analyze** how the threat may impact your leadership; and (3) **strategize** about the actions you need to take to overcome the challenges and preserve your leadership. Let's examine each of these steps to determine how best to conduct them and how negotiation and negotiation analysis can help.

Recognizing Threats to Leadership

Most threats to leadership are readily apparent. When an activist shareholder begins a proxy fight to take control of the corporation you head or a business rival joins a civic committee you chair, you know immediately, as soon as you learn of these events, that your leadership is challenged and may be in jeopardy. There are, however, other situations which at first glance do not have the appearance of a threat but may develop into one. In still others, the threat exists but is deliberately hidden from view like the Greek soldiers in the Trojan horse. The failure to perceive the threat itself or its implications can result in leadership loss, a situation that a friend of mine in Texas experienced several years ago.

In 1985, Joe Foran, then a young Texas lawyer, established Matador Petroleum Corporation to find and develop oil and gas deposits in the American Southwest. Starting in a one-room office with a single part-time employee, Foran, through a series of shrewd acquisitions, built Matador into one of the larger privately held petroleum firms in Texas. To raise capital, he gave wealthy investors seats on Matador's board of directors in return for their investment in the company. With a 10 percent interest in the company, chairman and CEO Foran remained Matador's largest individual investor.

In spring 2003, Tom Brown, Inc., a publicly traded oil company, offered to buy Matador for $388 million. Foran opposed the offer because he felt it did not take account of Matador's growth potential. At the board meeting to discuss the bid, Foran was astounded when the other directors voted to approve the sale. Too late, Foran realized that he had mistakenly believed that the other directors' interests were the same as his own. Foran, then in his early fifties, had the energy, talent, and time to build a company that would give him financial security in his retirement, still many years away. But most of the other directors were retired individuals who had been hurt by a falling stock market and declining investment returns. Their interest was not to build the company but to take the money and run—and that's exactly what they did. As Foran wryly described the board members to me, "They were so old they weren't even buying green bananas anymore."

The coalition of supporting directors so essential to maintaining Foran's control of the company was lost because the directors, while still friendly with Foran and appreciative of his efforts in building a company that attracted a handsome buyout offer, judged their financial interests at that particular time lay in selling the company rather than continuing to support Foran in maintaining the company's independence and pursuing its growth strategy. This story offers certain lessons to leaders who want to maintain their leadership positions. First, the interests of members of your supporting coalition are dependent on time and circumstances. When circumstances change, those interests can change dramatically and cause your coalition of support to fracture. Second, leaders need to be constantly alert to changes in circumstances that may have an impact on supporting coalition members' understanding of their interests. Third, leaders should be cautious about making unfounded assumptions about their followers' interests and not assume that their interests on a particular issue must necessarily be the same as the leaders'.

In order to understand the interests of coalition members, it is often necessary to get to know them as people and to develop a personal relationship with them, something that may be hard to do in the context of a formal board meeting. As Foran told me, "As chairman, I thought I had been leading the other directors in the boardroom at our quarterly meetings. I should have been trying to lead them one-on-one outside the boardroom a lot more frequently." A personal leadership relationship with each of the directors would have enabled him to stay informed of their concerns and prevent the formation of the coalition of directors that emerged at the meeting to accept the buyout offer.

Had Foran understood those interests earlier, he might have been able to structure an arrangement that gave the directors the cash they needed and still allowed him to keep control of his company. Also, had he understood those differences in interest between him and the other directors, he would have recognized immediately that the communication from Tom Brown was not just an offer to buy the company but a potential threat to his leadership of Matador Petroleum Company. Similarly, when Carly Fiorina successively orchestrated Hewlett Packard's (HP's) acquisition of Compaq, she may not have fully recognized that the new board members representing the former Compaq shareholders, as the buyout deal required, were a potential Trojan Horse that would cause her to lose her leadership of the corporation when they, with other board members, came to be believe that their fundamental interest of an increase in HP share value would not be achieved while she was at the company's helm. Had she succeed in raising the HP share price, she would of course have maintained the support of the new board members as well as the other directors and held on to her leadership of the corporation.

Analyzing Threats to Leadership

Having recognized a circumstance or situation as a potential leadership threat, a leader next has to analyze that situation in order to understand its actual and potential effects on and implications for his or her leadership. A leader might begin that analysis by identifying key supporters, that is, those people whose loss of support would put the leader's hold on power in jeopardy. In making that analysis, leaders have to recognize that the development of a new circumstance or situation may be a challenge or threat to their leadership by giving supporters new options to pursue their interests. In the new circumstance, their choices among options will be driven by their evaluation of how particular options will or will not advance those interests. Thus the Matador directors, as a result of the offer from Tom Brown, had a choice of two options: an immediate, specific payout at a good price if they accepted the offer or a delayed, uncertain, but potentially better payout if they rejected it and in doing so continued to support Foran's leadership. In view of their personal and financial situations, they chose the former. Similarly, the HP directors, faced with the situation of a persisting falling share price, had the option of sticking with Fiorina in the hope that her business strategy would eventually turn the company around or finding a new CEO with a fresh vision who might succeed in raising the HP share price a lot sooner. They evidently felt that the latter had greater potential to advance their financial interests so they voted to dump Fiorina.

Your analysis should also examine in depth the individual interests of each of your supporters, since their interests may not be as consolidated and united as they appear at first glance. Variations in interests among your supporters may enable you to stop them from acting as a block and instead permit the formation of a coalition that supports you and has the power to prevent your removal from leadership. It may also enable you to take certain actions that satisfy the interests of specific supporters and thereby retain their support. And if you believe that you have lost the support of certain key people in your institution or organization, you might extend your analysis to ask: From what other people might I get support and what do I have to do to get it?

Strategizing to Meet Leadership Threats and Challenges

Having analyzed and come to understand the nature and implications of the threat to your leadership, the next step is to formulate a *strategy*, a plan of action to address it. In former times, and even today in some countries, leaders meet threats to their leadership by murdering, imprisoning, and or banishing their presumed challengers. Thus, Queen Elizabeth I of England, viewing her cousin Mary Queen of Scots as a serious threat to her reign, had her imprisoned and then ultimately beheaded. In more recent times, the governments of Iran, Saudi Arabia, and Cuba, among others, seem to have regularly followed strategies of execution, imprisonment, and banishment in dealing with threats to their leadership. This book, however, is concerned with more gentle methods of leadership, specifically those that rely on negotiation. I will therefore consider only strategies for *negotiating* leadership threats and challenges.

A leader who has recognized and analyzed a challenge or threat to his or her leadership must then ask: What should I do about it? What should I do to maintain my leadership or, if I am to lose it, how best to negotiate a departure at least cost? Here are the top 10 negotiation strategies that embattled leaders rely on to preserve their power to lead.

Reaffirm and Strengthen Your Alliances

The reason you have the power to lead is that you have allies supporting you in your leadership position. As long as those alliances continue their support, you will remain in power. So when you are faced with a challenge to your leadership, it is important to verify that your supporting alliances remain intact. Thus when Joe Foran received the offer from Tom Brown to buy Matador Petroleum, he might have sought to affirm the support of his alliance with the company's board before its scheduled meeting by making phone calls to some of the more influential directors on his board to ask their opinion on the offer and so test how firm their support was for his desire to reject the offer. Had Foran discovered that certain directors were tempted to vote for the offer, he would have then through negotiation sought to understand their interests and shape a deal that would have caused them to reject the offer and instead continue their support for Foran in his leadership of the company.

Similarly, when I was dean of the Fletcher School, the most important allies supporting my leadership were the president and provost of the university, the faculty of the school, its board of visitors led by Charles Francis Adams, and the students. When the senior professor mentioned in Chapter 3 wrote to Adams and sought to start a student protest against my decision to renew the appointment of his *protégé,* he was seeking to undermine my leadership by weakening the support I was receiving from two of my important allies. By informing the president, provost, faculty and Adams of my decision to deny contract renewal, I was affirming the support of crucial supporting allies. When your soundings among allies reveal a weakening of support, you need to rely on negotiation to deal with possible defections. The meeting I had with students was intended to do precisely that and it resulted in the intended effect. In other situations, in order to maintain the support of a wavering ally, you may have to negotiate a deal that gives that person a desired benefit.

Make New Alliances

If you find that you have lost the support of important allies and that your leadership is therefore in danger, you need to negotiate new alliances that will keep you in power. This strategy is precisely the one used by heads of coalition governments when, because of changing political dynamics in a country, a political party that is a member of the coalition government announces its intent to quit the government because of policy differences with the coalition leadership, with the result that the government may fall due to a lack of sufficient support in parliament. The prime minister (PM) facing the loss of leadership will usually try to find other political parties with which to build a coalition and therefore remain in power. Thus, in the highly fragmented political landscape of Israel, Benjamin Netanyahu, its long-serving PM, was able to remain leader of the country by constantly forming new coalitions with increasingly conservative parties when more liberal parties, because of political disagreements with him, decided they could no longer serve in his government. So if you, as president of a foundation, seek to devote significant funds to new, but controversial, areas of activity, such as housing and support for immigrants and undocumented workers in rural areas, but discover that some of your strongest supporters are dead set against the idea, you might, instead of abandoning your proposed initiative, negotiate a new supporting coalition with other members of your governing board or bring onto the board new members who share your views.

Pay Off Challengers, Preferably with Other People's Money

Sometimes leaders can effectively remove challengers to their leadership by buying them off, by giving them a benefit that will cause them to end their challenge. To use this strategy successfully, you have to understand what the people challenging your leadership really want and then devise an offer they can't refuse. A case in point is the challenge that Ross Perot made to Roger Smith's leadership of General Motors (GM) in the mid-1980s.

In 1984, GM, faced with growing competition from the Japanese auto industry and seeking ways to end the decline in its market share, purchased Electronic Data Systems (EDS) for $2.5 billion, hoping that its technology and entrepreneurial culture would revive GM's fortunes. Founded in 1962 by Ross Perot, a feisty Texas entrepreneur, EDS, thanks to Perot's leadership and drive, grew into one of the most successful and lucrative computer services company in America. Perot was its chairman, CEO, and principal shareholder. The buyout acquisition called for EDS to remain an autonomous subsidiary within the GM organization with Perot at its head. A series of personal agreements between Smith and Perot set out the details of that arrangement.

To pay for the deal, GM issued a new class of shares that were given to EDS shareholders in return for their EDS stock, a deal valued at $33 per share. Perot received approximately $400 million in new GM shares, plus promised contingency payments, making him GM's largest shareholder. In addition, and equally important, he gained a seat on the GM board of directors.

Conflict between Perot and Smith arose soon after the acquisition was completed. Basically their dispute centered on three issues. First, Perot felt that GM was not respecting EDS's autonomy to operate as a separate business unit with its own policies on such matters as compensation, contrary to what Perot believed the two men had agreed. Second, Perot, who was strongly dedicated to a revival and renewal of GM as an automotive leader, came to the conclusion after serious study of GM operations, that Smith's policies for the company's development were wrong. The conflict over policy came to a head when Smith proposed that GM acquire Hughes Aircraft for $5.2 billion in 1985. As a GM board member, Perot argued vehemently against the deal. Unmoved, all the other GM directors followed Smith's lead and voted to approve it. A third cause of the conflict was the strong personality differences between Perot and Smith. Perot remained the free-wheeling entrepreneur, while Smith was the consummate corporate bureaucrat.

The conflict between the two men grew increasingly tense as Perot not only challenged Smith's policies but also his leadership style, charging that Smith was arrogant and autocratic. When their dispute became public and the subject of growing commentary in the financial media, Smith decided to adopt a two-step strategy to end Perot's challenge to his leadership: (1) to buy back the GM shares owned by Perot and (2) to remove him from the board. After lengthy negotiations between representatives of the two men, GM, invoking certain contingency clauses in the original sales agreement, repurchased Perot's shares for nearly $62 a share, paying him $750 million in 1986, nearly twice what it had paid for his interest in EDS just 18 months before. Shortly, afterwards Perot resigned from the GMC board, thus ending his challenge to Roger Smith's leadership of one of America's largest industrial corporations.[1]

In looking back on this incident, it is somewhat surprising that Smith was naïve enough to believe that Perot's EDS's entrepreneurial experience and spirit would somehow magically transform GMC's deep seated bureaucratic culture without wrenching conflict and upheaval. Indeed, it is surprising that Smith did not recognize that Perot, by virtue of the very nature of his

---

[1] Doran P. Levin, "G.M. v. Ross Perot: Breaking up is Hard to Do," *The New York Times*, March 26, 1989, Magazine, p. 1.

personality and entrepreneurial background, which Smith claimed to value, was ultimately going to challenge Smith's leadership, which was anything but entrepreneurial. In fact, one can argue that the only way to have brought a new entrepreneurial spirit to GM in the 1980s was to challenge and ultimately change its corporate leadership. Perhaps that was exactly what Perot had in mind when he joined the GM board. By personality and background, Ross Perot seemed to have a taste for challenging leaders to the point of seizing their leadership. Let's not forget that in 1992, Perot would make yet another challenge to established leadership when he mounted a third-party campaign to be elected president of the United States, gaining 19 percent of the votes cast, an effort that probably cost President George H. W. Bush the second term he desired.

Exclude Challengers

Another common strategy for dealing with leadership challenges from within an organization is either to exclude challengers from positions that allow them to threaten a leader's hold on power or to drive them completely from the organization itself. Normally, challengers' ability to threaten a leader depends very much on their place within the organization or indeed merely being part of it. So by excluding that person from that position, a leader deprives a challenger of the power to make a credible challenge. In theory, Roger Smith would not have had to orchestrate Perot's exclusion from the GM board had Perot, in return for the handsome buyback of his shares or other payment, simply agreed to stop criticizing Smith and to follow the lead of the other directors in supporting Smith and his policies. But of course the troubled relationship and lack of trust between the two men had deteriorated to the point that for Smith the only way to end Perot's leadership challenge was to exclude him definitively and permanently from the GM board.

Angela Merkel, a woman raised in East Germany who, after German reunification, rose in a predominately male culture to become a long-serving chancellor, was a consummate practitioner of exclusion both as a means to power and a way to preserve it. Early in her career when she first became minister for environmental matters, the top civil servant in the ministry condescendingly suggested that Merkel would need his help running things. She fired him shortly thereafter. His statement indicated to her that he would become a potential threat to her power to lead the ministry so he obviously had to go. Equally important, he had to go before he had developed supporters within the ministry in opposition to the young female minister.

Merkel would go on to force the exclusion of Helmut Kohl from his position as leader of the party and from the position of German chancellor along with many others. As a former US ambassador said about Angela Merkel,

"If you cross her, you end up dead. There's nothing cushy about her. There's a whole list of alpha males who thought they would get her out of the way, and they're all now in other walks of life."[2]

Merkel's ability to exclude rivals effectively is due to her skill in recognizing and analyzing a potential challenge, no doubt a result of her training as a scientist, her ability to exploit the weaknesses of her challenger, her patience in waiting for right moment to strike, and her calm in facing threats that would stimulate emotional reactions in other challenged leaders with less personal control. Current and potential leaders would do well to study her carefully.

In those situation in which you as leader do not have the authority to expel potential opponents from an organization by firing them as Merkel did, you may still have sufficient power to transfer them away from positions within the organization, such as memberships of key committees, and thereby reduce if not eliminate the challenge to your leadership. In short, use a strategy favored by kings of old to handle upstarts in the royal family—internal exile.

Agree to Yield Power...Later

Yet another way to deal with a competitor for leadership is to agree to give up the role at a later time and also to support or at least not oppose your competitor's subsequent rise to power. In return, your opponent's part of the deal is not to oppose your leadership for a fixed period of time. An example of such a negotiated deal was the so called "Granita Pact" between Tony Blair and Gordon Brown, allegedly made in the Granita restaurant in London in May of 1994, when both men were important, rising forces within the British Labour Party. Although the agreement was never written and its terms have been disputed over the years, it has been said that Brown agreed not to present himself in the next election for the leader of the Labour Party in order to give Blair a stronger chance of winning, that if Blair subsequently became PM then Brown would be given the post of chancellor of the Exchequer with wide powers over domestic policy, and finally that Blair

---

[2] George Packer, "The Quiet German: The Astonishing Rise of Angela Merkel, the Most Powerful Woman in the World" *The New Yorker*, December 1, 2014.

would serve only two terms as PM and then resign to allow Brown to succeed him. In fact, Blair led the Labour Party to a resounding victory in 1997 and Brown became chancellor of the Exchequer as a result. Labour would win again in 2001 and 2005 under Blair's leadership. But instead of resigning at that point immediately, according to their agreement, Blair, to the great annoyance of Brown, continued to serve as PM until 2007, at which time Brown became PM.[3]

Step Aside, but not Down

In certain situations, particularly strong leaders are able to negotiate an exit from leadership that requires them to give up the title and day-to-day responsibilities of leadership but hold onto a role and status within the institution that still gives them strong influence over major organizational policies and decisions. Thus, a chair and CEO of a corporation might give up the title and powers of a CEO but hold on to the role of chair in which he or she would have more or less defined powers in leading the company's board of directors, the institution's basic governing body. Similarly, Lee Kuan Yew, who was PM of Singapore from 1959 to 1990 and a dominant force in the modernization of that country, resigned but remained in the cabinet as "Senior Minister" (1990–2004) then "Minister Mentor" (2004–2011) where he continued to exert considerable influence.

University trustees, in negotiating the exit of a particularly strong and long-serving president, might seek to ease a leader's departure by appointing him or her "university chancellor." In such a situation, leaders see themselves not as "stepping down," but as "stepping aside." For example, John Silber served as the highly controversial president of Boston University from 1971 until 1996, when he resigned to assume the title of chancellor, holding that position until 2002. As chancellor, he continued to exercise a dominant role within the university. At Tufts University, when the trustees decided that the time had come to replace Jean Mayer after 16 transformative years as president, their negotiations also included a commitment to name Mayer chancellor of the university, a position with vaguely defined responsibilities for university development. While the trustees may have seen the position as purely honorific, it is not clear whether Mayer, who was both creative and

---

[3] Akifa Akbar, "Granita, a Byword for the Pact that Has Hung Over New Labour for a Decade," *Independent*, June 5, 2003, http://www.independent.co.uk/news/uk/politics/granita-a-byword-for-the-pact-that-has-hung-over-new-labour-for-a-decade-107817.html

crafty, viewed his new role in the same light. Unfortunately, he never had a chance to exercise his transformative powers as chancellor. Six months after leaving the presidency, he died of a massive heart attack.

Choose Your Successor

In certain situations, you may wish or be compelled to leave a formal position in an organization, yet still want to retain sufficient power to influence, if not control, the leadership decisions of your successor. Outgoing leaders seek to retain such influence by choosing or at least playing a role in the selection of their successor. They then use their power to pick someone who will be amenable to their suggestions and recommendations over key organizational decisions. In some countries without strong democratic traditions, leaders who, willingly or unwillingly must give up their leadership position, often arrange that a spouse, sibling or child will follow them as leaders. For example, Raoul Castro followed his brother as the leader of Cuba and Christina Fernandez di Kirchner succeeded her husband Nestor as president of Argentina.

Corporate CEOs sometimes also seek a role in the selection of their successors. Thus when Michael Eisner took responsibility for finding a new president for Disney, he also had an eye on the possibility of selecting someone who would have a high probability of succeeding him as chairman and CEO of the entire corporation. In other situations, outgoing leaders of corporations and non-profit organizations often attempt, sometimes successfully, to negotiate an agreement with the governing boards of those organizations that allows an outgoing leader to play a role in selecting a successor by advising, serving on, or even chairing the search committee.

When the trustees of Tufts University decided that it was time for Jean Mayer to step down as president, he negotiated a departure that not only gave him the position of chancellor with responsibilities for unspecified areas of institutional development projects but would also give him an undefined role in selecting his successor. He energetically set about trying to find a successor that he might influence, if not control. For example, he sent the university's provost, Sol Gittleman, down the road from the Tufts campus to Harvard to persuade a Nobel Prize winning scientist, a man with no experience in or desire for university administration, to become a candidate, seeing him as someone who, if chosen president, would certainly need the guidance of the experienced university chancellor.[4] Mayer, who had hired me

---

[4] Sol Gittleman, *An Entrepreneurial University.*

as dean of the Fletcher School and with whom I had developed a close working relationship, also urged me to be a candidate for the Tufts presidency. When I told him, after thinking about the issue for a week, that I really did not want to become a university president, he seemed genuinely disappointed. In fact, I was surprised at the depth of disappointment that he expressed. Only later did I come to realize that the cause of Mayer's disappointment was not that my refusal represented the loss of an opportunity for Tufts University or for me, but rather for him.

Share Leadership

Under special circumstances, two powerful contenders for leadership may negotiate an agreement to share the leadership of an organization by becoming its co-leaders. The history of such arrangements indicates that they are usually characterized by a continuing struggle for power, that they do not last long, and that ultimately one of the co-leaders drives out the other to become THE leader alone at the helm of the institution. In 1998, Citicorp led by John Reed and the Travelers Group led by Sanford Weill merged to form Citigroup, the largest corporate merger up to that time. Under the terms of the consolidation, Reed and Weill were to serve as co-chairmen and co-CEOs, a power-sharing arrangement. The personalities, backgrounds, and outlook of the two men were strongly different, Weill was a brash trader and deal maker, an instinctive decision maker, and skilled corporate in-fighter, while Reed was a cerebral strategist, corporate planner, experienced bureaucratic manager, and a reserved personality. Strong disputes about policy quickly arose between the two. Ultimately, in 2000, the board of Citigroup decided to entrust the leadership of the organization to Weill alone, so Reed retired.[5] It seems that while many leaders are effective deal makers in other domains, they have great difficulty negotiating successfully when it comes to sharing power.

Divide Leadership

Another strategy for resolving leadership challenges is to divide leadership responsibilities in a way that each contender has clear, autonomous power in a specific domain. One way to try to avoid continuing conflict is to divide the

---

[5] Charles Gasparino and Paul Beckett, "How John Reed Lost the Reins of Citigroup to his Co-Chairman," *The Wall Street Journal*, April 14, 2000.

organization structurally and convey responsibility over one part to one contender and the other part to the other contender. As we saw in Chapter 7, that was precisely the solution chosen in an effort to end the conflict between the two Ambani brothers that threatened the future of Reliance Industries in India. It was a special situation that few leaders and even fewer organizations would favor.

Collect Your Leadership Loss Insurance and Enjoy the Proceeds

Finally, when all other strategies to hold on to power fail in the face of a challenge, it may be wise to seek to negotiate the best deal you can to ease your departure. If you have had the foresight to negotiate some form of leadership loss insurance as Michael Ovitz did with Disney, you certainly want to collect the proceeds. However, there may be other benefits you may want to extract as part negotiating your departure, such as the use of an office, continued secretarial assistance, paid membership for a year or two of your favorite club, and an expense account to cover the costs of your transition to being a former leader. The time to negotiate for these things is before, not after, you have actually submitted your resignation. Before you resign you still have some leverage to secure these things from the governing board who may readily grant them to you as an acceptable cost for easing you from leadership. However, after you have resigned, the board, having achieved its goal, may see little reason to pay that cost. John Reed submitted his resignation from Citigroup and *then* asked for the same departure benefits that Weill would be given, including secretarial assistance and a car. The *Wall Street Journal* reported two months after he had resigned that "the board had yet to take up the request."[6]

Once you have collected the proceeds of your leadership loss insurance and the other perks and benefits you have managed to negotiate, you should enjoy them. You will find, as I did, that there is indeed life after leadership.

---

[6] Ibid.

Index

© The Author(s) 2017
J.W. Salacuse, *Real Leaders Negotiate!*,
DOI 10.1057/978-1-137-59115-9